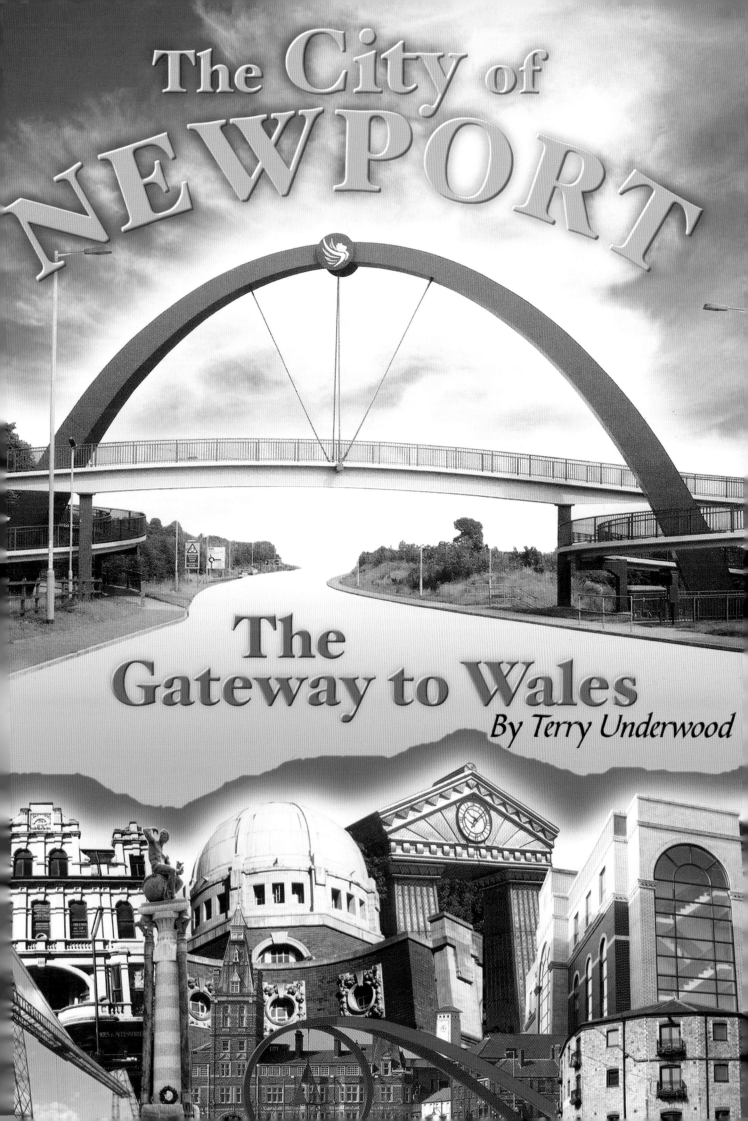

The City of NEWPORT

The Gateway to Wales

By Terry Underwood

ACKNOWLEDGMENTS

The South Wales Argus
John Davies Group
Jon Ross
The Welsh Museum (Cardiff)
Newport Civic Centre
Lonewolf Design Consultants
The Dolman Theatre, Staff
Trevor Brown, Abbeyfield
Patrick White
Tom & Marilyn Dart
Roman Reinactment Group
Peggy Baker (Ontario, Canada)
Jack & Rita Purnell
Jan Preece
Clive James (Newport Museum)
Ron McCormack (Save Our Ship Photographs)
Allen Markey

Special thanks to my wife Hazel who has willingly helped me with proof reading the text and supporting me at all times.

Published in 2005 by Rompdown Ltd, Unit 29 Leeway, Newport Industrial Estate NP19 4SL.
Tel: 01633 677710 Fax: 01633 677700 Email: sales@jdgroupuk.co.uk
Typesetting, design and make-up all by Rompdown Ltd. Printed in the UK. ISBN 978-0-9551641-0-1

CONTENTS

The City of Newport
The Gateway to Wales

Introduction

My Town, now a city

The Backdrop to My Life

My home Newport, the place of my birth, the city that lies just beyond the doorway that opens up the world to the land of song and beauty, and what lies beyond the gateway? Green hills and sparkling rivers of the Wye and the Usk, mountains and vales of Monmouthshire, Gwent and Newport, the land that's an overture leading to a grand symphony called Wales. Ah!

Wales, home sweet home, that's Wales, till death do us part my love shall last, my longing, my yearning for Wales, sang the choir. The stage is set but each backdrop to my life is changing, enriching and enhancing an already beautiful landscape, the green green grass of home stretching as far as the eye can see, beautifying an already a most green and pleasant land.

We as people need homes, shops, churches, factories and offices, together with places of entertainment, sports ground, schools, libraries, museums and riverside walks, parks to laze about in and roads to connect us. There are many statues in and around Newport to remind us of the past history of the town, WH Davies the super tramp poet who wrote, "What is this life if full of care, We have no time to stand and stare," and the chartist statue representing the last armed insurrection in the UK. That took place in 1839 in Newports Westgate Square, to name just two, but there are many more springing up like magic mushrooms.

My city is changing, each year new factories and shops are being attracted to the town, the Newport University of Wales is now on our doorstep at Caerleon, the Wetlands Bird Sanctuary at Nash, Leeway and other industrial and shopping estates are still growing in size year by year and the banks of the River Usk are being enhanced with walkways, trees and seating for those of us that just want to stand and stare. Newport's city Centre is changing too, there are plans for a number of major redevelopments such as the Spires shopping centre, the Westgate development now in its final stages, an Arts and Theatre to be built on the banks of the River Usk together with waterfront housing planned for the east side of the river, more development at the Celtic Manor Hotel and Golf Club and with the possibility of space being made available with the part closure Llanwern Steelworks, Newport could have an international Airport right on our doorstep.

Author Terry Underwood with Sir Harry Jones, Leader of Newport's City Council.

My town Newport, now crowned a city, because Newport to me is the gateway to Wales.

Terry Underwood

The contribution of industry to Newport

Newport Docks, Great Western Railway, Llanwern Steel Works and many other factories have contributed to turning the town into a city, the University of Wales Caerleon, The Celtic Manor and Golf Course has also had an effect on us achieving city status, as has I'm sure so many others too numerous to mention.
To have acquired city status is one thing, talking it up is another, let us all continue to build on what we have today, a city can be proud of.
The future is bright.

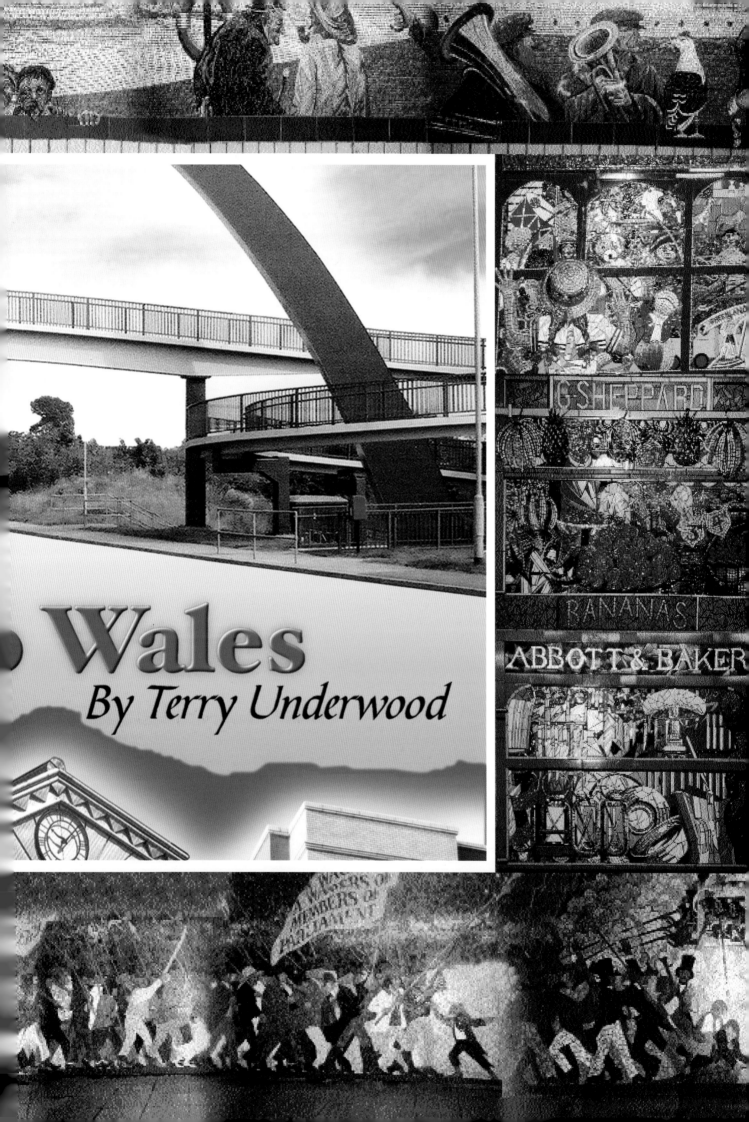

Wales

By Terry Underwood

Newport City Gateway Logo.

The Gateway to Wales. The second River Severn crossing leading to the city of Newport.

The second Severn Crossing or the Gateway to Wales.

Exit Cardiff - Enter Newport. Archway near the LG Factory. (Now closed) and other major factories between the city of Newport and Cardiff, capital of Wales.

Foreword by Sir Harry Jones

In the central entrance hall of Newport's Civic Centre, the history of Newport and its hinterland is depicted in 11 splendid full length murals conceived and painted by Hans Feibusch from 1961 to 1964.

The murals show in graphic detail that Newport, its people and its communities, have been shaped by, and have often played a prominent part in the major social and economic events and changes through the course of our national history.

The sequence extends from the early Celtic and Roman settlements, through the coming of Christianity, the centuries of border conflict and strife following the Norman period in the Civil War. The accelerating progress and change of the modern era is reflected in images of the Chartist uprising, the arrival of the Americans in the second world war and the opening of the huge, integrated Llanwern steelworks.

Just thirty years later, Newport once again occupies centre stage in the transformation from the old to the new social and economic order. The announcement of the end steel-making at Llanwern presages the passing of the traditional heavy engineering and metals industries which have sustained national prosperity since the industrial revolution.

At the same time, Newport has been in the forefront of the modern electronics and information revolution, attracting international inward investment in high technology from North America, Korea, Japan and Europe. If Hans Feibusch could paint a 12th mural at the turn of the century, it would surely be based on the semiconductor and the micro-chip.

Newport's history has been eventful, sometimes turbulent, often portending fundamental social change. Terry Underwood has earned his esteemed reputation as a local historian with the capacity to interpret the events of Newport's past and their impact on the lives of its people.

Councillor Sir Harry G Jones CBE
Leader of Newport County Borough Council
with author Terry Underwood, inside the Civic
Centre.

The Building of a City

See Newport today as a jigsaw puzzle with the missing pieces gradually coming into place to complete the picture. Newport City will be enhanced in the very near future with riverside walks, lined with trees and seats. A new arts theatre complex to be built near "The Wave". Riverside flats and houses for people with a love for water front views, our beloved Transporter Bridge being preserved and promoted as a major tourist attraction, the completion of the Southern distributor Road with an additional bridge over the River Usk, the road is expected to reduce heavy traffic travelling through the city and should be completed by the year 2004.

The Ryder Golf Tournament will be staged at the Celtic Manor golf course in the year 2010. The Waterfront Theatre and arts centre is now under construction and should be completed by 2004. With many other jigsaw pieces waiting to be slotted into place thus completing the picture.

This book, the City of Newport, Gateway to Wales has been compiled for the future to remember 'The Way We Were' and 'The Newport of Yesterday' together with hopes and dreams of the year to come.

If one has the time to 'Stand and Stare', to discover and appreciate how Newport has developed from a village to a Town, and now into a City, then two fine places to view our city can be found at Ridgeway and Christchurch. Looking down at Newport from these two good vantage points one sees the tremendous growth that has taken place from its early beginnings to its present day City Status.

In 75AD the Augustan Legion of Romans invaded this area building a fortress three miles from the mouth of the River Usk where they called the Ians Isca (now Caerleon). This land was found suitable to the construction of the fortress, unlike other parts which were covered in swamps and marshy ground.
About 400 years later when the Romans left Caerleon to return to Italy the fortress was demolished, leaving the amphitheatre and the foundations of the Barracks which can still be seen today.

Terry Underwood.

Some Notable Dates
In the year 500AD St Woolos on the Hill was built which attracted people to move downstream.
Newport Castle was built in 1145 or there abouts and the population of the new town was just a few hundred.
Recently the boundary of Newport has been extended to include Penhow and Castleton. The castle at Penhow was once the home of Sir Roger de Maur in 1129.

A charter to the borough of Newport was given to the town by James I, and in 1643, Oliver Cromwell paid a visit to the town and knocked it about a bit!
Between c1664 and 1672 the Morgan Family of Tredegar built a mansion on the west side of the town they names Tredegar House. For over 500 years the Morgans gave Newport an almost 'Royal' image, but with it came many stories of historic events that fired the people of Newport and beyond, with regards to Captain Henry Morgan, the notorious Buccaneer (Pirate) and Godfrey the second Lord Tredegar who survived the charge of the Light Brigade battle of Balaclava.

In 1792 the first Monmouthshire canal act was passed and by 1796 the canal development cuts through the moat of Newport Castle. By 1801 the population of the town was 1,087. In the year 1800 the construction of the wooden bridge near the castle was demolished and replaced by the first stone bridge.
In 1839 Newport had a riot, the ex mayor of the town John Frost led 5,000 angry men and women down the valleys of Monmouthshire into the heart of Newport, their aim, to change the laws of the land to give people a free vote thus stopping the poverty that existed at the time.

A confrontation took place outside the Westgate Hotel where 32 sldiers inside the hotel faced the thousands of rioters outside and still streaming down the hill.
22 rioters where killed, Frost and two other leaders, Jones and Williams were sentenced and escaped hanging but were exiled to Tasmania.

In more recent years W.H. Davies was born in Newport. He wrote one of my favourite poems, "Leisure".
"What is this life if full of care. We have no time to stand and stare" he wrote more than 700 poems giving tremendous pleasure then and now to many people in Newport and many countries around the world.

Roman Remains

The Roman empire was expanding. It's armies were everywhere, Britain was one of the last provinces to be added to the Roman Empire, and it proved to be one of the most troublesome.

Britain was invaded in AD 43 by an army of about 45,000 Roman Soldiers led by Aulus Plautius. The name Newport did not exist at this time, but a town or cities under different names did. Castletown and Novus Burgus or Castell Newydd, or Casnewydd for short, to name but a few, Pendan was another name used long before Newport came about, but the names used were wat before the Romans invaded Britain, so Pendan sometimes spelt Pendunville or Pentonville was a town that had an existence long before the rise of Newport. Pentonville still stands today as a silent witness to the fact that Pendan has its origin in the dim and far off past.

When the Romans came in AD 74 or 75 they dismissed the area where Pendan had stood due to low lying water-logged land that made it impossible to build upon. The level of the River Isca (now the Usk) being at times the highest and lowest rise and fall in the world, and so the Romans chose Caerleon three miles farther upstream, Pendan was gradually declining. While under the Romans, Caerleon, now renamed as Isca, became a grand place, second only to Roman in all its splendour, it drew of the population of other towns, Pendan included, so that Pendan became quite deserted. The Caerleon Fortress, now Isca, was occupied for over 200 years, there the Romans kept three legions on permanent standby, the sixth legion was stationed at York, the twentieth legion stationed at Chester, and the second legion stationed at Isca Silurum (Caerleon).

When the second legion arrived at Caerleon they brought an army of about 5,000 men and 1,000 civilians, men and women who were mostly tradespeople. The building of the fortress included six areas of Barrack accommodation, Hospital, Fortress, Baths, workshops, Headquarters, Granceries etc with a high defence wall built around an area of over 48 acres, outside they built an additional Baths and a magnificent Amphitheatre, plus Parade Ground, much of this can be seen today or at least where they once stood.

The Caerleon Fortress "City of the Legion" was occupied by the Romans for over 200 years, when Rome itself got into trouble these Romans went to the rescue - in AD 322 Britain was once more an independent Kingdom.
Geoffrey of Monmouth, when writing of Caerleon wrote...
For besides its wealth beyond all other cities, its situation was most pleasant and fit for the great solemnities.

On one side it was washed by the noble river, The Usk, so that the Kings and Princes from countries beyond the seas might have the conveniences of sailing along its courses, and on the other side, the beauty of the meadows and the groves with magnificence of its Palaces make it even rival Rome in all its grandeur..

Ermine Street Guard Roman Re-enactment Group on the steps of Caerleon Museum.
(Photograph by kind permission of the Welsh Museum).

view of the Roman Amphitheatre, Caerleon.

Ermine St Guard prepares for battle. (Dressing to kill) at Caerleon, Newport.

A torchlight procession at Caerleon Amphitheatre, Newport.

Roman soldiers roll call at the amphitheatre. Caerleon in the city of Newport Ermine Street Guard, Roman re-enactment group.

An elder of the Roman Empire with a Commanding Officer of the Roman Empire

Preparing for battle

Waiting for orders.

Commanding Officer leading Roman Elders from the Amphitheatre.

Preparing for battle.

Call to Arms

Centurians having a respite.

Centurians on the march.

7

Caerleon Museum

Caerleon Amphitheatre, Today the scene of many roman re-enactment events.

Remains of the Roman Barracks, Caerleon.

The Garden of Arthur in the Ffwrwm High Street, Caerleon

Dr Russel Rees, Historian.

In the art and sculpture at the Ffwrwm.

Scenes at the Art and Sculpture Ffwrwm Caerleon.

Doctor Russel Rhys   Ancient Royal Links at Caerleon

Doctor Russel Rhys has been living in Caerleon since 1969. He has been a practicing GP, a Gwent County Councillor, an antiques dealer and latterly the creator of Ffwrwm Arts Centre. The Centre is a testament to his passion for the mediaeval legends of Wales, such as the Mabinogion (Arthurian Sagas). Tales relevant to Caerleon's history, but sadly unknown and unappreciated by the modern day Welsh. Russel Rhys' crusade is to teach the modern Welsh the brilliance of their cultural past and the joy of their heritage.

Dr Russell Rhys of the Ffwrwn Art and Craft Centre, Caerleon, has recently acquired a set of plaques depicting King Arthur and other characters from the legend. Perhaps one of Newport's most celebrated Royal links is with King Arthur – the legendary ruler of Britain whose name has become a watchword for Honour and Chivalry.

Some historians believe Arthur was crowned King in Caerleon and according to Dr Russell Rhys of the Ffwrwn Art and Craft Centre, "There is documented proof that the famous King was there". In an account by the historian Geoffrey of Monmouth, it is stated that King Arthur was crowned in Caerleon. The site of King Arthur's round table is believed to be at Caerleon's Roman Amphitheatre, and a possible site of the cave where the King and his knights are said to have slept is also thought to be there.

If all this is true, then Caerleon must be Camelot.

When Isca Became Caerleon

In 410 AD the Romans left Britain to return to Rome leaving behind only a few who were no longer a part of the army. These Romans in time married Silurian women and the race from which we sprang was born and the Isca of the Romans which had suffered numerous Invasions being ransacked and burned was reclaimed and rebuilt as Caerleon, and it was famed throughout the roman Empire, ships laden with supplies and newcomers traversed their way up the River Usk and many settled in the new Roman City of Caerleon, 'or was it Camelot'?

King Arthur was crowned here and held court, and while living in Caerleon no Saxon or Dane would ever dare to set foot in Caerleon or anywhere in the surrounding district.

Reconstruction of the Roman Amphitheatre as it was. (by kind permission of the Welsh Museum

King Arthur's Army preparing to attack.

So This Is Camelot
by Terry Underwood

Looking down upon Caerleon
From Christchurch on the hill,
A place where history comes alive
Where Romans wander still

Standing there one moonlit night
With clouds and winds much calmer,
Did I see more than a thousand men
All dressed in shining armour?

Is this place where Arthur lived?
A place that we've forgot,
Was this King Arthur's resting place
Can this be Camelot?

When Arthur took Excalibur
Embedded in Welsh stone,
With ease he drew the mighty blade
To make the sword his own.

With Lancelot, Sir Galahad, and
Merlin in the plot,
There is no doubt, when I look out
That Caerleon is Camelot.

The Mynde or Mound in Caerleon

Legend tells us that King Arthur and his knights lay sleeping in Caerleon awaiting the call to arms for their beloved country and what better place to lie undisturbed than beneath the green mound, flow surrounded by a turreted wall, this wall wasn't always there, it was built in 1820 by Mr John Jenkins, the owner of the Caerleon Tin Plate works.

It was prior to this that a Caerleon man experienced an unusual adventure, winding his way down Mill Street after a night out at the Red Lion he was amazed to hear sounds of music and revelry coming from the direction of the mound, being curious he went to investigate only to be arrested by a soldier in an ancient type uniform. He was led to a great iron doorway leading into the mound, where he was welcomed by men in armour and bidden to partake of the excellent food and wine with which the tables were laden, also on the table were heaps of gold and silver, and to his amazement he discovered that he was sitting at the table of King Arthur and his Knights where he was made to feel well at home, when he had enough and decided to leave he was given a bag of gold coins and bade 'God Speed'.

In the morning he was found lying dead drunk on the roadside near the Mynde, although he had no gold on him, he insisted that his story was true, the effect of which made him become a teetotaller who persisted in telling his story until his death.

Caerleon, Once King Arthur's Camelot

I first learnt the stories of King Arthur as a child, by the time I was ten years old I was re-enacting every story to the rest of the boy's in the street where I lived. I was told that Arthur lived just over Christchurch Hill in a place called Camelot.

My Mum and Dad would take the family up Royal Oak Hill every Saturday walking over to a small Village just beyond Christchiirch Hill called Caerleon sometimes known as Camelot, walking all the way and finally stopping at a pub called The King's Arms for liquid refreshment.

"So this is Camelot" I would say, "Well", my Dad would reply, "it used to be Camelot in King Arthur's days and he certainly held court here many times", then he would say, "this is where Arthur as a young boy first saw the sword buried almost to the hilt in stone, it was inlaid with precious jewels that glittered in the sunlight, at the base of the stone were words which read, "whoever pulls this sword out of the stone is the rightful King of Britain'.

Many tried and failed, but young Arthur on his first and only attempt succeeded in removing the sword from its resting place.

Holding the sword high above his head a loud cheer went up from the watching crowd, and many knights fell to their knees and proclaimed Arthur King - promising their loyalty to him as he held high his proclaimed Excalibur and Kingship.

Geoffrey of Monmouth

Geoffrey of Monmouth was the Welsh author of History of the Kings of Britain written in Latin around 1136. Geoffrey's History consists of a patch of source material embroidered with a true storyteller's imagination. In writing History, Geoffrey gave Britain a glorious and heroic past, and most of all he gave England Arthur. In fact it was Geoffrey who gave the first full account of the origins and life of Arthur and exalted him to the   status of King.

He provided him with a powerful court at Caerleon also known as Camelot, giving him Merlin as his advisor.

Sir Henry Morgan Buccaneer 1635 - 1688

Sir Henry was born around 1635 and was reported to be the younger brother of Sir Thomas Morgan a short and fiery Welshman, if we accept the relationship between himself and Sir Thomas, he was the eldest son of Lewis Morgan a cadet of the Tredegar Family who was a younger son of Henry Morgan of Rhiwbina in Whitchurch Glamorgan. The late Lord Tredegar, Head of the great Monmouthshire family of Morgan, always claimed kinship with him.

As a lad Henry was fascinated by sailing ships moored on the banks of the River Usk and often stayed at Tredegar House with his cousins. Later he journeyed to Bristol where rumour has it he was kidnapped at the seaport and sold as a servant when the ship reached Barbados.

It was on reaching Jamaica that he threw in his lot with the Buccaneers, a more wild and villainous lot it would be difficult to find, Henry very soon became a master of his craft, made money and was successful in all that he did enabling him to but his first small boat.

Henry went from strength to strength following many swashbuckling years at sea he was a force to be reckoned with.

In 1668 Morgan was asked by Sir Thomas Modyford the Governor of Jamaica to levy a force as an expedition to ascertain whether the rumour of an impending Spanish invasion of Jamaica was true. This is one account… another account states that it was Morgan who brought the report to Sir Thomas. The outcome being that a fleet of ships commanded by Morgan set sail for Cuba to rendezvous near to the mouth of The San Pedro River where they landed and marched inland to Puerto Principi. They gained control with disastrous results, killing the Governor and leaving few survivors they plundered and looted everything of value, but Morgan refused to let them burn the town. All of this made Henry Morgan much richer and infamous, now the owner of many large ships and commander of thousands of men he led them into many more such escapades.

One such escapade was the invasion of Panama where they were met with a well equipped force of Spanish Infantry and Cavalry numbering about 3000. Battle raged and the city burned. The outcome of which Morgan was sent home to face charges.

His Majesty King Charles II himself a brave man recognised a grave man when he met Morgan who was soon high in Royal favour, consequently after three years his disgrace was turned into favour and he was eventually knighted and given the title of Colonel Henry Morgan, to be made Lieutenant Governor of Jamaica where he finally returned.

Captain Henry Morgan, Prince of Buccaneers died in 1688.

His memory has been stained by the cruelty of which he had been responsible, conspicuously that of the burning of Panama, we can whitewash him, but it must be remembered that he lived in a cruel age, he would often speak of the days of his youth when in Newport as a 15 year old he wandered down the banks of the River Usk fascinated by the ships and the seafaring people that gave adventure and purpose to his life.

Sir Henry Morgan

John Frost and the Chartist Riots (1839)

In the early 1800's, Newport witnessed the sowing of the seeds of discontent which finally lead to the now famous Chartist Riots and the attack on Newport's Westgate Hotel, resulting in the loss of many lives, and a change in the laws of the land.

Monmouthshire, as Gwent was then known, had an abundance of Iron Works and Goal Mines that were scattered throughout the valleys.

The Town of Newport, being the nearest Port, was well equipped to handle the produce from the coal and iron industries. The position of Newport was clear; like the narrow end of a tun-dish, with the coal and iron being fed down through the valleys by canal, road and later, railways, to a single point, Newport, and with it, evidence of the appaling work conditions of its labour force. Not only were men employed at these works, but also women and children, some as young as five years old, and working as long as fourteen hours a day, for little money, a miner's wage being about twelve shillings a week.

Disturbances in the valleys were all too frequent with rioters plundering shops and houses, only to be quelled by soldiers. Leaders were arrested, and conditions made worse by the closure of many pits.

To add to the misery, the industry operated what was known as a truck system - the workers being paid a small wage and the balance made up of Company Tokens, which could only be spent in the Company shops. This of course meant that huge profits from sometimes inferior goods went straight back into the coffers of the Company, and many a poor worker would be forced to mortgage his wages in advance in order that his family could eat.

As early as 1802 the South Wales Ironmasters had formed their own organisation to confer on matters of interest to all owners. Their meetings took place at Abergavenny four times a year.

Strenuous efforts were made by the aggrieved workers to improve their conditions of work, only to be rejected by the Masters, using as their basis the Combination Law, passed in 1799. This Law, until repealed in 1824, was designed to prevent other groups of people (the workers) from forming similar organisations to protect their interests.

John Frost Leader of the Chartists

The men became incensed by such repressive measures and took the law into their own hands, forming secret societies and lodges, which met in public houses, private houses, and on remote hill-tops, in fact anywhere away from the informants eyes and ears.

The lesson of the Merthyr Riots in 1831, and the hanging of the unfortunate Dic Penderyn, was to become in later years the keystone of their security precautions.

In the absence of good law, rules were made by the workers, only to be broken time and time again or amended beyond all recognition. After verbal and sometimes physical conflict with their employers one thing became apparent - that a plentiful supply of labour was detrimental to their claim for higher wages.

The following rules were formulated by the workmen:-

(a) Limit the amount of labour;

(b)   No children other than the worker's own should be permitted to work in the mines without the agreement of the membership of the Lodge.

(c)   A person seeking employment for the first time was compelled to pay a certain sum of money into the Lodge Fund before being allowed to start work.

Anyone who infringed the rules would receive a warning. Should the warning be ignored, they would be paid.a nocturnal visit by a gang of men called "Scotch Cattle", who would deal out punishment according to the magnitude of the transgression. The Scotch Cattle roamed the valleys from Risca to Tredegar and over to Pontypool, in fact anywhere in the industrial areas. The gangs or "Herds" would receive instructions from another "Herd" to punish a transgressor in their own area. To avoid identification, the most powerful and pugnacious terrorist in each "Herd" was called the "Bull". Disguised in the skins of beasts and with blackened faces, the "Cattle" set out on their punitive expeditions under cover of darkness, heralding their approach to the house of a 'scotched' victim by imitating the lowings and bellowings of cows. They would enter the victims' homes through forced entry and inflict serious physical injury, destroy furniture, then set fire to the house. Rape and murder were committed in the name of Scotch Cattle.

The most active Herd was that of Blackwood, although in Monmouthshire there were many.

During the campaign of terror, people were afraid to leave their homes after dark.

A writer of the day states in the "Monmouthshire Merlin" - "No person can travel from Risca to Tredegar without shuddering at the work of violent and wanton devastation that presents itself to the eye". Such events caused great mistrust of workmen's unions and pressure was brought to bear on the Welsh Calvinistic Methodist Association at Tredegar, by the Iron and Pit Owners, not to allow unionists to become members of the church, and that all members should refrain from associating themselves with workmen's unions.

This was the disturbed state of industrial Monmouthshire at the advent of Chartism.

Reformers marched in torchlight processions to attend midnight meetings held in some remote place; such assemblies made peaceful people very uneasy. Chartist songs were sung by marchers on their way to and from these nocturnal meetings, Chartist newspapers appeared on the streets and ears were cocked in readiness to hear the message from the silk-like tongues of impetuous orators.

One such agitator was Henry Vincent, a member of the London Workingmen's Association and one of the finest orators of the day. At the age of 25 he was much travelled and sought after by every radical group in the country. His visits to Newport were frequent and the meetings he attended large. On the same platform usually appeared another imposing figure and although much older he served to temper the meetings with a somewhat statesman-like approach. This man was John Frost.

Frost, a Newport-born businessman, and Ex-Mayor of the town, was well liked by the townspeople and had been a leader in the fight for the people's reform.

The marriage certificate of John Frost and Mary Geach on the 21st October 1812.

Jones of Pontypool

Zephaniah Williams

John Frost

Thomas Phillips
Mayor of Newport

Henry Vincent

Sketches of the leaders of the Chartists Insurrection at Newport

John Frost was born on 25th May 1784 in the Royal Oak Inn, Thomas Street, Newport. The town in those days had a population of just a few hundred, but Frost was to witness the growth of his native town from a small tidal river port to a sea-port and commercial centre of great importance by the year 1800.

The inhabitants were over a thousand and Frost was now old enough to play his part in the events of the town. After serving his apprenticeship with a Cardiff tailor as a draper's assistant, Frost took employment with a Bristol shop and finally moved to London. It was during his working spell in London that Frost attended many political meetings to hear prominent politicians speak and such events were to influence the rest of his life. It was at one such meeting that Frost met and befriended Henry Vincent.

Frost's mother, widowed some years earlier, begged her son to return to Newport. In 1811 he did so and opened his own business, a modest shop in Mill Street. He married a widow named Geach and settled down to being not only a respected businessman and leading citizen of Newport, but also its Mayor.

That was in the year 1836 when as a councillor Frost served the people of Newport, but his great passion was to raise the living standards of the working class by peaceful means. He addressed meetings up and down the country, and with Vincent and Frost on the same platform it was difficult to maintain order and arrests were often made.

On one such occasion Vincent concluded an eloquent speech at the Bush Inn, Commercial Street, Newport, with these words, 'Perish the Privileged Orders. Death to Aristocracy".

Similar meetings were held at the Parrot Hotel at the corner of Charles Street, at Pentonville and Christchurch, Newport, and generally throughout Monmouthshire, mainly Risca, Tredegar, Pontypool and Blackwood, - the Coach and Horses, Blackwood, being the chief workingmen's lodge in the county.

Nantyglo was a hot bed for using force to achieve its aims, much of this being generated by their leader, Zephaniah Williams, who, together with William Jones of Pontypool, became Lieutenants to the Chartist leader, Frost.

John Frost's birthplace, Thomas Street, Newport.

In March 1839 Henry Vincent was arrested at Monmouth for inciting people to riot. This was the spark that lit the fuse of the November riots that were to take place later that year. Preparations for armed revolt took place and weapons of all kinds were being forged in the county. Newport's own Cordes Dos Works contributed the Lion's share and secret arms drillings were actively carried out.

The unlawful conduct of the Chartists was brought to the attention of the Lord Lieutenant of the county and the Secretary of State. Anti-Chartist meetings were held in Newport and at Christchurch. A Newport surgeon, Harry Fry, son-in-law of John Frost, spoke openly against the Chartists and a group of highly trained horsemen who called themselves the Christchurch Cavalry gave physical opposition to the Chartists.

The imprisonment of Vincent and his fellow workers was the immediate cause of the Newport Riot. Newport people were terrified and stopped work for a day, they felt that they were on the verge of a civil war.

A detachment of soldiers moved into Newport, 120 or more strong, and London Policemen were sent down to organise the special constables who had enrolled in Newport.

A Newport printer, John Partridge, whose printing shop was at Devon Place, was responsible for the Chartist publications and immediately flooded the town with Chartist pamphlets.

The Mayor, Thomas Phillips, asked the people to remain calm and then requested that troops now stationed at the Union Workhouse, Stow Hill, be transferred to a more central position at the Westgate Hotel. The Commanding Officer of the 29th Regiment, Captain Stack, obliged and a detachment of one officer, Lieutenant Grey, and one sergeant, with thirty men, were sent to the Westgate without delay. They were admitted to the Hotel through the stable yard, the gates of which were afterwards securely locked. The soldiers were then placed in the eastern wing, chosen as the best position for defence. Shutters were closed so that the appearance of the soldiers would not be construed as a challenge by the Chartists.

However, the drastic action by the Borough authorities caused tension among the townspeople and Newport held its breath.

On Friday 1st November 1839, Frost held his final meeting at the Coach and Horses Inn, Blackwood.

Williams and Jones, with about thirty delegates, assembled to make final arrangements for the attack on Newport. They planned to march in three separate groups down the Valley and meet at the Cefn, Rogerstone.

Frost would lead the western division from Blackwood, Zephaniah Williams would lead the Nantyglo contingent, and William Jones would lead his men from Pontypool.

Their purpose was to appear in strength on the streets of Newport, to bring nationwide attention to their grievances, to destroy Newport's only bridge and its main link with London, (thus preventing the mail getting through), and to march to Monmouth and secure the release of Henry Vincent from Monmouth Gaol.

The marchers would be in groups of ten, with a supervisor called a Deacon or Corporal. Five groups would march together under the command of an officer, making 51 in all. This was repeated many times and the whole operation was organised with a military-like approach.

To identify between friend and foe the password "Beanswell' was agreed upon. A stranger greeted with the first syllable "Beans" responding with the second "well' would be considered to be a friend; if he failed to give the proper reply he would be taken prisoner as an enemy of the cause.

Blackwood was the scene of great excitement and activity. Frost had spent several days in the town, preparing for the appointed day, Sunday 3rd November 1839.

This day, the men of Monmouthshire would rally and march, to arrive at Newport at about 2 o'clock on Monday the 4th, take the town by surprise and blow up the bridge.

To arrive at Newport in the early hours of Monday, the Chartists, about 10,000 in all, mustered at appointed places and began their march at 8 o'clock that evening under the cover of darkness. Slowly they made their way down through the valleys, singing Chartist songs, and armed with the crudest of weapons, billhooks, pikes, swords and a smattering of guns. Most men had been drinking to help their courage, and when the rain started (for it rained heavily all night) the inns were filled with unruly men in rain sodden clothes, downing even more drink.

By the time they reached the Welsh Oak, great numbers were incapable of carrying out any orders that might have been given. Murder and rape had been committed, houses ransacked, and general disorder was apparent.

Frost had lost some control and delayed the attack until daylight, thus giving his men time to rest and sober up, whilst giving Jones and his men time to join up with the marchers at the Cefn.

But it also gave the soldiers at the Westgate time to consolidate their positions and this was relayed to Frost by insurgents.

The march continued at about 7.00 am. and with the coming of dawn, the rain eased, leaving heavy clouds hanging over the town. The sun was trying to break through, and this gave the Chartists new heart.

The men of Pontypool who were to have assembled at the Greenhouse, Cwmbran, failed to join the main column but still the marchers were strong enough numerically to "eat" Newport.

Frost gave the final order "To the Westgate", and the men, now in some semblance of order, cheered as they marched in close formation down Stow Hill.

The Attack on the Westgate

At about 8.30 a.m. on Monday, 4th November, 1839, the Chartists marched down Stow Hill in Newport.

The leading marchers gathered in front of the Westgate Hotel shouting for the release of some Newport Chartists imprisoned in the cellars.

It appears that a 'special constable' tried to grab a gun from one of the Chartists, a shot was fired which started a general melee.

The Chartists forced open the door of the hotel and entered the passage. Unknown to the rioters, thirty soldiers with their officers who had been brought from Bristol by Packet boat, were concealed within the

The attack of the Chartists on Newport's Westgate Hotel, 4th November, 1839.

hotel with the Mayor. As the situation worsened, the soldiers opened fire on the crowd. The concentrated fire had a devastating effect, the crowd fled in confusion, the riot was over.

According to the 'Merlin' newspaper twenty-two bodies were recovered but the Register of Deaths kept at Newport lists only ten dead persons.

The townspeople fled in all directions at the sight of the rain-soaked mob. Building workers on the new Catholic Church (now St. Mary's) left the site hurriedly as they feared for their lives. The sheer numbers of the marchers alone were quite frightening, and the shouting and banging of sticks increased the deafening levels as the mob wheeled into the Westgate Square.

The shops had been closed and shopkeepers peered expectantly through half open doors and shutter chinks. Small groups of onlookers stood in Skinner Street at safe distances from the front of the Hotel.

Frost stood ahead of the men whilst firearms were pointed in a threatening manner towards the Hotel, when a loud voice called out, "It's the Mayor!" The Mayor, Thomas Phillips, viewed the menacing mob from an upstairs window.

For a moment an awful silence filled the Square. Another voice cried out, "We've come a long way for this" and the silence was no more. The mob cried out "Reform!" and Frost seemed lost in the tidal wave of revolt that followed.

It has been said that the first shot was fired accidentally. A Chartist that had reached the Westgate doors, who considered himself lucky because he had managed to obtain a firearm, found that his way into the hotel foyer was barred by a special constable. In the struggle that took place to gain entry the insurgent's gun was fired into the air. The mob, thinking the shot had been fired by the troops, immediately returned the firing in retaliation; many shots were fired and the battle was on. The Westgate Square was filled with smoke, and the smell of burnt gunpowder soon reached the nostrils of those in the vicinity.

Commander Jack Lovell called out "In, my men!" and in seconds the hotel entrance and passage became choked with assailants; several fell wounded, together with the proprieter Hallen. The mob outside fired shots into the windows,

while the rioters inside smashed glass and furniture as they moved further into the hallway. The defenders up to this point had not retaliated. The Mayor anxious to stop the fighting called out from an inner room, "Lay down your arms" but the words were lost in the noise of battle. Lieutenant Grey decided the soldiers must be brought into action and the order to load their guns was given as more shots were fired into the hotel.

The door to the inside room containing the Mayor and troops had been securely locked in an attempt to stop the riot. Mayor Phillips and Lieutenant Grey opened the windows to address the crowd, but before a word was uttered a shot rang out and Mayor Phillips fell back into the arms of the officer, with flesh wounds to his arm and groin. The soldiers moved forward to the windows and commenced   firing into the mob outside. Instantly the shrieks of the wounded and dying caused further panic among the rioters who fled in confusion from the scene of the disaster. Even those who had not been involved in the riot retreated at full speed.

Thomas Phillips
The Mayor of Newport at the time of the riots who helped to defend the Westgate with Lieutenant Grey and thirty soldiers of the Queen.

THE CHARTISTS ATTACK
John Frost leading the assault on the Westgate. Mayor Phillips can be seen standing in the window.

The same night a warrant was issued by the police for the arrest of Frost and the other leaders of the riot. Sightings of Frost had been reported over a wide area, but he had hardly left the town, hiding at Tredegar Park till dusk. Frost then jt&jnped aboard a coal truck bound for Newport and returned to the home of his friend and Chartist printer, John Partridge.

It was late and it appeared that the Partridges had retired to bed for the house was in complete darkness. Constables arrived and demanded that the door be opened; this was not done and force was used to gain entry. A lamp was held high up and down the passage; the face of Partridge could be clearly seen and beyond Partridge was the unmistakeable figure of Frost and another man. Both were carrying weapons.

A Police Superintendant called out, "We represent the law", to which Frost replied, "The law demands so much. To break it is to adjust to a changing world. The people demand adjustment in their time".

"Hold your fire" cried the superintendant.

Then Frost said, "Let the tongue replace the pistol. No more bloodshed". and with that Frost was led away quietly.

The scene at the Westgate was tense as Frost was led through ranks of tired soldiers and town officials to be searched, charged and committed for trial. Together with other rebels, Frost was taken under military escort to Monmouth.

It was over a week before William Jones was arrested at Crumlin and even longer for Zephaniah Williams to be captured on board a ship at Cardiff.

Ty Hallen House

After the Assault

When all Newport was left wondering

At Monmouth Crown Court in December 1839, the trial for high treason began which carried the death penalty. The judges were the Lord Chief Justice Sir N.C. Tindal, the Right Honourable Baron Parke and the Honourable Sir John Williams.

During the trial, the town was filled with soldiers to prevent Chartists from making further attacks due to newspaper reports and prominent people demanding the full punishment for treason. The case was handled badly and Frost, Williams and Jones were found guilty with a recommendation for mercy.

Henry Vincent carried on the fight for the lives of the three leaders from an adjacent cell, mainly through the newspaper 'The Western Vindicator".

Their execution seemed certain as the sound of workmen erecting the gallows could be heard daily. A plea had been lodged by Judge Tindal to the Home Secretary for mercy and suggested that their lives should be spared. Weeks later the three leaders were awakened from their sleep to be told of the Government decision. Their sentences were commuted to transportation for life.

Early in February 1840 the prisoners were taken to Chepstow under a strong military escort and there they boarded the steamer "USk" bound for Portsmouth from which they eventually sailed to Australia on the convict ship "MANDARIN".

Frost at the age of 54 was to spend the next 14 years away from these shores and his family.

This was the final scene of one of the greatest political tragedies in British history. In March 1854 the three men were pardoned, but only Frost returned to this country. Jones and Williams remained in Australia, where Williams became a wealthy man through his coal mining activities.

John Frost went to reside at Stapleton, Bristol, where he died on 28th July 1877 at the advanced age of 93 years. But on his first visit to Newport after his banishment, he received a tremendous welcome when he was drawn through the town in a flower-decked open carriage. Crowds lined the streets and brought tears to his eyes once more as he left the carriage to re-enter the same hotel that has given Newport - sad as it may seem - a permanent place in history - The Westgate.

Henry Vincent

Henry Vincent attracted large audiences at open air meetings throughout Monmouthshire, and his eloquence always roused the crowd to a high pitch of enthusiasm. He was not a native of Monmouthshire, but a 'missionary' sent by the London Working Men's Association to spread the gospel of Chartism in the provinces. He was twenty-five years old, handsome and very popular with female audiences. Unlike many of the other Chartist leaders he believed strongly in the political equality of the sexes. He also edited a Chartist newspaper "The Western Vindicator".

In May 1839, Vincent together with three other Chartists, was charged by the local magistrates with conspiring to produce discontent and unlawfully assembling in breach of the peace. He had deliberately courted martyrdom. In a broadsheet he wrote "Your local rulers are anxious to arrest me tonight, let them take me... at the worst my detention can be for a few days." Vincent received twelve months imprisonment and he played no part in the November events. However, his trial and sentence raised the temperature of discontent and gave weight to the arguments of those who advocated force as the only answer to repressive authority.

Henry Vincent

John Frost

Frost strove to serve the public interest. He became a Justice of the Peace, a Poor Law Guardian, a Harbour Commissioner and during 1836 served as the Corporation's second Mayor. He fulfiled all these offices with dignity, diligence and impartiality at a time when corruption commonplace. It was his passionate concern for the rights of the people and the hatred of privilege and self-seeking that led him into the Chartist Movement and to exile in Tasmania. By nature he was conciliatory, but he rode a tide of discontent that he was unable to control. At the time of the Chartist march to Newport, John Frost was 55 years old: he was born in Newport at the Royal Oak Inn on 25th May 1784.

It is very unlikely that his radical political ideas were formed during the short time he worked in London as a shopman to a merchant tailor. It is certain that he returned to Newport with a good knowledge of the causes and course of the French Revolution derived from discussions discussions held in the radical clubs of the London coffee houses.

In 1811, he acquired his own drapery business in High Street. Newport and proved to be a very successful businessman. It is true that he was declared bankrupt in 1821. but this was deliberately contrived to avoid payment of further libel damages to Thomas Prothero. His business remained prosperous and his wife and seven children never appear to have been in want.

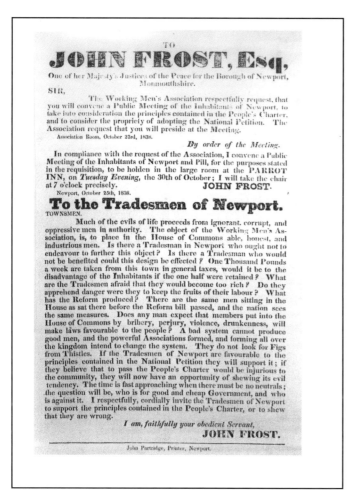

Printed informaion handed out to the people of Newport before the riot.

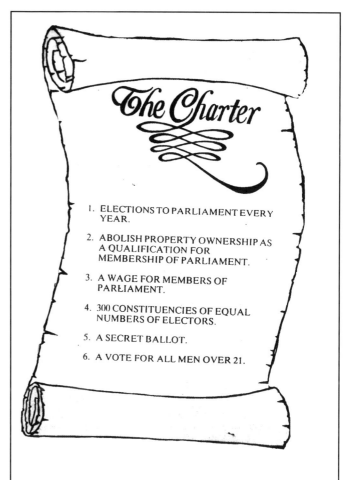

The Charter

He was a longstanding member of the Hope Chapel and throughout his life, his Nonconformist faith was one of the mainsprings of his concern for the rights of the people.

For although he was the acknowledged leader of the South Wales Chartists, he did not have a firm grasp upon the local Chartist lodges. A very large part of his time during 1839 was spent outside Wales. He served as a delegate to the Chartist Convention in London and later Birmingham, and he played a very active role in its proceedings, acting on occasions as its President and travelling to many parts of the country. His absence from South Wales meant that men like William Jones and William Edwards were able to build up support for an aggressive strategy.

Zephaniah Williams

Zephaniah Williams was a native of Argoed (Bedwellty) and was forty four years old in 1839.

He had been mineral agent for the Sirhowy Company. In 1839 he kept the Royal Oak Inn, Nantyglo, which was used a Chartist meeting place. For many years, he had been involved in agitation for the reform of Parliament and during the summer of 1839, he put all his energy into building up support for the Chartist cause in the northern parts of the Sirhowy and Ebbw valleys.

John Frost

He was detested by Chartist opponents. The Rev. Benjamin Williams asserted that he was a blasphemer, who held no belief in God or eternity. Zephaniah William certainly held unorthodox religious views, but he steadfastly refused to debate such issues, as he could not see how his difficulty in accepting the doctrine of revelation invalidated in any way the argument for acceptance of the Charter. He was no rabble rouser; his speeches presented reasoned arguments, explaining the Charter, its necessity and its justification. He never advocated the use of force to gain political ends and frantically endeavoured during the night of the march to Newport to impress upon his men that there most be no bloodshed and that the arms they insisted in bringing should only be used for self defence.

William Jones

William Jones had been a watchmaker at Pontypool since 1833 and he owned a beer shop which was used as the local Chartist headquarters. In his earlier years, he had been a member of a travelling company of actors and the Chartist move-ment gave him the opportunity to employ his histrionic talents to the full Through-out the weeks before she march to Newport, together with Zephaniah Williams, he toured the lodges "to stir them up". His message was very different from that of Williams:

He attacked the law because it protected money, not persons. He dwelt upon the hardships of his audience; the colliers did not know in the morning whether they

Zephaniah Williams

would return home alive or dead, and they ought to earn more money than any one else. It was their intention, he said, to liberate Henry Vincent from gaol and put Lord John Russell, the Home Secretary in his place.

Other Chartists

Three Newport men were tried with Vincent: John Dickenson, a butcher and William Townshend, son of a wine merchant, who were sentenced to six months imprisonment, and William Edwards, a baker, who was gaoled for nine months.

The important role William Edwards played in building up the Chartist movement in Monmouthshire has too often been overlooked.

He had helped to set up the Newport branch of the Working Men's Association and he chaired its meetings at the Bush and Parrot Inns. Prior to his arrest, he tirelessly toured the valleys, explaining the Charter. recruiting support and organising Henry Vincent's speaking tours. He recognised the bitter feelings held by those in authority and in the ranks of the Chartists and was reported to have said that no doubt many lives would be lost before the Charter was gained and that he was prepared to sacrifice his own.

William Jones

Samuel Etheridge , a well known Newport radical and printer, played an active part in the local W.M.A. as its secretary. He was 61 years old and his press was now run by his previous foreman and Chartist sympathiser, John Partridge. Etheridge objected to the violent language employed by Edwards and seeing that the movement was drifting towards violence, he opted. None the less both he and Partridge were brought to trial after the Westgate riot.

The Trial

As soon as the riot was over, the Magistrates started hunting out suspects. John FROST was soon arrested, William JONES was captured three weeks later on board a ship in Cardiff due to sail for Portugal.

John Frost, Zephaniah Williams and William Jones were indicted with nine others on a charge of High Treason. The trial opened at Monmouth on 31st December, 1839 before Lord Chief Justice Tindal. A large number of other defendants appeared on lesser charges.

The three ring leaders were sentenced to be hanged and quartered, however, the Lord Chief Justice stressed to the Home Secretary that whatever offence they had committed it was not Treason. Reluctantly the Government commuted their sentences to transportation for life.

They were taken from Monmouth under strong escort to Chepstow, where they were taken by boat to Portsmouth. Within a week they were bound for Port Arthur the convict settlement in Tasmania.
In March, 1854, all three were pardoned conditionally, a year later they received an unconditional pardon.

Jones and Williams stayed in Australia.
Frost eventually returned to Newport wehere he received a magnificent welcome. He later settled in Stapleton, Bristol, where he died on 28th July, 1887 aged 93 years .

John Frost after his return from Tasmania at the age of 93.

After the attack of the Chartists on Newport's Westgate Hotel, 4th November, 1839. The courtroom at Monmouth, 31st December 1839.

Exile

They were removed under strong escort from Monmouth gaol and taken from Chepstow by boat to Portsmouth. Within a week they were on the convict ship 'Mandarin', bound for Port Arthur, the convict settlement in Tasmania.

Both Frost and Williams found themselves subjected to a period of hard labour breaking stones in a quarry. In contrast, Jones proved more obedient and did not suffer such ignomiry.

In March 1854, all three men were pardoned conditionally and a year later they received unconditional pardon.

Both Jones and Williams remained in Australia - Williams became a wealthy man through his coal mining activities - but Frost eventually returned to Newport. Here he received a tremendous welcome and was drawn through the streets in a flower decked carriage. He then went to reside at Stapleton, Bristol, and here he died on 28th July 1997 at the advanced age of 93 years.

A FULL AND

PARTICULAR ACCOUNT

OF THE

Dreadful Riot !

Which took Place at NEWPORT, MONMOUTHSHIRE,

On Monday, November 4th, 1839,

Whereby Twenty Lives were Lost, and above Fifty Wounded

Many of which is thought Dangerous.

It appears that the Chartists, at Newport, Merthyr, Abergavenny, and the adjoining neighbourhoods had previously concerted a plan of assembling together at Newport, as those already there had ordered the Merthyr Chartists to come to Newport to join them armed; the plan was,—they first intended disarming the Soldiers as only forty remained at Newport, to go then with those in a strong body to Monmouth, accordingly on Monday November 4th, as early as 7 o'clock in the Morning they at Newport began to assemble together intending to put these plans into execution in defiance of the Law, About seven o'clock a considerable mob was assembling together, in Commercial Street. The Soldiers and Magistrates were at the Waistcoat Inn, and the Chartists collected in a great body, in front of the House, when the Mayor came to read the Riot act and desire the Chartist to disperse, but to no effect, they were immediately dreadfully assaulted pelted and even fired at by the Chartists and the Inn threatened to be demolished, which threat they afterwards fulfilled leaving the House in complete ruins, when the Magistrates ordered a Detatchment of Ten of the Soldiers to fire upon the mob, but to fire over them, which they did; Ten fired at a time, three times; during which time the Chartists continued firing at the Soldiers the Magistrates so whereby many were Killed and Wounded, among others two of the Soldiers were dangerously wounded. Consequently the Soldiers were ordered to fire actually into the mob, with ball cartridge; which they did for several rounds in detatchments of ten at a time, until the streets were cleared, about twenty were Killed, and above fifty wounded, after which the Melancholy appearance of the streets cannot be well conceived, Persons carrying away the Killed and wounded, and quantities of blood remaining in the streets, presenting a picture of desolation and one truly heart reading.

Further account .—Tuesday evening, the town seems still and peaceable, excepting a great talk about the killed, wounded, and unfortunate desperate transaction ; some of the ring leaders are apprehended. The Mayor was reading the Riot Act at the Inn Window when the Chartist fired at him and wounded his shoulder and wrist.

W. BYAN, Printer, No 25, Garden street, Swansea.

Leaflet handed out to the people of the town giving details of the dreadful riot.

A meeting of discontented iron workers and coalminers.

John Partridge printer of York Place, Newport with John Frost studying broadsheets.

A London orator, Henry Vincent at Gold Tops, Newport takes a stand for justice.

Soldiers based near to Woolastow House, Stow Hill as the rioters march past.

One of the many midnight meetings in preparation of riots.

Rioters marching down Stow Hill to Westgate Square watched by stonemasons on St Mary's Church tower, Stow Hill.

Troops at the window of the Westgate Hotel fire at the rioting mob.

Mayor of Newport, Thomas Phillips, wounded inside the Westgate Hotel.

The arrest of John Frost from the home of John Partridge Printers.

The Chartists secretly burying their dead at midnight.

The trial ot John Frost, Zephaniah Williams and William Jones at a court in Monmouth.

Transportation to the convict settlememnt Port Arthur in Tasmania.

John Frost returns to Newport in 1856 to a rapturous welcome from the crowds.

33

A Man Betrayed
by Terry Underwood

A rebel wind was blowing, round the hills of Nantyglo,
A thousand men did muster, against a common foe.
John Frost the Chartist leader had set out to rebel,
To fight the Queen's authority, and deliver Wales from hell.

From Blackwood and from Ponty, the Chartist raiders came,
To congregate in Newport, once there to die in vain.
"To the Westgate!" cried their leader, "and be prepared to die".
"Are you with me?" asked their leader, and a thousand men said "Aye".

With pikes and pick axe handles, a musket here and there,
Frost led the men in marching, as thunder filled the air.
They marched at eight towards the light,
In blinding rain all through the night.

"Don't let the rain defeat us," John Frost gave out a cry,
"So make alive your spirits and keep your powder dry".
The singing of the rebels filled the valley to begin,
But the rain brought them to shelter, and forced them in to every inn.

Five thousand men by this time, had mustered in the rain,
To march like hell to Newport, to break the poor man's chain.
With each turn of the weather, sober men were but a few,
Each man became a victim of the mighty devil's brew.

It took the leader's courage, with careful gentle prods,
To keep those rebels marching, soon a band of drunken sots.
With every clap of thunder, the men took an ape-like shape,
Forgot why they were marching, murdered men with wives to rape.

The looting of the homesteads, the ravishing of the maids,
Molesting of the children, a mask of ugly shades.
They marched at eight towards the light,
In blinding rain all through the night.

They straggled down the valley, tired, wet and spirit broke,
The troop became mere rabble till they reached the old Welsh Oak.
There Frost and Jones and Williams had forced the men to rally,
They stood them there till sober, then continued down the valley.

The coming of the sunrise, the easing of the rain,
Made victory almost certain and voices sang again.
The Monmouth caps were drying, the smell of steaming wool,
The sound of squelching boots afoot, and stomachs that should be full.

Bill Jones and Zephaniah Williams were marching ten feet tall,
John Frost, a little nervous, who would be the first to fall?
The passing of the Handpost, St. Woolos on the hill,
The tramping of ten thousand feet descending down Stow Hill.

The Newport streets were shining, the cobbles standing proud,
The sunlight caught in pools of rain, reflecting heavy clouds.
Their singing turned to anger as they marched on to their fate,
For shutters sealed the Westgate where the militia 'lay in wait.

Inside with muskets ready, stood the Mayor and Captain Grey,
With thirty soldiers of the Queen, to keep the mob at bay.
Bewildered Newport townsfolk took cover from the band,
And the only thing that stayed, a dog, who did not understand.

They milled around the Westgate, their sticks and muskets high,
Ten thousand angry voices were echoing in the sky.
John Frost was still the leader and stood there, feet astride,
Waiting for the mob to cool and tempers to subside.

"Lay down your arms, Mayor Phillips," the Chartist leader said,
"Come out, let's talk surrender, too many already are dead".
The silence that came was broken, with the creaking of the gate,
For the Mayor had come to talk of peace, but the crowd just couldn't wait.

A shot rang out, resounding, the mob gave out a roar,
The fight was on, more shots rang out as they battled through the door.
By now the blood was running, and many had to fall,
In waves the mob kept coming, answering the Chartist call.

John Frost was soon forgotten, stood lost in his command,
Swept aside by a sea of Welshmen, once more an ugly band.
A flash, and then another, burnt powder filled the air,
As the men, without then leader, ran riot in the Square.

They charged the Westgate staircase, guns firing as they went,
And the firing was continued 'till every gun was spent,
Mayor Phillips gave an order, "Shoot to kill the rebels, Grey!"
And the hall was filled with a blinding flash, as every man obeyed.

The flashing of the muskets knocked the rebels of f their feet,
And those that were left standing, turned and ran in full retreat.
Frost, the naked leader, stands there alone, afraid,
The tear-wet eye, the trembling lip, depict a man betrayed.

"To the Westgate!" cried their leader, "and be prepared to die".
"Are you with me?" asked their leader, a thousand men said "Aye".
Where are the men of Ponty that marched to town this day?
The echo of their voices is like them - gone far away.

GONE...GONE...
FROST STOOD ALONE, AFRAID.
GONE...AYE, GONE...
THUS WAS A MAN BETRAYED.

Terry Underwood

37

Viscount Tredegar (Newport's First Freeman)
Balaclava October 25th 1854

Godfrey Charles Morgan was born at Ruperra Castle in Glamorganshire on 28th April 1830, and succeeded his father the Right Hon Viscount Tredegar as the 2nd Baron in 1875.

As plain Godfrey Charles Morgan he left college to join the army, at the age of 23 Charles joined the 17th Lancers Brigade and rose to the rank of Captain where he did his duty on the field at the battle of Balaclava in Southern Russia, which was the scene of the one of the most heroic achievements of the British Army, when the Light Brigade, now known as the "Six Hundred" greatly distinguished itself heading its way past the guns in the fore and routing the enemies cavalry.

This unparalleled cavalry charge was performed on 25th October during the early days of the Crimean War.

> While all the world with bated breath
> Wondered! at the charge they'd made
> Who bravely rode that 'Vale of death'
> To great renown that will not fade.

Captain Godfrey Morgan's horse Sir Briggs' carried his master to victory in the most heroic war contest and feat of arms ever witnessed in the world's history at the time.

When his horse 'Sir Briggs' died he was buried in the grounds of Tredegar House Newport where a memorial Stone was erected to commemorate the memory of 'Sir Briggs. A favourite Charger, he carried his master, the Right Hon. Godfrey Morgan, Captain 17th Lancers boldly and confidently at the battle of Alma, in the front line of the Light Cavalry charge of Balaclava, and at the battle of Inkerman 1854, this brave steed died on 29th February 1874 at Tredegar park aged 28. In 1885 Viscount Tredegar became Colonel of the Royal Monmouthshire Engineers Militia and a member of Parliament for Breconshire from 1858 to 1875.

He was formerly an Alderman and Chairman in local parliament - the Monmouthshire County Council, Lord Lieutenant of Monmouthshire, a Justice of the Peace, and as a land proprietor he owned over 40,000 acres.
In 1909 on 9th June, Viscount Tredegar (Godfrey Charles Morgan) 2nd Baron, 1st Viscount was given the freedom of Newport at a ceremonial held at the great Central Hall in Commercial Street, Newport.

Viscount Tredegar died on 14th July 1937.

Scenes from the Battle of Balaclava, October 25th 1854.

Defence at Rorkes Drift, January 22nd 1879.

Wounded by Mark Churns

Pinned Like Rats

Rorke's Drift

On January 22nd 1879 at Rorke's Drift in South Africa, a small outpost manned by British troops, came under siege from between three and four thousand Zulu's. Warriors armed with spears, knives and a small number of rifles taken from dead British Soldiers at the massacre which took place at Isandhlwana the previous day, where over 400 British soldiers had been slaughtered and disembowelled.

At Rorke's Drift a small unit of 95 Officers and men of the 3rd Company of the 2nd Battalion of the 24th of foot soldiers under the command of Lieutenant Gonville-Bromhead, and Lieutenant John Chard of the Royal Engineers were preparing to make a stand. The officers and men had been notified that a large force of British troops had been in conflict with a Zulu settlement some miles away, they had however received no further information so were not aware a massacre had taken place and that the same force of blood thirsty warriors were on their way to Rorke's Drift.

The outpost at Rorke's Drift contained a small hospital unit that was filled to capacity with sick men of the 24th of the foot Battalion, as the remainder were preparing defenses when two army Scouts rode into camp on horseback from Isandhlwana to inform Lieutenant's Bromhead and Chard of the devastation news of the Zulu's massacre of Isandhlwana. Orders were immediately given to the men to man each wall of the outpost placing the whole force of 95 sick and able were on a state of active alert.

For several hours they sat there in the blazing African sun watching and waiting until at about 3.30pm a Zulu Warrior appeared on the top of a hill some half a mile away shield and spear in hand's. He raised his spear to signal the others who were behind him out of sight to signal they had reached their target at Rorke's Drift.

The besieged troops at Rorke's gasped in horror, some were bold and brazen, while others sick and fearful awaited their fate. The Zulu's filled the skyline on top of the hill raising their spears and stomping to a Zulu war chant as they prepared for another slaughter of the British.

Taking control the company Sergeant Major shouted out the orders for "every man to remain still and quiet, and you will not, I repeat not, fire your rifles until I give the order, understood." Some nodded their approval, while others just stared as more and more Zulu's filled the skyline, estimated to be between 3 - 4 thousand.

Lieutenant Bromhead gave orders to the Sergeant Major for the troops facing the Zulu's to form three ranks of fifteen, the first rank lying down, the second rank kneeling and the third rank standing behind a barricade of timber and mealie sacks, this would give them the continuous fire power needed to quell the attack by firing in rotation, one rank firing while other ranks were re-loading.

At about 3.40pm the blood thirsty warriors charged down the hillside towards Rorke's Drift screaming and shouting the war cries as they ran.

"Steady man", shouted the sergeant Major, "hold your fire", as the hoard came within firing range. The Zulu's stopped suddenly and silence filled the air, but the raising spears and the stomping of feet, with the beating of their shields spread terror throughout the valley, but still the men of the 24th of foot held their silence and not a shot was fired.

A final chant from the Zulu's and about a thousand came charging forward running with hatred in their hearts towards the gallant 95 men at the outpost still holding off their fire, from the three rows of 15 to others posted at every strategic point awaiting orders to fire. Then the order came, "Right men, front rank fire!". Several Zulu's fell to the ground, but the main force continued racing onwards towards the mission station, then they were quickly joined by thousands of warriors coming from the rear.

The hospital unit was situated in the centre of the station where a number of very sick soldiers lay, some of which were completely capacitated, leaving only the company cook, Private Alfred Hook from Chepstow, and Joseph Williams from Newport, to defend the hospital ward.

The Zulu's were now flooding over the defence walls at the station climbing over dead warriors who had fallen in battle, the gun fire was deafening , while thick smoke filled the air and the hospital unit was set on fire. Hand to hand fighting was now being fought and the screams of men being killed could be heard above the chants of Zulu's and gunfire. The Zulu's were everywhere and making their way through the smoke of the blazing hospital they found the inner room where Private Williams opened fire as they entered, he was finally overpowered and killed, then private Hook defended the area single handed and killed a large number of the foe.

So fierce was the fighting that the Zulu's began to retreat but the voice of Lieutennant Bromhead giving orders to the men could be heard above the carnage taking place.

"First rank fire!', "Second rank fire!". This was shouted time and again until the Zulu's that were left went into retreat.
At 4.30am on the 23rd January firing ceased with the light of dawn bringing in a new day.

Bloodied and battered the brave heroes watched from Rorke's Drift as the beaten Zulu's reached the top of the hill where around 200 turned to face the station, raising their shields and spears in a salute to the courageous men of foot before disappearing over the hill.

Victory was secured.

Private John Williams of Cwmbran together with 10 others were awarded the Victoria Cross and 16 British Troops lost their lives, with 12 wounded.

Among those fighting at Rorke's Drift were the following men from Newport;
Corporal Alfred Saxty
Private Joseph Williams
Corporal John Lyons
Private John Murphy

To them and their comrades we owe an unfailing debt of gratitude for their courage and stance against so many by so few. History was made to the glory and honour of this fine Welsh regiment, and today 123 years later some Welsh people are proud to own a picture of these brave men, an historic Painting reproduced in the hundreds and purchased to commemorate this historic event, so too do we still read with pride the awesome story of their heroic victory over the rampaging Zulu's.

And once more Newport can be proud that it's sons played their part in this Historic Campaign.

May 8th. The First Monmouthshire Regiment of the Second Battle of Ypres, 1915.

The picture commemorates the part taken by the first, second and third Battalion of the Monmouthshire regiment in the second battle of Ypres, when regiments suffered overwhelming casualties in helping to reconstitute an army in an effort to capture Ypres and the channel ports. It was a proud day for the county of Monmouth but the saddest of the war for the country as a whole. The incident depicted concerns "D" company of the first Monmouthshire regiment commanded by Captain Harold Ford Edwards the officer standing up and firing a revolver the only person identified. The British campaign in France and Flanders in 1915, Sir Arthur Conan Doyle wrote, "This first Monmouth company were outflanked and attacked in the rear after the Germans had taken to the trenches, to the right still under their gallant Colonel Robinson preserved In what was already a hopeless existence. The Germans trained a machine gun upon them from a house that over looked their trenches but nothing could shift the gallant miners who formed the greater part of the regiment. Colonel Robinson was shot dead while passing his men down the trench one by one in the hope of forming a new front. Half the officers and men were already on the ground, the Germans saw this and were on top of them with cries of "Surrender, Surrender," Surrender be damned, shouted Captain Edwards, and died still firing his revolver into the grey of them. It was a fine feat of arms.

In retrospect of the battle, the official history of the war said, "pinned down as they were in the narrow salient on hill 60 shelled night and day from three sides the conduct of the troops was magnificent."

May 8th 1915 was before the days of steel helmets and gas respirators, and the rifles used by territorial force were long pattered Lee Enfields. The small dragon on Captain Harold Ford Edwards back shows the identification mark worn by the first Monmouthshire officers so they could be readily distinguished by their men in battle, all ranks wore the same webbing equipment. The time of day is noon, by this time the British artillery had ceased to fire through the lack of ammunition and casualties, while the only aeroplanes on the battle front were German, part of the German forces consists of German marines which account for the presence of sailors in the picture. The German officer on the right of the picture holding up a disc painted black for the British side and white for the german side, this was in order that the German artillery could distinguish the position of their foremost infantry.

The picture was painted by Fred Roe and presented to the Newport Museum and Art gallery on December 19th 1935 by the South Wales Argus who opened a subscription list for the purchase of the painting.

The magnificent effort of the Monmouthshire Regiment at Ypres on May 8th 1915 must go down in history as one of the finest feats of courage in World War One. It has already been recorded they wrote the saddest yet most glorious chapter in Newport's history, when in a heroic stand against great odds before Ypres, the Monmouthshires helped to bar the Germans from the vital channel ports. Of their strength of nearly 500, only 129 officers and men survived. On a wall just above St. Mary's Church plaque reads, here stood Stow Hill Drill Hall from which sallied Newport's own Territorial Soldiers, The First (Rifle) Battalion the Monmouthshires Regiment to fight for Britain at the outbreak of two world wars.

The Cenotaph that stands in Clarence Place is there to remind us daily of the great courage and supreme price the men of Newport had to pay for our peace and freedom that we enjoy today.

Going home - thank you Jesus -

Author's Father (marked with XX), Victor Charles Underwood, recovering at Newtown Mid Wales from wounds following his involvement in the Battle of Ypres on May 8th 1915.

Private V.C. Underwood
3rd Battallion,
Monmouthshire Regiment

The First Battalion Monmouthshire Regiment in the battle of Ypres, May 8th 1915.

The First Battalion Monmouthshire Regiment marching down Stow Hill, 1914.

The 'Mons' marching down Chepstow Road, 1914.

Plaques on a wall on Stow Hill where the Drill Hall stood in 1915.

43

The Right Honourable James Thomas of Pill

One of the widest streets in Newport is George Street, with its friendly little red bricked houses nestling up close to each other, and each house sporting a gaily painted front door. The street is still a busy one, usually filled with fast moving vehicles, but in the late 1800's those little red houses flanked a great western railway line that linked a goods yard and Dock Street Railway Station.

So, it is little wonder that young Jimmy Thomas, who was born at No. 51 George Street, fell asleep each night with the clanging of railway wagons in his ears, and that when he reached the age of fourteen, went to work for them as a call boy and eventually moved on to become one of the most colourful characters in British Parliamentary history.

James Henry Thomas was born in 1874, a small child in stature, and came from very poor circumstances. When other children in George Street were invited to the Whitsun treat, young Jimmy would have to stay at home, his clothes too shabby and totally unsuitable for any celebration. Illness was the excuse given when such invitations were forthcoming.

At the age of five, Jimmy could be seen running along to the Newport National School on a Monday morning with little or no footwear, clutching in his hand a penny - that being the weekly fee one had to pay to attend the infants department.

When he was seven, he was transferred to the older boys section and the fee then became tuppence a week.

The school, because of its location, was often called St. Paul's Church School. This was the only school Jimmy was to attend and it was at this school that Jimmy probably had his basic training as an orator - he being so small it was easier to talk his way out of an argument than a fight, but he was not afraid of anyone.

At the age of nine, Jimmy started work for Mr. John Phillips who kept a Chemist shop in Commercial Street. He was paid the princely sum of four shillings a week. Arriving at 7.00 a.m., he had to sweep out the premises, clean the windows and polish the brass until 9.00 a.m. He would then leave for school, return to the shop at lunchtime, and again after school to make deliveries of medicines and generally carry out messages. He worked all day on a Saturday, and would rarely see his home much before midnight. Sunday was spent helping his grandmother by turning the mangle, and assisting with the household chores before attending St. Paul's Sunday School.

Jimmy's father, a railway worker, died when he was young leaving Jimmy in the care of his grandmother. He could scarcely remember his mother as she had died some time earlier.

Jimmy left school at the age of twelve and became an errand boy for the High Street Drapers, Baker and Manhire earning six shillings a week - a vast difference from the kind of salary he was to earn as a Government Cabinet Minister.

At fourteen, Jimmy joined the Great Western Railway. Although his ambition, like most other boys in his day, was to become an Engine driver, he started work as a call boy. This sometimes meant walking the streets of Newport in the small hours of night with a lantern in one hand and knocking the doors with the other. He once said: "As a call boy, I had to go around in the dead of night, rousing drivers, fireman and guards who were due out at different hours. I was rather a nervous little chap and taught myself to whistle to keep up my courage."

When he was fifteen, he became an Engine cleaner and worked at the Dock Street Railway Station. He was very popular amongst the other boys and soon established himself as a leader. It was at this time that Jimmy organised his first strike.

The cleaners were allowed 3ozs. of tallow a day to ensure the paintwork on the engines were kept in tip top condition. The company, in an effort to save money, reduced the allowance by a third and the cleaners' pride in their work took a tumble. Jimmy, leading a deputation, went to the Superintendent's office and presented their ultimatum "No more tallow, no more work". He then led the cleaners away from the engine sheds.

Within a day, Jimmy had won the fight, the tallow ration was restored and the conscientious cleaners regained their pride. To Jimmy, it was the first lesson in the value of collective action.

As a cleaner, his wage was seven shillings a week and conditions were not good. This led him to take a more active part in Union matters and his natural ability as a "talker" was used to its full extent. He would often dominate a meeting between the Union and the bosses, bulldozing his way through discussions until he achieved the wishes of his branch members.

At twenty, Jimmy became interested in politics and was an active member of the Newport Trade Union Council.

Jimmy became a fireman and then an engine driver, thus achieving his childhood ambition.

In 1898 he married Agnes Hill, his life long sweetheart, who was almost the "girl next door" as she lived only a few streets away from George Street, growing up as a typical Pill girl.

Jimmy and Agnes brought up a young family living in two rooms and knew the hardship of earning little money. They lived a short distance from the line and when Jimmy worked at night, he would often sound a blast on the engine whistle as the mail train passed his home, letting Agnes know that all was well.

To improve his standard of living, Jimmy was invited to Swindon, but assumed that his removal was not unconnected with his local political activities.

Wherever Jimmy Thomas spoke, he impressed his audience greatly and before long became Chairman of his branch of the Amalgamated Society of Railways Servants.

In early life his age and wages occasionally coincided. At eighteen he earned eighteen shillings a week, and at twenty-four this had risen to twenty-four shillings, enough to start a home and keep a family, but only just enough.

Thirty five years later, he was to refuse a Government post at a salary of £5,000 per annum, a substantial wage for any man in 1933.

Later, if Mrs. Thomas had forgotten the difficulty of making ends meet on twenty-four shillings a week, her memory was refreshed by some of the knick-knacks she had retained in her home from the earlier days, reminding her of the joy in acquiring them to help adorn her two rooms in the early days of her marriage.

In 1904 Jimmy was elected President of the Associated Societies of Railway Servants, and in 1909 was invited to stand as labour candidate for Cardiff. However, before the election, his party requested him to contest the Derby Division. He eventually won the seat and was to retain it until his untimely resignation.

On 8th May, 1924, he became Mayor of Swindon and the freedom of the Borough of Newport was conferred on him. As the Member of Parliaments for Derby, Jimmy Thomas, the shabby little errand boy from Newport, was enjoying his fame, power and influential friends, of which he had many. He laughed with Kings and Queens, rubbed shoulders with Princes and usually argued with Prime Ministers, but he was generous and never forgot his own poor circumstances when he was young.

When in Cardiff, he and his wife would each year organise a joyous beanfeast for the poor. One year alone, 3,000 children took part, many without shoes and stockings, and he never forgot Newport.

In later years, an association of the old boys of the National School was formed for pupils attending between 1880 and 1890. Jimmy Thomas, as one of the founders, attended most of the reunions. When speaking at dinners, he would recall his happy memories of opening up his lunch box on the footplate of his engine and finding there a pound of steak and frying it on his shovel. He then said"

"...There is a great contrast between that sort of thing and dining off the gold plate of Buckingham Palace, or ending a City Banquet with the loving cup passed around from hand to hand...I have tried all three and I can honestly say that for sheer good appetite, give me the wife's basket, a nippy morning and a well heated shovel."

When he became a Cabinet Minister with the title of State for the Dominions, he attended a dinner with the Prince of Wales (the late Duke of Windsor) at which a speaker was labouring with a rather boring speech at the Prince's elbow, and just as fed up as the Royal guest was Jimmy Thomas.

"I wish you could get him to sit down, Jim" said the Prince.

"Leave it to me, Sir", replied Jimmy, whereupon he scribbled a not and gave it to the toastmaster to pass on to the speaker. No sooner had he read it that he sat down abruptly. The Prince was puzzled. "What did you put in the note?" he asked. Jimmy leaned over confidently; "I wrote. 'sit down you b****** fool, your fly front is open."

One thing is certain, Jimmy Thomas was a great personality and was loved by a great many people, but in the end no one could save his political career.

In 1936, Jimmy was Colonial Secretary to Lord Baldwin's National Government. It was also budget time and he stood accused of betraying government secrets. Jimmy denied emphatically that he had deliberately made disclosures of information to a friend and another parliamentary member.

Jimmy resigned his ministerial post and described his position as "The darkest hour of my life". In his final speech, his last sentence referred to the one who had shared all his trials and sorrows, and who still believed in him - his wife Agnes. Agnes Thomas, the one time little girl that lived a few streets away from Jimmy's poor beginnings, was in the House of Commons to hear her husband make a personal statement and to reiterate that he never consciously gave away a budget secret. Then, as Jimmy Thomas, the boy from Pill, walked away, he paused at the Bar of the House, turned and bowed to the Speaker, and with tears streaming down his face left the historic Chamber which had seen so much of his success.

For the next ten years, Jimmy shared his retirement with Agnes in their country home at Sussex. He went on to write articles for newspapers and magazines.

In 1946, the Thomas' returned to South Wales and settled in Porthcawl where he and his wife could be seen taking long walks along the sea front and coastal paths.

Jimmy Thomas always felt that he was doing the right thing for his country and fellow workers. The last time he visited the House of Commons was in May 1948 where he watched the Speakers Procession on its way to the Chamber. He stood with the general public watching the nostalgia. Memories of the long and fiery debates and encouraging applause of fellow members came flooding back.

For Jimmy, the man who might have become Prime Minister of this country, it was the end of the line.

He died the following January.

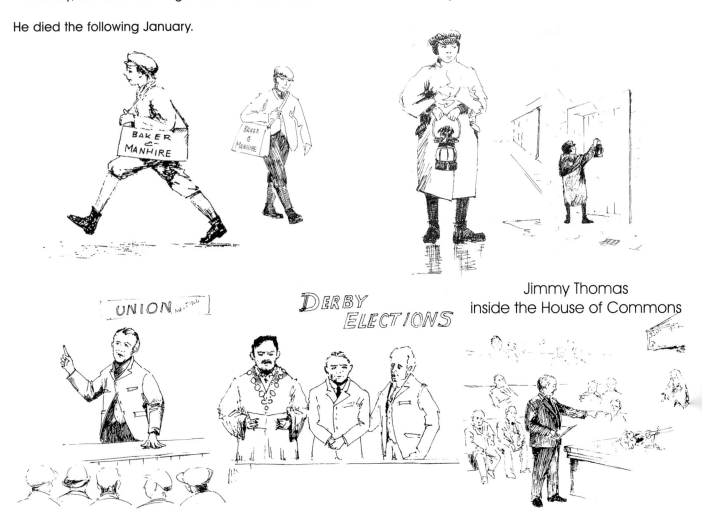

The active life of Newport born Jimmy Thomas

Freemen of the City

If John Frost, Newport's Freedom Fighter, could be seen looking down on our town today, he would probably be wearing a smile on his face as wide as the River Usk. He fought for Freedom and was deported from Freedom, but the Freedom of Newport was never to be his. The nearest it came to John Frost was on a sunny day in August 1865, when he rode through the streets in an open landau back to the Westgate Inn, the scene of his 'crime' some sixteen years earlier. He was given a rapturous reception, cheered on route by the hat-throwing crowd that the lined the Newport streets. His love for Newport, together with the memories of his fight for Freedom, had to stay behind in the town that day for his people to remember with pride. Frost was never to return to the place of his birth: No honours for this man.

It should, however, be pointed out that receiving the Freedom of Newport was, at the time, out of the question. The power of the Town Council to bestow such an honour was not available until the Honourary Freedom of Boroughs Act, 1885. Remember also that opinion in the town was divided on Frost: whilst some saw him as a hero, many still despised him.

Receiving the Freedom of any town or city is an honour of which one can be proud. It represents the epitome of public recognition, irrespective of occupation, sex, race or religion.

Newport has been sparing in granting this accolade. It is right that a town with such fine traditions should guard its powers jealousy in this regard if the honour is not to be devalued. Since June 1909, there have been fifteen recipients, mainly politicians, council officials, industrialists and military personnel.

In the early days, the making of a Freeman was a grand affair. Bands played and thousands cheered as they stood in Commercial Street to watch the passing of the parade. Flags and bunting were in plenty, and Newport's Great Central Hall was the venue. Anyone who was anybody in the town had an official invitation and no expense was spared to ensure that the occasion went off without a hitch.

The first Freeman of the Town in the 20th Century was the Rt. Hon. Viscount Tredegar, Lord Lieutenant of Monmouthshire, described as a 'pillar of the community', landlord, and a soldier of distinction. His exploits at the Battle of Balaclava in (c)1854 are well-documented and his interest in the town as a benefactor, even then was in evidence. That day in June 1909, was long remembered by all those people who had the time to stand and cheer.

Again in 1909, with 44 years of service to the public, Alderman John Moses, J.P, known as the Father of the Corporation, was the second man to have the Freedom conferred on him. A Newport man born and bred, he was a former Mayor, owner of a shipbroking firm with a fine record of public service that began way back in 1865.

Thirteen years passed before the next occasion. This time the honour went to Albert Newman, Newport's Town Clerk, retiring after 40 years service. Freedom conferred was considered a great honour for a council officer in 1922.

In 1924 another Newport man, the Rt. Hon. James 'Jimmy' Thomas, M.P., received the Freedom of the town. Jimmy was a Pill boy, born at 51, George Street in 1874. He had started working life as an errand boy for the Newport High Street drapers, Baker and Manhire, and then as a call-boy for the Great Western Railway and achieved his childhood ambitions of becoming first a Fireman and then an Engine Driver. He soon became interested in politics and became active as a local union official, impressing his audiences greatly wherever he spoke. In 1904, he became President of the Association Societies of Railway Servants and went on to become Member of Parliament for Derby.

Jimmy Thomas, the shabby little boy from Newport, enjoyed his fame, power and influential friends, of which he had many. As a member of Parliament, he became a Cabinet Minister and between 1924 and 1936 held various posts including Lord Privy Seal and Secretary of State for the Dominions. He wined, dined and laughed with Kings and Queens, rubbed shoulders with Princes and argued with Prime Ministers, but he was generous and never forgot the poor circumstances of his own youth.

Newport's Freemen

June 1909	Rt. Hon. Godfrey Charles Morgan, Lord Tredegar, Lord Lieutenant of the County of Monmouthshire
October 1909	Alderman John Moses JP
June 1922	Albert Augustus Newman
May 1924	Rt. Hon. James Henry Thomas MP
February 1927	Alderman John Parry JP
April 1934	Horace Sampson Lyne MBE
March 1935	Alderman John Moxon OBE
September 1936	William Royse Lysaught CBE, JP
September 1936	Alderman Frederick Phillips JP
September 1936	Alderman John Lloyd Davies JP
September 1945	Field Marshall Sir Bernard Law Montgomery
April 1947	Corps of the South Wales Borders 24th Foot
April 1954	Mrs. Mary Ann Hart OBE, JP
July 1969	Royal Regiment of Wales (24th / 41st Foot)
May 1978	104th Air Defence Regiment Royal Artillery (Volunteers)
February 1998	Aubrey Hames
September 2001	Royal Welsh Fusiliers
April 2002	Merchant Navy Association. (Red Duster)
May 2004	Sir Harry Jones

Mayors of Newport 1314 to 2004

1314 - 1315	Ralph and Phillip Dory
1401 - 1402	Roger Thomas
1406 - 1407	John Clerk
1407 - 1408	John Wakins
1431 - 1432	Jenkin Vethkyn
1433	Richard Batten
1434 - 1435	Williams Berne
1444	Williams Kemeys
1446 - 1447	Williams Kemeys
1447 - 1448	Richard Adam
1448 - 1453	Williams Kemeys
1453 - 1454	Williams Kemeys and/or William Berne
1454 - 1455	Richard Adam
1455 - 1456	William Berne
1457	Hugh Mantell
1459	Thomas Vaughan
1463	David Gwillim Merick
1464	John Merick
1465	Thomas or Richard Vaughan ap Rosser
1491	Morgan David ap Gwillim
1497	Griffith Taillour
1499 - 1501	Llywelyn ap Ieuan Vaughan
1501 - 1503	Thomas Bulke
1503 - 1504	Roger Kemeys
1510	John Morgan
1514	John ap Thomas ap Gwilym
1515	Jevan Ralphe
1516	John ap Thomas ap Gwilym
1519	Thomas ap Hopkin
1521 - 1522	Thomas ap Hopkin
1513	William Huws
1524 - 1525	Thomas ap Hopkin
1525	Thomas ap John
1527	William Watkins
1528	William Huws
1528 - 1533	William Llewellin
1533 - 1534	Thomas ap Robert (alias Thomas Boytre)
1534 - 1535	Richard ap Howell
1535	William Llewellin
1535 - 1536	Maurice Vaughan (alias Baker)
1536 - 1537	Henry Vaughan (alias Baker) and/or Thomas Boytre
1537 - 1538	Morgan ap Howell
1538 - 1539	John Taylor
1539	Thomas Boytre
1540	John Taylor
1541 - 1542	Richard ap Howell
1545	Thomas Boytre
1545 - 1546	ap Hopkyn
1548	John Lloyd
1550 - 1551	Richard ap Hopkin
1551 - 1552	John Lloyd
1552 - 1553	William Morgan ap Morris
1556 - 1557	Rowland Morgan
1561 - 1562	Morgan Griffith
1562 - 1563	Henry Parowe
1563 - 1564	Morgan Edward
1564 - 1565	Lewis Thomas
1565 - 1566	Morgan Griffith

1566 - 1567	Morris Thomas
1567 - 1568	Giles Morgan
1568 - 1569	Morgan Griffith
1569 - 1570	Thomas Morgan
1570 - 1571	Morgan Griffith
1571 - 1572	William Watkyn
1572 - 1573	Edmund Morgan
1573 - 1574	Lewis Thomas
1574 - 1575	William Phillip
1575 - 1576	Morgan Griffith
1576 - 1577	Thomas John Lloyd
1577 - 1578	Roger Williams
1578 - 1579	William Pritchard
1579 - 1580	Giles Kemeys
1580 - 1581	Miles Herbert
1581 - 1582	Miles Herbert
1589	John Hollis
1590 - 1591	Miles Herbert
1591 - 1592	Miles Herbert
1594	John Jones
1599	Thomas Morgan
1605 - 1606	Morice Nicholas
1607	Thomas James
1614	Rowland Morgan
1614 - 1615	John Jones
1619	Morice Nicholas
1623 - 1625	John Priddy
1625 - 1626	Morice Nicholas
1626 - 1627	John Jones
1627	Roger Williams
1628 - 1629	John Plumley
1629 - 1630	Morgan Meyrick
1630 - 1631	Richard Williams
1631 - 1632	Thomas Abrahall
1632 - 1633	Henry Nicholas
1633 - 1634	Walter Jenkins
1634	William Rees
1635 - 1636	Thomas Harris
1636 - 1637	Thomas Young
1638	James Williams
1646	William Woolph
1656	James Young
1658	Thomas Young
1667	William Morgan (of Friars)
1669	Charles Williams
1676	George Morgan
1682	Charles Williams
1685	Francis Pettingall
1689	Nehemiah Williams
1690	Thomas Bassett
1695 - 1596	Nehemiah Williams
1697	Charles Williams
1698	Charles Williams
1698 - 1699	Nehemiah Williams
1699 - 1700	John Morgan
1701	Roger Williams
1701 - 1702	Henry Herbert
1702 - 1703	Francis Pettingall
1703 - 1704	Charles Ward

1704 - 1705	Charles Ward	1815	William Williams
1705 - 1706	Charles Morgan	1816	John Williams
1706 - 1707	Thomas Morgan	1817	William Foster
1707 - 1708	John Plumley	1818	John Owen
1708 - 1709	John Plumley	1819	William Brewer
1709 - 1710	Nehemiah Williams	1820	Abraham Jones
1710 - 1711	Lewis Morgan (of Friars)	1821	David Harrhy
1711 - 1712	Henry Herbert	1822	Thomas Jones Phillips
1712 - 1713	Charles Herbert	1823	William Williams
1713 - 1714	John Jones	1824	George Griffiths
1714 - 1715	Roger Williams	1825	William Brewer
1715 - 1716	Charles Morgan	1826	Abraham Jones
1716 - 1722	Charles Ward	1827	David Harrhy
1722 - 1723	John Jones	1828	Benjamin Thomas
1723 - 1726	Richard Pettingall	1829	Richard Rogers
1726 - 1727	Thomas Williams	1830	Edward Jones
1727 - 1730	Thomas Edwards	1831	John Owen
1730 - 1732	Charles Morgan	1832	John Williams
1732 - 1733	Francis Jenkins	1833	John Jones
1733 - 1734	Thomas Morgan	1834	John Owen
1734 - 1735	David Seys	1835	Joseph Latch
1735 - 1736	William Seys	1836	John Frost
1736 - 1740	Thomas Williams	1837	Lewis Edwards
1741 - 1746	Thomas Morgan	1838	Sir Thomas Phillips
1746 - 1747	William Seys	1839	Thomas Hawkins
1747 - 1750	John Cadogan	1840	Thomas Hughes
1750 - 1754	Thomas Dumayne (Scott lists Dumayne	1841	Lewis Edwards
as Mayor 1748 - 54		1842	Richard Mullock
1755 - 1758	John Cobb	1843	John Stening Allfrey
1759	Adam Barber	1844	Edward Dowling
1762	John Cobb	1845	Joseph Latch
1764 - 1766	John Blethin	1846	Thomas Morgan Llewellin
1766 - 1767	William Keene	1847	William Jenkins
1769 - 1722	Andrew Weaver	1848	William Evans
1773 - 1777	William Kenne	1849	T.B. Batchelor
1778 - 1781	Thomas Richards	1850	William Childs Webb
1782	John Thomas	1851	Henry John Davies
1783	Thomas Morgan	1852	Stephen Iggulden
1784	Thomas Griffiths	1853	James Brown
1785	John Morgan	1854	Samuel Homfrey
1786	Charles Morgan	1855	James Nelson Knapp
1787	Robert Darch	1856	Charles Lyne
1789	Edward Harries	1857	William Williams
1790	Richard Griffiths	1858	Henry Shepherd
1791	John Thomas	1859	Thomas Gratrex
1792	Edward Bliss	1860	James Brown
1793	Thomas Morgan	1861	James Brown
1794	Robert Darch (died)	1862	George William Jones
1794	Charles Price	1863	William Williams Morgan
1795	Edward Harries	1864	Edward J. Phillips
1796	Richard Griffiths	1865	Thomas Floyd Lewis
1797	Charles Morgan	1866	William Graham
1798 - 1800	Sir Robert Salusbury	1867	Thomas M. Llewellin
1800	Rev. Thomas Leyson	1868	James Murphy
1801	William Phillips	1869	Thomas Beynon
1802	Edmund Harris	1870	L.A. Homfrey
1803	John Thomas	1871	David Harrhy
1804	William Foster	1872	Wyndham Jones
1805 - 1808	Morgan Williams	1873	Nelson Hewertson
1808	Sir Robert Salusbury	1874	Benjamin Evans
1809 - 1812	Robert Jones	1875	Henry Pearce Bolt
1812	William Foster	1876	George Fothergill
1814	George Griffiths	1877	John Moses

1878	Joseph Gibbs
1879	Henry Russel Evans
1880	John Rosser Jacob
1881	Thomas Beynon
1881	Oliver Gross
1883	John William Jones
1884	Charles Lyne
1885	Edwin James Grice
1886	George Hoskins
1887	Thomas Pugsley
1888	Henry Faulkner
1889	Mark Mordey
1890	Samuel Batchelor
1891	Henry John Davis
1892	Thomas Jones
1893	Frederick Phillips
1894	James C. Sanders
1895	John R. Richards
1896	Thomas Goldsworthy
1897	Alfred Robert Bear
1898	Thomas Henry Howell
1899	George Greenland
1900	William H. Brown
1901	Henry John Davies
1902	John Holman Dunn
1903	W. Clifford Phillips
1904	Robert Wilkinson
1905	John Liscombe
1906	Frederick Phillips
1907	Thomas Parry
1908	Graham W. White
1909	William Miles Blackburn
1910	John Henry Williams
1911	John McGinn
1912	Charles P. Simmonds
1913	John Lloyd Davies
1914	Frederick Pring Robjent
1915	Charles Thomas
1916	Alfred Swash
1917	William Evans
1918	Henry Charles Parfitt
1919	Peter Wright
1920	William Augustus Lintin
1921	Edwin Ambrose Charles
1922	Edward Davies
1923	Charles F. Williams
1924	William Ellis Robertson
1925	Cyrus Thomas Clissitt
1926	Arthur Thomas William James
1927	Frank Quick
1928	Walter Thomas Griffiths
1929	W.H.B. Williams
1930	Thomas Crowther
1931	Griffith A. Jones
1932	Walter J. Wall
1933	Frank J. Humphries
1934	William F.E. Smith
1935	William Casey
1936	Isaiah Cameron Vincent
1937	Mary Ann Hart
1938	John Robert Wardell
1939	Richard Davies
1940	John Henry Swallows
1941	William George Rudd

1942	George Scott
1943	Henry Godfrey Barter
1943 +	Alfred Henry Pursey
1944	George William Armstead
1945	Sarah Jane Hayward
1946	Reginald Silas Tyack
1947 - 1949	Thomas Francis Mooney
1949	Mary Josephine Dunn
1950 - 1951	Albert Edward Willis
1951 - 1952	Albert Edwain Pugh
1952 - 1953	Arthur F. Dolman
1953 - 1954	William Pinnell
1954 - 1955	Maurice Selby
1955 - 1956	Letitia Bell
1956 - 1957	Frederick V. Cornford
1957 - 1958	Frederick G. Hopton
1958 - 1959	Herbert R. Nock
1959 - 1960	Edwin Aston
1960 - 1961	George H. Coulson
1961 - 1962	Herbert H. Jones
1962 - 1963	Reginald Pook
1963 - 1964	William T. Vaughan
1964 - 1965	Percy C. Jones
1965 - 1966	Alfred G. Lovell
1966 - 1967	Thomas L. Pardoe
1967 - 1968	Cecil A. Stone
1968 - 1969	William . Huckle
1969 - 1970	Lilian Mabel Bowen
1970 - 1971	Sidney Teece Miller
1971 - 1972	Stewart McDougamm Watson
1972 - 1973	Frederick Arthur Edwards
1973 - 1974	Eric William Rowthorn
1975 - 1976	Roger Williams
1976 - 1977	Stanley Pritchard
1977 - 1978	Aubrey Hames
1978 - 1979	Edna Bosley
1979 - 1980	G. Mathias
1980 - 1981	Roy Morris
1981 - 1982	Leslie J. Knight
1982 - 1983	Ruby Kehmstedt
1983 - 1984	Betty Clifford
1984 - 1985	Rev. Cyril Summers
1985 - 1986	Trevor Warren
1986 - 1987	Reginald Lloyd
1987 - 1988	Robert F. Allen
1988 - 1989	Veronica J. Brydon
1989 - 1990	Rosemary J.M. Butler
1990 - 1991	Harry G. Jones
1991 - 1992	Harry Williams
1992 - 1993	Alan J. Perry
1993 - 1994	Joan W. Jepps
1994 -1995	Edward J. Travers
1995 - 1996	W. John Jenkins
1996 - 1997	Lloyd R. Turnbull
1997 - 1998	Robert Charles Bright C.B.E.
1998 - 1999	Kenneth Powell
1999 - 2000	Frederick Sweeting
2000 - 2001	Graham Dally
2001 - 2002	Ronald Morris
2002 - 2003	Bob Poole
2002 - 2004	Ray Truman
2004 - 2005	Paul Cockeram
2005 - 2006	Ken Critchley

The Chartist Riot

The scene is at the top of Stow Hill, with a corner of St. Woolos Cathedral on the left. Angry crowds converge and make their way down the road. John Frost harangues the crowd, while next to him a supporter using a primitive loudspeaker (on display in the Newport Museum) calls for their attention.

▲ Steelworks

On the left is an open furnace. A workman is pulling a white-hot bar of steel across the floor, while behind him another man pulls the next bar out of the fire. On the right, men are handling a still glowing sheet through the mill in which the steel bars are rolled out to sheets. Two men on either side of the mill regulate the pressure. At the back on the right is a small crane, while a larger one in the centre handles a load of steel sheets on a trolley.

The Arrival of the ▲ Americans

The third panel depicts the arrival of the Americans on a troop-carrier at Newport Docks during World War II. Soldiers are coming down the gangway. A big crane handles a light tank. On the right is an Officer and a group of soldiers carrying their kit. Below are more soldiers being directed by a British Liaison Officer.

Building of the George Street Bridge ▲

Returning to the head of the stars, (depicted in the first set of panels) is the last full-size mural, showing the building of George Street Bridge, opened in April 1964. The two ends of the Bridge are moving towards each other across the river. Everywhere are cranes, scaffolding and men engaged in work. On the left is a group of people who have come to see the progress of construction. In this group, the artist painted portraits of (left-right) Mr J G Iles, the Town Clerk, Alderman Arthur Dolman, Alderman Cornford and Alderman Tyack. In doing so, the artist has followed the tradition of including portraits of friends and sponsors of his work. As the Corporation or the whole Council could not be included, the artist chose the four men intimately connected with the commissioning of the murals as representatives.

52

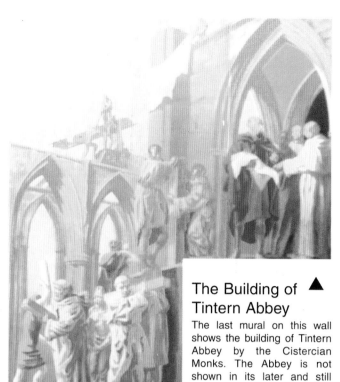

The Building of ▲ Tintern Abbey

The last mural on this wall shows the building of Tintern Abbey by the Cistercian Monks. The Abbey is not shown in its later and still existing shape, as can be seen today in the Wye Valley. On the right, a master builder explains the plan to the Abbot, while in the centre and on the left, monks and bondsmen are busy carrying and setting up beams and stones.

The Burning of ▲ Newport Castle

The first scene depicted on this wall is the burning of Newport Castle. On the left, Owain Glyndwr, the attacker, and his Standard Bearer, beckon to his troops who are jumping into the shallow water from a barge and attacking the castle through the watergate and the windows.

The Battle of Agincourt

In this panel, King Henry V stands astride his fallen horse defending himself against a French Knight who bears down on him. To the King's assistance comes a Welsh Knight, Sir Dafydd Gam, who rides up behind him with sword aloft. Around this group the battle rages. The French, among whom are two men in the blue coats of the Dauphin, are falling back. Welsh Archers, standing firmly on the hill on the left, are forcing the French Knights to flee. ▼

The Surrender of Raglan Castle

This panel depicts a scene from the Civil War. In the background is the castle, very much as it looks today. Out of the main entrance march the garrison, in full battledress, guns primed, flags flying - honours which had been granted to them in the Articles of Surrender. In the left foreground the Earl of Worcester, owner of the castle, with two ladies of his family, talks to General Fairfax, leader of the Cromwellian soldiers. The Earl is wearing Elizabethan clothes, a fashion he was to follow all his life. Both his and General Fairfax's features are taken from contemporary portraits in the National Portrait Gallery, London.

Civic Centre Murals, 1994.

We are privileged to here reproduce photographs of the Feibusch murals, the originals of which grace the interior of Newport's Civic Centre. These giant works of art depict milestones in the history of Newport and Gwent from Roman times until the near present and are the brilliant work of celebrated artist Hans Feibusch. Mr Feibusch painted them thirty years ago and although now 96 years old he is happily still active and living in London.

Our thanks to Newport Borough Council for their permission to reproduce them.

Celtic Settlement ▲

In the background can be seen a few round thatched huts and the outline of a stockade flanked by banks of earth and stone. These banks, which are connected by a wooden bridge, dominate and protect the approach to the village. Along the road, a group of traders are travelling. An old soldier with pike and shield, his hair brushed up into a stiff crown, leads the way. On the left are armed men guarding the entrance to the village.

The Roman Settlement at Caerleon ▲

The First panel shows an Imperial Legate, standing with his officials under a purple canopy, saluting the troops. Two sacrificial rams are led past; standard bearers, legionnaires and cavalry follow. On the left, a group of Britons look on sullenly. The winged figure on the column (right) is not an angel, but a Goddess of Victory.

The Coming of Christianity to South Wales ▶

In this centre panel a Saint, perhaps St. Tathan, steps ashore with his disciples and is received by a local King, Caradoc, whose soldiers, together with some other people, look on with suspicion or perhaps welcome.

Now and then . . .

Royal Oak Pub Chepstow Road

Rebuilt in 2000, The Royal Oak pub now renamed Tobey''s Restaurant.

Clarence Place, showing the top end of Corporation Road with the Coliseum Cinema on the right.

The Coliseum Cinema now demolished in 2000, and replaced by a three storey block of flats.

Clarence Place showing the Cenotaph with the Regal Cinema to the left of the cinema.

Clarence Place in 2001 with Clarence House office block and multi storey car park in the centre and the Odeon Cinema behind the Cenotaph.

Maindee Square - Chepstow Road c1908

Maindee Square, Chepstow Road c2001

Newport Castle in the days when it was used for storage and a brewery.

Newport Castle 2002

Savoy Restaurant and the general post office that stoop on the corner of Station Approach c1912.

Office block, car park and café with the now restored post office front premises which are now used as offices c2002

High Street, Newport, showing the Corn Exchange Clock Tower on the left and the Market Arcade on the right c1903.

High Street, Newport, with the reserved frontage of the general post office on the left. The new office block and car park at centre, with part of Newport Castle in the far centre.

Westgate Square in c1908 showing the Town Hall Clock in the centre. The Westgate Hotel on the far right.

Westgate Square 2002.

A view from Llanarth Street showing Lloyds Bank and the Talbot Inn. On the right situated at the bottom of Charles Street.

Commercial Street 2002.

Commercial Street c1910. Newport Central Hall on the extreme right, and the YMCA on the left of the picture.

Commercial Street in 2001.

Commercial Street c1905. Looking up Commercial Street from the junction of Cardiff Road and Kingsway.

Commercial Street 2001.

Commercial Road c1908, leading to Pill.

Commercial Road c2001 as it is today.

Caerleon Road c1920. Photograph taken from the corner of Duckpool Road on the right looking towards Caerleon.

Caerleon Road in the year 2001.

The Ship Inn c1900 photograph taken from Caerleon Bridge and looking towards Christchurch on the hill, in the distance.

The Ship Inn, Caerleon as it looked in 2001.

High Street c1920 looking towards the Westgate Hotel in Westgate Square

High Street, Newport in 2001.

Bridge Street c1908. Looking towards the Queen Hotel. Photograph taken from the corner of Bridge Street and High Street.

Bridge Street 2001. Note the doorway to the bank moved to the corner from High Street.

70

Westgate Square c1906 taken at the bottom of Stow Hill and looking towards High Street.

Westgate Square in 2001.

Commercial Street c1920's, Charles Street on the left of the picture with Reynolds Department store on corner left, Llanarth Street is on the right with Wildings as Bee-Hive Store.

Commercial Street 2001 with the Trustee Savings bank on the corner of Charles Street, to the left, and Clarke's shoe shop on the corner of Llanarth Street on the right.

The Handpost, photograph taken from the junction of Risca Road and Bassaleg Road

The Handpost in 2001.

The Handpost c1908 looking towards Risca Road

The Handpost, showing the Handpost Hotel on the left, Risca Road in the centre of the picture 2001.

Maindee Square c1922 leading to Clarence Place, Maindee School to the right in the far distance.

Maindee Square 2001. From the junction of Wharf Road and Victoria Avenue.

Caerleon Road c1920 taken from the corner of Mordern Road, showing shops galore, butchers, bakers, sweets and spuds, but not a supermarket in sight.

Caerleon Road 2001, taken from the same spot but a different view point. In time everything changes, you can bank on it.

Chepstow Road c1910 with Maindee School on the left.

Chepstow Road 2002, Maindee School demolished the site is now a car park.

Chepstow Road c1922. Maindee Square looking towards the city centre, of course it was town centre in those days. The George Hotel on the right, corner of Victoria Avenue.

Chepstow Road c2001. The George Hotel still on the corner of Victoria Avenue. Photograph taken from the junction of Wharf Road and Victoria Avenue.

Church Road c1910. Showing Duckpool Road to the left, Christchurch Hill Centre and Fairoak Avenue to the right, note the tramlines came to an end at this junction

Church Road c2001, same view roundabout here.

The Ship Hotel, Caerleon, c1930's just before Caerleon Bridge and the road leading to Belmont Hill and Christchurch.

The Ship Hotel, Caerleon, in the late sixties and early seventies, the hotel was run by Bill and Murial Hopkins, the parents of Sir Anthony Hopkins, actor And film star.

Clarence Place c1912. Looking towards Caerleon Road to the left and Chepstow Road to the right, photograph taken before the cenotaph was built.

Clarence Place 2001. Behind the cenotaph is the tax office.

The Post Office, High Cross, Newport.

82

Cross Hands Hotel in the thirties on the corner of Chepstow Road and Somerton Road.

Cross Hands Hotel 2001 on the corner of Somerton Road

Tom (Toya) Lewis

Tom Lewis, the boy hero from Pill, Newport, who at the age of fifteen risked his life , time and time again in efforts to rescue workmen trapped beneath the timber shutterings that had collapsed during the workings of the South Dock extensions in July 1909.

A POSTCARD ISSUED IN JULY 1909 OF THE NEWPORT DOCK DISASTER AND THE BOY HERO, TOM LEWIS, AGE 15

The Newport Dock Disaster

Young Tom (Toya) Lewis on horseback

W H Davies 1871-1940

Newport's Tramp Poet

To Stand and Stare

The exact place of birth of William Henry Davies is somewhat vague; we know that he was born in 1871 at Portland Street, Newport, either in the Church House Inn or a few doors away, to Mary and Francis Davies who had borne four other sons. Sadly, three by this time had died leaving at the time of William's birth only one son, Francis, who was retarded.

Three years later a sister, Matilda, was born and in the same year, 1874, his father died. Soon after, William's mother re-married and went away leaving all three children in the care of their grandfather, Captain Francis Davies, the landlord of the Church House Inn, who felt it his duty to bring up the children.

William Henry's birth was registered on 3rd July 1871, but for unknown reasons, he always celebrated his birthday on 20th April each year.

Young Davies spent his early days in a street with trains and shops at one end and the glass-like waters of the town Dock at the other. Pillgwently in the 1870's was nothing more than a dockside village surrounded by green fields and rows of little grey houses—popping up like mushrooms. In those days there was plenty of room for expansion in Pill.

William Henry lived in a world where to survive, one had to "do it yourself" or perish. One had to stand with feet firmly planted on the ground, wave your arms for elbow room and use the brain to pull oneself out of the mud.

From the start, W.H. did just that. He learnt to run hard and as an energetic youngster would often lead other boys in games, etc., which took great vitality. He was taught the art of boxing and there were times when he certainly needed that. Often as a boy, Davies would arrive on the doorstep of "The Church House" proving to everyone that his blood was of the common variety, deep red.

In 1879 Captain Davies surrendered his publican's license and went to live at 38 Raglan Street. Young Davies then attended Temple Street school, that is, as often as they could catch him, for more often than not, at every opportunity he would play truant and was sometimes found making mud castles on the banks of the Usk.

Frequently he was led down Commercial Street by their maidservant, one hand holding his and the other taking him by the scruff of the neck.

He also learned to steal - one is not sure whether he was taught this futile activity by other boys or whether, in fact, he taught them.

During one of these escapades, Davies and some other boys of school age were stealing articles from a grocery shop when, suddenly a bottle of perfume fell to the floor. The lads ran from the shop, half way up Commercial Street, the air scented with the tell tale smell of Jasmine. Davies, with a clean pair of heels ran to make it for home but on this occasion, his running ability didn't help him. With half of Pill shouting "Stop Thief", he had little chance of making good his escape. He was caught, the house was duly searched and enough goods were found for Davies to have his own stall in Newport market.

In an attempt to save his grandson from punishment, Captain Davies offered to settle for goods stolen and to pay fines imposed upon him. Six boys were charged, Davies being one of them and the police proceedings were published in the Merlin in January 1884.

Davies assumed the role of ringleader and in his autobiography states:

"I and my Lieutenant were sentenced to 12 strokes of the birch, whilst the other four, not being caught red handed, each received 6 strokes."

Young Davies had brought terrible disgrace to his grandparents and to make amends immediately took after-school work in an ironmongers shop where he earned 5/- a week from running errands. Because of the stricter regime imposed on him by his grandfather, he had become a virtual prisoner of "The House" being allowed out of doors only to attend day school, Sunday school and to work at the ironmongers.

To console himself during the long winter evenings he began to sketch, mainly pictures of ships, for which he soon found a ready market from sympathetic neighbours who would purchase his drawings for 6d. each. This told him two things - he could sell and had an artistic ability.

Young William read books far into the night and soon began to dream of literary fame as well as artistic acclaim. He wrote many essays and was a frequent visitor to the local beauty spots, often leaving an energetic game to seek solitude at Tredegar Park where he would sit and watch the deer lazily grazing and derive inspiration for further writings.

With a school friend, David Rees, he joined the mutual Improvement Class at a Baptist church. In Rees, William Henry gained not only a friend and classmate, but an avid reader of classical poetry. Soon, Davies was also writing and reciting his own works and at the age of fourteen had written a poem on Death.

On leaving school, his first full time job was as an apprentice to a Picture Frame Maker and later he moved to Bristol where he learnt the art of drinking.

Without doubt, W H Davies has brought to the lives of many, past and present, the joy of poetry, to read him is to know him, and to know him is to love him (ask my wife!). Here is one of his many poems which is a favourite of ours.

Forgiveness

Stung by a spiteful wasp,
I let him go life free;
That proved the difference
In him and me.

For had I killed my foe,
It had proved to me at once;
The stronger wasp, and no
More difference.

Davies had a yen to travel and often dreamed of far off lands. Eventually he made trips to Canada and America, mainly by cattle boat. When in America, he walked in the sun by day and slept under the stars at night.

W. H. had little money and was considered by most to be a tramp. He was once jailed for vagrancy, together with other Hobos, usually in a state of drunkenness, and he often picked up prostitutes.

As he walked through life, he observed and recorded in verse what he saw and felt. Determined to find fame and fortune, he sailed back home to the cold, wet land of his birth. He vowed never to leave Newport again, but his stay lasted for only two months. He was depressed beyond words to find his school chums had grown into dull husbands, struggling against poverty and failure. During those two months Davies was drinking hard, when, one day he saw a newspaper headline - 'Canada, The Land of Gold". Determined to join the goldrush in the Klondyke, he returned to Canada and planned to ride freight trains to his destination.

On Sunday, 20th March 1899 in a town called Renfrew, Davies and a companion called Three-fingered Jack decided to jump a train going direct to Winnipeg. The jump was successfully made by Jack, but William missed his footing as the train gathered speed and he fell to the track as the train moved out of sight. For a moment he lay there not feeling any pain, but on his second attempt to raise his body he discovered his right foot had been severed at the ankle.

Finally, after long periods in hospitals, his leg was amputated at the knee. Davies returned to England on crutches, but quickly had a false leg fitted. His tramping days were far from over.

For a while he lived in London and moved around with other poets of the day. His poems were being read by a much wider circle, but were earning him little or no money. He paid for copies of his work to be printed and very often gave them away. On one occasion, he sent copies of his poems through the mail in small batches to people listed in "Who's Who" and asked for the princely sum of 2/6d. Not all sent him money, but one reacted to his work.

George Bernard Shaw sent Davies a letter which included a pound, saying that Davies, the author, was a real poet whose simplicity was "Like a draught of water in the desert". Shaw also wrote that he would not earn any money by selling poetry, but should use the pound to send copies to influential critics.

Davies continued his work and to eke out a living, went from door to door selling 'boot laces'.

He made a number of visits to Gwent and sometimes avoided Newport like the plague— (he was not always welcomed by his relatives). On one occasion, W.H. arrived at Chepstow with the intention of seeing his relatives, thought about it, lost his nerve and spent the next few weeks stumping about Gwent. He stayed at Tintern all day, long enough to see the Abbey by moonlight; he walked the Wye Valley with the beautiful Wye River as his only companion. He became a familiar sight all over Gwent — Monmouth, Abergavenny, Pontypool, Crumlin — for he could be seen coming a mile off. His slightly theatrical attire, his soft black hat, red handkerchief (to hide his grubby collar), walking stick and wooden leg made it almost impossible not to take notice of this limping stranger, and wherever he went in this pleasant land, he wrote about it.

Leisure

What is this life, if full of care,
We have no time to stand and stare.

No time to stand beneath the boughs
and stare as long as sheep or cows.

No time to see when woods we pass,
when squirrels hide their nuts in grass.

No time to see in broad daylight,
streams full of stars like skies at night.

No time to turn at beauties glance,
and watch her feet, how they can dance.

No time to wait till her mouth can
enrich that smile her eyes began.

A poor life this, if full of care,
We have no time to stand and stare.

Davies paid for more of his poems to be published and some of them found their way to Sir John Adcock, a famous critic of the day, who gave his poems enthusiastic reviews.

The tide had turned, a certain fame had come his way and he often made newspaper headlines as the miraculous "Tramp Poet".

Edward Thomas, the welsh poet, advised him to write his life story. G. B. Shaw agreed and declared it must be called "The Autobiography of a Super Tramp".

William Henry decided to return to Newport and spent many months looking for a suitable house in which to live. Daily he would walk from his mother's home at 6 Llanwern Street, in search of his perfect retreat. This he found on a hill over-looking the town—No. 1 Woodland Road.

Davies began writing in a top floor room where he enjoyed panoramic views of the River Usk meeting the Severn Channel. It seemed that he had found his "Shangri-la", but after only one week he was given notice to relinquish his tenancy. He discovered that his eccentric landlady was notoriously fond of evicting her tenants. He left Woodland Road and moved to 42 Dudley Street, this time convinced he could write his book there.

He eventually left Newport in February 1906 — never again to try and set up house in Gwent.
Davies completed his book "The Autobiography of a Super Tramp" which was finally published in 1908. It has since become a classic.

On further visits to Newport, Davies praised the town for its remarkable beauty despite its dockland canvas. He recommended visitors to climb Stow Hill or Christchurch Hill to admire the view over the ships and islands in the Channel.

When he revisited Allt-yr-yn, Davies wrote of it:

The most beautiful part of Newport is the green country called Allt-yr-yn, which has a clear canal coming down lock by lock with Twin Barlwm mountain in the distance.

"I had not been in Newport long before I was walking in that direction, when I was well out of town and stood on a hillside road where I could see down into that wonderful green valley, I became deeply affected at the sight, for there was not the least change .. . In a little while I began to feel tantalised and tormented that it was still the same whereas, I myself, had undergone so many serious changes."

Davies had visited Allt-yr-yn many times as a boy, visits which inspired him to write poetry like:

'DAYS THAT HAVE BEEN'

Can I forget the sweet days that have been,
When poetry first began to warm my blood;
When from the hills of Gwent I saw the earth,
Burned into two by Severn's silver flood.

When I would go alone at night to see
The moonlight, like a big white Butterfly,
Dreaming on that old castle near Caerleon,
While at its side the Usk went softly by.

When I would stare at lovely clouds in heaven,
Or watch them when reported by deep streams;
When feeling pressed like thunder, but would not
Break into that grand music of my dreams?

Can I forget the sweet days that have been,
The villages so green I have been in;
Llantarnam, Magor, Malpas and Llanwern,
Lliswerry, Old Caerleon and Alteryn?

Can I forget the banks of Malpas brook,
Or Ebbw's voice in such a wild delight,
As on he dashed with pebbles in his throat,
Gurgling towards the sea with all his might?

Ah, when I see a leafy village now,
I sigh and ask it for Llantarnam's Green;
I ask each river where is Ebbw's voice -
In memory of the sweet days that have been.

Davies, at the age of fifty-one, having already lost his mother, was growing tired of the bachelor existence he had been living.

In London he met a young woman over thirty years his junior. Her name was Helen Payne. Davies had been her lover for over three months when he calmly announced to all that he intended to marry his Helen.

His relatives were shocked and did not attend the ceremony which took place in East Grinstead on the 5th February, 1923. His great romance is the subject of a recent novel "Dear Emma".

Davies decided to move out of London. He needed a place to live where he could find solitude and be within easy reach of Newport and his relatives. They chose to live in the Cotswold village of Nailsworth and stayed happily married for seventeen years.

His writing continued, his books were published and his poems amounted to no less than seven hundred and forty-nine which appear in a book published by Jonathan Cape "The Complete Poems of W. H. Davies".

Davies was honoured in his native town. In 1930 a civic luncheon was arranged by the people of Newport.

Again, in 1938, he visited the town bringing with him his wife, Helen. On that occasion the meal was delayed whilst the Mayor and Davies visited the Church House Inn in Portland Street.

The B.B.C. discovered that Davies was a talented broadcaster, but one of his programmes ended in disaster. The poet had a habit of leaning back on his chair whilst he read. On this occasion he lost his balance - down

Newport born poet, William Henry Davies.

he went, wooden leg and all. The broadcast ended abruptly with a cry of "Oh Damn".

In the spring of 1938, he suffered a slight stroke but he recovered. On 21st September the same year, Newport unveiled a plaque in honour of the poet's achievements. The ceremony took place outside the Church House Inn. Davies had warned the organisers that he was too ill to make a speech, so it was left to John Masefield, the Poet Laureate, to reply on his behalf. Davies was seen to be shaking and perspiring with nerves throughout the speeches, but he expressed a determination to do something for the town, "If only time and energy allowed". He then asked to be driven to Ridgeway to look at Allt-yr-yn and was also taken to the Amphitheatre at Caerleon.

During 1939, after a series of severe heart attacks, he was warned by doctors to avoid all excitement and exertion. He was told that the constant dragging of his wooden leg had weakened his heart.

Davies loved his Newport and childhood memories came flooding back to him when he wrote:

'THE RICHEST STONES'

My wandering days have run their course,
and Age is in my flesh and bones;
Of all the temples, domes and towers,
Where have I found the richest stones?

The little house where I was born,
And where my early childhood lies,
Was built with solid blocks of gold,
And all its walls had diamond eyes!

W.H. Davies died on 26th September, 1940. He loved life and he loved Newport.

The Super Tramp has left his work for all to see, and while its possible to take a book from a shelf, it's easy to get the feeling that he is not far away... but just for the moment, he has stopped writing.

His roof, the stars, were jewels set in the crown,
His bag, laid bare, no jewels were ever found,
His wealth, his words, are there for all to see,
We shared his house, now left, for you and me.

Royal visit to Newport

In 1937, King George VI and Queen Elizabeth came to Newport and were greeted by hundreds of well wishers giving them an overwhelming reception. They left Newport Railway Station to be greeted by pavements filled with cheering crowds, from Station Approach, High Street and Bridge Street. The purpose of their visit was to cut the first sod in St. Mary's Garden, near to Fields Road and Gold Tops for the building of the of the new Civic Centre.

Banners were raised to welcome the King and Queen to Newport, a Banner reading 'Good Luck to our Majesties' King George VI and Queen Elizabeth was raised on Cardiff Road near Tredegar House and Park, also on the site near to the bridge that crossed over the Ebbw river.

Flags filled the air over the railway Bridge at the top of Bridge Street, to the left of the picture above are a small group of early morning well wishers making sure of their place for a good view of the proceedings.

The South Wales Argus offices at the top of High Street was all decked up with loyal greetings to their Majesties, while a early morning crowd soon began to fill up the Station Approach to secure a right royal view of the King and Queen.

Newport Town folk go up in the world to get the best possible view, sitting comfortably on the National Provincial Bank window ledge at the corner of Bridge Street, they were banking on a first class viewing from top to bottom. I hope the brought cushions for the long wait.

At Station Approach a huge welcome sign flutters in the breeze, perhaps the sign itself is getting excited at the possibility of a first class view of the King and Queen.

Newport Station, platform 1. Their Majesties have arrived and are being welcomed by the Lord Lieutenant of Monmouthshire, the Mayor of Newport, Major Vincent and Newport Councillors.

As the royal party leave Newport Station and enters Station approach, the sun begins to shine and crowd's give out a tremendous roar, it's 'Welcome to Newport' all the way.

Music fills the air and with cheering crowd's of flag waving Newportonians the King and Queen make their way through the sunshine to the guard of honour

The band played the National Anthem and the Crowd's sang along with them, 'God save our gracious King', then all was silent as King George inspected the troops. Then another tremendous roar came from the crowd's as the King joined the Queen making their way to an awaiting vehicle.

Crowd's fill the High Street and with the old General Post Office building in the background, some Newport folk went up the wall to get the best view, and if you found yourself in the middle of the crowd by bringing your own step ladder you placed yourself head and shoulders above the rest.

Any moment now, it's a tight squeeze but it's worth it, the things we do for a couple of coppers'.

Troops line up for the Royals to make their exit from Station Approach and into High Street. The soldiers present arms as the King and Queen pass by.

Order arms from the men as field Marshal's, Generals, and Councillors walk behind the Royal Couple.

The scene at Westgate Square and High Street as the Royal car turns into Bridge Street followed by other vehicles on their way to St. Mary's Gardens.

Spectators still banking on a first class view of a right Royal visit to the town.

"Who will buy a nice coloured ribbon, red white and blue if you like", it's not every year that Royalty comes to Newport.

Newportonians patiently waiting for the arrival of the King and Queen on their visit to Newport Civic Centre

Crowds of privileged dignitarys, councillors, Justice of the peace and men of the church were waiting in the grounds of St. Mary's House for the Royal couple to arrive. The moment has come.

While the Lord Lieutenant of Monmouthshire looks on with other top Councillors, the Mayor of Newport, Councillor Major Vincent hands the spade to King George.

The Mayor together with Queen Elizabeth watch as the King cuts the first sod for the foundation s of the new Civic Centre.

Newport in the mist of time

Newport Town bridge and castle in 1890's.

Newport Town bridge and castle in 1910.

Newport Bridge looking towards Clarence Place with the Dome of Newport Technical College showing centre c1912.

Commercial Street. Charles Street to the left with Reynolds Departmental Store on the corner and Wildings Bee-Hive store on the corner of Llanarth Street to the right. c1920's.

Commercial Road looking towards Pill. Photograph taken from the junction of Commercial Street and Cardiff Road near the railway crossing. c1912.

Looking up Commercial Street from the junction of Cardiff Road to the left and Kingsway to the right (c) 1905.

Photograph taken from Newport Bridge looking towards High Street with the Corn Exchange standing proud with Clock Tower c1914.

High Street looking towards the Westgate Hotel in the centre of picture. (c) 1930's.

Clarence Place, showing the top end of Corporation Road with the Coliseum Cinema on the right c1920's.

Clarence Place near the Cenotaph and the junction of Caerleon Road to the left of the war memorial and Chepstow Road to the right c1925.

Clarence Place c1915 looking towards Caerleon Road to the left with Railway Bridge and Chepstow Road to the right.

Clarence Place in the 1930's with the Regal Cinema just to the left of the cenotaph.

Chepstow Road from the junction of Victoria Avenue and Wharf Road looking towards Eveswell. Early 1900's.

Chepstow Road again near Maindee Square looking towards Eveswell about 1912.

Looking down High Street from the top of a tram. Old Green pub on the left, Corn Exchange with Clock Tower c1910.

High Street again in the 1920's. Photograph taken from the Old Green crossing.

Members of Newport Town council in Chepstow Road on a Sunday morning Mayors Parade in 1906.

King George V with Lord Tredegar on Caerleon Road c1910.

Queen's Square, Bridge Street, showing the Queen's Hotel left and the Lyceum Theatre on the right 1908.

Queen's Square again, early 1900's.

The Lyceum Theatre, Bridge Street.

Queen's Square, in the twenties.

The Old Green Crossing, looking towards Clarence Place.

Commercial Street, looking towards Westgate Square.

Westgate Square with the Town Hall Clock ticking away. Westgate Hotel on the right of photograph.

High Street from the corner of Station Approach in the 1930's.

Woodland Road, off Victoria Avenue.

Carrisbrook Road, off Chepstow Road.

Maindee Square, Chepslow Road.

Maindee Baths, Victoria Avenue c1938.

The Town Bridge, Newport Castle on the left with a row of shops on the right, Jay's, John Hall, Singer's Sewing Machine Shop, J. Kyrle Fletcher, Godfrey's Music Shop. c1950.

High Street looking towards the Station Approach c1949.

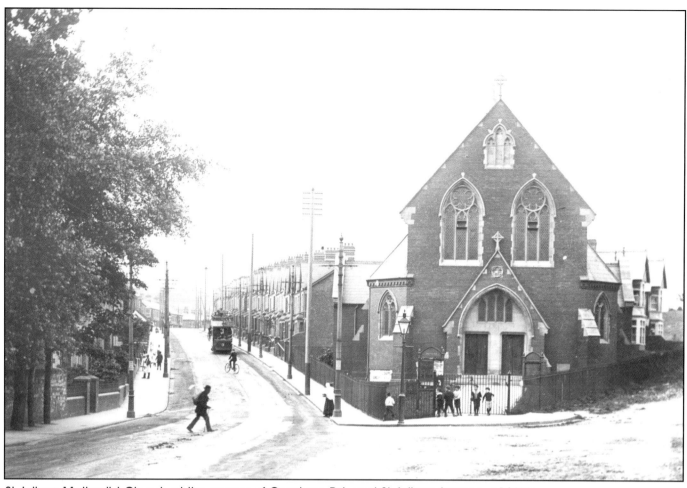

St Julians Methodist Church at the corner of Caerleon Rd. and St Julians Avenue. c1920's.

Christchurch Road with St Julians Road to the right.

Barrack Hill early 1900's.

The Handpost to the left and Risca Road.

Shops at Maindee Square c1908.

Shops in Maindee Square, Chepstow Road c1908.

Kingsway snowed under. Newport Market on the left.

The canal Fourteen Locks.

Station Approach taxi rank.

Newport Station at an earlier time.

Maindee School Chepstow Road. Since demolished.

Lysaughts Club and Institute, Corporation Road.

The museum at Caerleon. c1906.

The Square, High Street, Caerleon.

High Street, Caerleon. c1906.

High Street, Caerleon. c1910.

Ship Inn and Toll House, corner of Belmont Road, Caerleon.

High Street, Caerleon.

A view from Caerleon Bridge looking up the Approach Road to Christchurch on the hill.

Charles Williams' house on the corner.

Caerleon Museum and extension.

Newport Technical College, Clarence Place.

Queen's School, Stow Hill (now demolished).

Statue of Charles Morgan of the Tredegar family in Bridge Street.

Chartist memorial statues in Westgate Square to commemorate the uprising in 1839.

Civic Centre, Newport.

Floral elegance at the Civic Centre.

128

Public walkway to the embankment of the River Usk. 2002.

The Wave situated near the Town Bridge and Newport Castle.

Masonic Hall, Dock Street.

The Kings Church, Lower Dock Street, Newport.

Market Building Upper Dock Street.

Snowed up at the junction of Commercial Street.

Cold Storage, Shaftesbury Street, now demolished.

131

Newport Train station.

Midland Bank, corner of Stow Hill and Bridge Street, now HSBC bank.

Newport Arcade, High Street.

High Street near Kings Head Hotel now pedestrianised.

Elevated view of Macey's Bar at Queenway.

Another view of High Street.

133

Argus Office that was on the left and showing an elevated view of High Street.

Looking across Queensway with a view of the Civic Centre Clock Tower.

Looking across Queensway.

John Frost Square

A view from Newport Station looking towards Cambrian Road.

Cambrian Road and Ferris's Restaurant.

Carnegie Library, Corporation Road.

Aerial view of John Frost Square.

Dock's Way leading to the Newport Transporter Bridge.

Virgin Cinema Leeway Trading Estate (now UGC Cinema).

Virgin Cinema (now UGC Cinema).

Mechanical clock from Ebbw Vale Garden
Festival Site; now in John Frost Square. Named
'The Nick of Time'.

River Usk Embankment public walkway 2002.

The Wave on the River Usk bank at Newport.

River Walk - 2002.

City carpark & high rise building near Kingsway.

Refurbishment of the Old Town Dock.

Riverside Old Town Dock.

Refurbishment area of Old Town Dock.

Gatehouse at Belvue Park on the Cardiff Road.

Corn Exchange car park, near the old green roundabout.

Victoria Place off Stow Hill

STC Electronics Division, now Fitness Centre, Corporation Road.

Aerial view of Newport Athletic Grounds.

Old Green roundabout near town, bridge and castle.

Clarence Place and Cenotaph, Tax Office in background.

Newport Art College , Clarence Place.

The Lighthouse near the mouth of the River Usk.

Further view of Newport Lighthouse, mouth of River Usk.

The Walkway of Newport Transporter Bridge - looking down on the west side of Newport.

"Hi everybody, it's me, the Trannie talking to you"

It seems like only yesterday that I was born and my feet were planted firmly on both sides of the River Usk. But to most people, who have the time to stand and stare at my majestic height, I have lived more than their lifetime and for many years I have

been an accepted part of the Newport skyline, that busy town near the Bristol Channel that forms the Gateway to Wales.

Newport, a town divided by its fast flowing river, has always accepted me as part of its image. Time has been good to me, the warmth of the sun invigorates me and constantly brings back my youth.

I was born on the 12th September 1906, but the idea of me becoming a Transporter Bridge was conceived in 1889 and I am still standing and in full working order with just five short years to achieve my centenary. I am considered to be the finest example of a Transporter Bridge in the United Kingdom and perhaps the world and for that I must thank my designer and engineer, Ferdinand Arnodin. Of course, there are other bridges over the Usk but none as grand and exciting as me, if you pardon my modesty. I have been told the River Usk had nothing but stepping stones to cross over the high tidal river but that was before the year 1158, afterwards the Normans came and built a wooden structure near that ruin of a Castle.

This and subsequent bridges constructed at the same spot remained the only way to cross the river for over 700 years, then things started to happen.

In 1799, the wooden bridge was demolished to make way for Newport's first stone bridge. It was made ready in 1800 at a cost of £10,864. Nice, but it had a hump back which irritated horses and carts trying to cross over it and later motor vehicles when they finally arrived.

Then I came along to put matters right. Towards the last part of the 1800s, the east side of the river started to enjoy a period of rapid development when a steel manufacturing company called Lysaghts decided to build a factory on the east side of the town and, because of this, I was born.

The people who lived around me and those who lived near my left leg in an area called Pill needed me and the service that I could offer them.

I made it easier for those who worked in the steelworks to get to work and home again in no time at all and the people of Pill loved me for that. From my great height, I have seen history passing by as the town grew larger, buildings reaching up to the sky trying to outgrow me.

New roads developing like a spider weaving its web, and ships large and small, passing through my ever open gateway and making ripples in the Usk, making waves over my sunlit image that reflects me on the water.

I have cherished memories of my many friends in Newport, for I am their guiding sign that welcomes them home. Newport people travelling on trains look out from their carriage windows for the first sight of me. It is then they realise that they are home. I believe that my Gondola is my hand, gently I carry people across the Usk – taking great care as if they are my very own children.

Members of our Royal Family paid many a visit to me, looked me up and down and, with a nod of approval, boarded my gondola knowing that they are safe in my hand. There are times when I allow people to walk up my stairways, right up to the top, almost to the stars, to reach my overhead main span.
Often I have heard hysterical laughter from happy children and sometimes from grown-ups, too, as they mount my stairway. I hear them gasp when they reach the top and scream with delight on seeing the panoramic views of Newport.

The banks of the River Usk have changed beyond all recognition from the days when I was young. I have seen the town growing from where I stand, places like John Frost Square, The Royal Gwent Hospital (now five times its original size), the re-building of Pill, a clock tower being added to the Town's Civic Centre and Llanwern Steelworks stretching from Newport almost to Caldicot and now each day without fail I get an early morning wave from my friend 'The Wave' that stands proudly on the River bank near the Old Town Bridge and the Castle. I have had my moments, of course, some happy, some sad. In 1923, I saw the Town Bridge being pulled down and that made me sad. In 1927, I saw the new Town Bridge and to me it looked great and that made me happy. Around 1961, and then without warning, another new bridge appeared on the horizon, which started to be erected further up stream. When I saw the four towers reaching up to their full height, I thought to myself, "Oi, Oi, look out, what's going on up there, they are building another Transporter Bridge and its going to be taller than me". But relief came when it turned out to be just another road bridge by the name of George, but I must not be jealous of him. Since 1964, when he was born, George and I have become very good friends and that made me happy.

I have had many moments of fame. I have starred in movies, not Hollywood ones of course, but films like 'Tiger Bay'. To watch a young Hayley Mills pretending to cling for dear life as she hung on to the outside of my gondola as I moved it slowly over the river still haunts me to this day, but then that was in 1959 and I still get a buzz from it. Oh, and then there was 'The film that never was', "Flight to Freedom" - it was going to be called, starring Newport's own John Cortez alias Tommy Evans, a Pill lad with a great tenor voice, but it never made the big screen. I can still visualise an old red London bus boarding my caring hand with a dozen or so German soldiers with fixed bayonets following in hot pursuit, acting of course. Oh, I nearly forgot to mention this, in 1985 I had a nervous breakdown. I just could not operate up to my usual standard and I was ordered to have a complete rest. I knew things were happening to me as early as 1968 when a local councillor suggested that I was too expensive to maintain and described me as being a white elephant. In 1970, an American businessman by the name of Douglas Jones offered to buy me for a million pounds, dismantle me and ship me off to the States. Once there, re-erect me somewhere near Hollywood and, of all things, he said, "If we put it up near Hollywood and there is no water to go under it, we'll divert some". The cheek of it was enough to make me shake, rattle and roll. The rattling of my girders were heard as far away as Newport Council Chambers. It was then that the council decided that I should stay in my birthplace - Newport.

Hooray for that! I was instructed to see a doctor which I did and, thank goodness, I was now on the road to recovery, but first, I had to undergo major surgery. While I was waiting for my operation, due to my rusting girders and worn-out cables, the council came and hung some light bulbs on me. Yes, they hung thousands of light bulbs all over me just to remind people that I was still the star attraction that I have always been. At night, people would look up at me and say "What a sight, look, it's Newport's Standard Lamp".

In 1985, my hospital appointment was still a long way off, so everything stopped. It was then that I decided to go privately. Excitement filled the air and in 1992, my first surgery was carried out. After many further operations I was finally declared fit for work and signed off the sick in 1995.

Today, everyone holds their celebrations around me, from Royal Occasions to Carnivals and Pill Festivals and, of course, there are my open days. At least twice a year, I open my heart and welcome everyone to visit me. In 1998, Newport Corporation invited the public to form a group called 'The Friends of the Newport Transporter Bridge'. What an honour for me to have a very supportive group around me, but then I'm worth it, and with my 100th Birthday coming up, I really do need them.

At my age, I am still very good looking, elegant and terribly fit and I am all set to become even more impressive in the years to come.

To conclude, a Newport writer once wrote a poem about me.

Iron cradle gliding through a misty morn,
Trellised legs straddle the water's edge,
Razor breeze softens the seagull sounds,
Transporter linking up both sides of town.

Gentle monster in the still of night,
Poised, waiting for the day's first light,
Moving slowly to the other land,
People huddled on its gentle hand.

Rusting giant with its arm out-stretched,
Rumbling bogey with its lines below,
Casts its shadow on the Usk itself,
Little people on a moving shelf.

Sweeping fog to ride the highest tide,
Moving Pill closer to the other side,
In time we hear with misty eyes your haunting bell,
Oh! Trannie, Trannie, you serve us well.

Terry Underwood

Thank you for that. Yours sincerely, The Trannie

The Car Transporter Bridge, Newport Mon.

Joe Shepphard - Mechanical Engineer for the bridge - right
Cliff Hammett - assistant - left

University of Wales at Caerleon.

Alt-yr-yn College University of Wales' extension.

John Lysaght Limited

Directors, Managers, Staff, Operatives and their Relatives jointly welcomed Their Majesty The King and Queen and Her Royal Highness Princess Elizabeth to Orb Iron Works on March 29th, 1944.

A gathering of some thousands of people gave a rousing reception to the Royal Visitors, who were able to see the various products of the Works in course of manufacture.

The visit made history in two ways. It was the beginnibg of Princess Elizabethis first industrial tour, and also the first visit of Royaly to the Newport Works of the Company.

These photographs are being published to meet a wish expressed in many quarters for a fitting souvenir to commemorate the honour of the occasion.

John Lysaghts company of Home Guard presenting arms at the entrance of Orb Iron works, Corporation Road, Newport to welcome the Royal Family, March 29th 1944.

His Majesty King George arriving at John Lysaght Ltd.

Their arrival at Newport Civic Centre on March 29th 1944. Her Majesty , Queen Elizabeth and her Royal Highness Princess Elizabeth being welcomed by the Mayor of Newport.

Their majesties the King and Queen and her Royal Highness Princess Elizabeth leaving a section of the OBE factory.

The King stops again for a chat with members of the crowd, while daughter Princess Elizabeth (now) pauses to listen.

King George VI stops the tour of the factory to talk to a group of ex-employees.

Queen Elizabeth accompanied by the Managing Director leaving the Orb Iron Works with a round of applause and cheers from the workforce.

Mai Jones

Song Writer, Variety Producer, Star Maker
Creator of the BBC's Radio Show "Welsh Rarebit"

Take any Sunday evening in 1911, walk up Hill Street, off Newport's Commercial Street, and stop outside the Myndd Sion Welsh Chapel. Standing there you would have heard organ music of a rare quality, and had you opened the door and looked beyond the congregation you would have been astonished to see a little girl with long fair hair and wearing a long white dress, sitting at the organ allowing her fingers to dance gracefully over the keyboard, no one would have guessed that this little girl would achieve the fame that would set the whole nation singing.

Mai Jones

Young Mai Jones, born twelve years earlier and living in Harrow Road off Corporation Road, would be leading the whole congregation as they sang with gusto the popular Welsh hymns. This she would continue to do for the next 49 years despite the pressures of the national fame she was to achieve, for Mai developed her musical talent far beyond the dreams of most musicians.
The whole world loves a success story today, her fame was achieved by her hard work and her experience in the musical world. Playing the piano at concerts and cabarets, she also provided background music for the silent movies shown at the Coliseum Cinema that stood in Clarence Place, but busy as she may have been there was always one place, at one time of the week where Mai could be found, on Sunday at 6.30pm in the Myndd Sion Welsh Chapel, Hill Street, Newport.
In 1994 with Britain at war many welshmen were called up to the armed forces and were serving their country abroad.

Thoughtfully BBC planned a radio show with welsh humour as the main ingredient, and of, course music. The job of presenting a weekly programme as a reminder of home to those faraway from Wales went to the unknown Producer Mai Jones, and armed with an abundance of enthusiasm she assembled a group of artistes from the ranks of factory workers, shop assistants, housewives, clerks, farm and mine workers. She auditioned, rehearsed, mused and moulded the into a show that was destined to become a firm favourite with British Forces everywhere. The show was called "Welsh Rarebit".

A show filled with Welsh flavoured material needed a song to create an idealistic opening for the programme, a poem which Mai had read written by a Welsh poet Lyn Joshua, began with the words "We'll keep a welcome in the Hillsides". Seated at her piano she wrote them into a manuscript but needed additional lyrics she approached a Newport man James Harper who was manager of the London Hosiery, a shop in High Street, working around the lyrics, Mai composed a lovely melody that eventually would be sung by countless millions. "We'll Keep a Welcome" resounds wherever there is a crowd of Welshmen feeling patriotic and is often sung alongside the Welsh National Anthem.

Mai Jones' Radio Shows became favourites throughout Britain with programmes like "Silver Chords", "Teatime Variety", "Out For Fun", "Welsh Music Hall", "Merry Go Round", "Just Plain", "Cuckoo", "Never A Dull Moment" and "Open House". Through these she established a core of Welsh and international entertainers many of whom became household names.

There were Comedians Harry Secombe, Stan Stennett, Wyn Calvin, Ossie Morris, Albert and Les Ward, Ossie Woble, Beryl Orde, Maudie Edwards, together with two Newport men Donald Wells and Frank James, who latterly and prior to his retirement was secretary to their Worships, the Mayor's of Newport.
There were singers: Donald Pierce, Dan Donovan, Dorothy Squires, Tessi O'Shea, Petula Clarke, David Hughes, Meryl Waite, The Lyrian Singers: The Welcome Singers, The Girls in Harmony, she even recognised the singing talents of Shirley Bassey but never actually engaged her for radio.
Mai Jones died on 7th May 1960 at the age of 61, she collapsed and died at her home in St. Marks Crescent in Newport while entertaining friends with her husband Mr Davey Davies.
At her funeral thousands lined Hill Street to say farewell outside the small Welsh Congregational Church in Newport.
Her full life had been spent continually giving of her time and talent to a nation of people that had time for her.

On June 4th 2002, while the nation was watching Queen Elizabeth's Golden Jubilee celebrations on television, the scene at the mall and the surrounding area of Buckingham Palace was packed shoulder to shoulder with well wishes estimated to number a million people, when suddenly the massed voices burst into song as the Queen, Prince Phillip and family appeared on the balcony. The music that filled the air on that memorable day was "We'll Keep A Welcome" which served as a tribute not only to Her Majesty the Queen but also to Mai Jones a reminder to us all how it began with a little girl who played the chapel organ at Mynydd Sion, the small Welsh Chapel that is still standing in Hill Street, Newport.

JOHN CASHMORE - NEWPORT - LIMITED
Shipbrokers

Part of the workforce at John Cashmore Ltd.c 1910

The Port of Newport has had many achievements over the years of which it can justly be proud of, and one of the foremost establishments on the banks of the high tidal River Usk was one of the largest privately-owned shipbreaking yards in Great Britain.

Founded in 1872, John Cashmore opened his small ship repair business with great success. By 1912, the company turned to shipbreaking, and soon took the lead in this field for the whole of Great Britain. Over the years, hundreds of war ships, steamships and submarines have been dismantled at the Newport site.

Here is a short list of vessels dismantled by John Cashmore Ltd.

Warships   - H.M.S. Collingwood
- H.M.S. Terrible
- H.M.S. Gibraltar
- H.M.S. Birkenhead
- H.M.S. Inconstant
- H.M.S. Royalist

Steamships   - Doric
- Welsh Prince
- Rosslare

Plus a large number of submarines and smaller vessels.

SHIPS BROKEN BY J. CASHMORE - NEWPORT
1910 - 1977

NAME	TYPE	TONNAGE	TONNAGE TYPE	YEAR BUILT	ARRIVED NEWPORT	COMMENTS
T.B. 106	Torpedo boat	95	D	1889	1910	J Collidge list ,not in Cashmores books
SALMON	Destroyer	310	D	1895	1912	
DRAGON	Destroyer	330	D	1895	1912	
DEVONIA	Steamer	1327	G	1879	1913	Iron
ELDORADO	Steamer	1514	G	1886	1913	Iron
BRUZIER	Destroyer	280	D	1895	1914	
CARDIFF No.1	Dredger	121	FT		Mar-15	
V.125	Destroyer	920	D	1917	Oct-21	German, scuttled Scapa
BIRKENHEAD	Crusier	5235	D	1915	Feb-22	
PERESGINE	Destroyer	1025	D	1916	Feb-22	
PHOEBE	Destroyer	1025	D	1916	Apr-22	
MUNSTER	Destroyer	1025	D	1916	Apr-22	
OBDURATE	Destroyer	1025	D,	1916	May-22	
PARKER	Destroyer	1670	D	1916	Jul-22	
NEREUS	Destroyer	1025	D	1916	Jul-22	
NERISSA	Destroyer	1025	D	1916	Aug-22	
LURCHER	Destroyer	765	D	1912	Aug-22	
LYSANDER	Destroyer	970	D	1913	Aug-22	
N.1	Submarine	1440	S	1917	Aug-22	Ex Nautilus
INCONSTANT	Crusier	3500	D	1915	Sep-22	
E.27	Submarine	660	S	1917	Nov-22	
T.B 33	Torpedo boat	300	D	1909	Nov-22	
T.B 35	Torpedo boat	300	D	1909	Nov-22	
ROYALIST	Crusier	3500	D	1915	Dec-22	
E.33	Submarine	660	S	1916	Dec-22	
G.5	Submarine	700	S	1916	Dec-22	
COLLINGWOOD	Battleship	13250	D	1910	Mar-23	
N	Destroyer	1025	D	1916	Mar-23	
P.6	Patrol boat	580	D	1917	Jun-23	
TIRADE	Destroyer	1080	D	1917	Jul-23	
LUCY	Dredger	430	G	1900	Aug-23	Llanelli
PC.63	Patrol boat	680	D	1917	Aug-23	
P.14	Patrol boat	570	D	1916	Sep-23	
CORDELIA	Crusier	3750	D	1915	Sep-23	
VESUVIUS	Torpedo boat	245	D	1874	Sep-23	
UNDAUNTED	Crusier	3500	D	1914	Nov-23	
GIBRALTA	Deport ship	7700	D	1894	Dec-23	Ex Crusier
BARRY BARGE	Barge	36	G		Dec-23	
CARDIFF BARGE	Barge	140	M		Dec-23	
CLAN KENNEDY	Cargo liner	5086	G	1907	Jul-24	
HOLDERNESS	Minesweeper	750	D	1917	Sep-24	
CAISSON Q	Dock gate	96	FT		Oct-24	
CAISSON M	Dock gate	96	FT		Dec-24	
LIVERPOOL	Steamer	686	G	1892	Dec-24	
LEON PANCALDO	Cargo	2418	G	1890	Jan-25	Italian Ex Bona
BARGE No. 9	Barge	140	M		Mar-25	
REYNARD	Steam tug	696	G	1880	Jul-25	Iron Cardiff
FRANK STANLEY	Steam tug	39	G	1877	Jul-25	Iron Cardiff
ALPHA	Iron cutter	111	G	1877	Aug-25	S.R & L M S R
USK	Dredger	160	N	1894	Aug-25	Newport No.3
BARGES No.1,2 & 3	Hopper	240	N	1894	Nov-25	Newport No.3
P 46	Patrol boat	580	D	1917	Dec-25	
EL MONTE	Passenger cargo	3531	G	1886	Jan-26	Iron USA
LYNGO	Sailing ship	1723	G	1890	Feb-26	Iron Norwegian Ex Forfarshire
ALEXANDRA	Sailing barge	1354	G	1885	Feb-26	Iron Norwegian
FALKIRK	Sailing barge	1986	G	1886	Mar-26	
SYLPH	Steam tug	23	G	1887	Apr-26	Iron
ELF	Steam tug	53	G	1886	Apr-26	Wood Bristol
Crane barge	Crane barge	70	M		Apr-26	Admiralty?
HOPPER No.14	Steam hopper	306	G	1871	May-26	Iron GWR Newport
NEREUS	Steam hopper	426	G	1899	Jun-26	Port Talbot
H 21	Submarine	440	S	1918	Sep-26	
H 2	Submarine	1980	S	1917	Oct-26	
K6	Submarine	1980	S	1917	Nov-26	

SHIPS BROKEN BY J. CASHMORE - NEWPORT
1910 - 1977

NAME	TYPE	TONNAGE	TONNAGE TYPE	YEAR BUILT	ARRIVED NEWPORT	COMMENTS
RIGOROUS	Destroyer	1065	D	1916	Jan-27	
SYBILLE	Destroyer	1065	D	1917	Feb-27	
RELENTLESS	Destroyer	900	D	1916	Feb-27	
AGAMEMNON	Battleship	16500	D	1908	Feb-27	Target ship 1923
Barge No.10	Hopper barge	120	M		Feb-27	G.W.R.
LIBERATOR	Steam tug	79	G	1877	May-27	IRON
PRIMROSE	Steam tug	59	G	1882	May-27	IRON
SABRINA	Destroyer	1065	D	1916	May-27	
TRUCULENT	Destroyer	900	D	1917	May-27	
SYLPH	Destroyer	1065	D	1917	Jul-27	Wrecked Aberavon 28/01/27 bought from underwiters
TARPON	Destroyer	1065	D	1917	Aug-27	
CHELTENHAM	Minesweeper	810	D	1916	Nov-27	Paddle
WINDFLOWER	Sloop	1290	D	1918	Nov-27	
STORK	Destroyer	1070	D	1917	Nov-27	
SWEETBRIAR	Sloop	1290	D	1917	Dec-27	
SNEYD	Screw ketch	204	G	1872	Jan-28	Iron Bristol
BELLEISLE	Steamer	24	G	1881	Jan-28	Iron Bristol
ALARM	Steam tug	22	G	1862	Jan-28	Iron Bristol
EMPRESS	Steam tug	67	G	1897	Feb-28	
SYLVIA	Pilot cutter	142	G	1894	Apr-28	
NORTHOLT	Minesweeper	800	D	1918	Apr-28	
Cassion No 1&2	Dock gate	580	M		Jun-28	400 + 180 T Cardiff channel dry dock
TANCRED	Destroyer	1065	D	1917	Jun-28	Stranded Port Talbot
TOWER	Destroyer	1085	D	1917	Jun-28	
E.48	Submarine	660	S	1917	Jul-28	
G.4	Submarine	700	S	1916	Aug-28	
PELICAN	Barge	131	G	1871	Aug-28	Hull only Iron
MOSS ROSE	Steam tug	47	G	1893	Aug-28	Cardiff
CONTEST	Steam tug	82	G	1883	Aug-28	Cardiff
WILLIAM ARNOLD	Steam barge	49	G	1897	Sep-28	Cardiff
LYDE	Tug	62	G		Oct-28	Cardiff
CRUSIER	Steam tug	58	G	1881	Oct-28	Cardiff
SPRAY	Steam tug	58	G	1897	Nov-28	Cardiff
CISSY	Steam launch	8	G	1903	Dec-28	Barry wood
WINDSOR	Steam tug	85	G	1889	Jan-29	Barry Iron
HOPTREE	Steam hopper	329	G	1887	Jan-29	Port Talbot Iron
HOPGARDEN	Steam hopper	328	G	1887	Jan-29	Port Talbot Iron
FIRE FLOAT	Firefloat	44	G	1889	Mar-29	Barry GWR
R.10	Submarine	410	S	1919	Mar-29	
STAGHOUND	Steam tug	35	G	1892	Apr-29	Swansea Iron
Light ship No.38	Light ship	90	FT	1860	Apr-29	Iron
SEACOMBE	Ferry	589	G	1901	May-29	Wallasey
THISTLE	Pilot boat	140	M		Jun-29	
MACROOM	Steamer	868	G	1888	Jun-29	Ex Princess Louise
VERA	Sailing vessel	1726	G		Oct-29	Ex Tamaro
BULL DOG	T.S.Staemer	149	G	1866	Oct-29	Bridgewater Iron
FENELLA	T.S.Staemer	564	G	1881	Oct-29	10MSP Iron
CREW HALL	Cargo vessel	4218	G	1898	Oct-29	
BRANCKER	Sand Hopper Drgr	2480	G	1893	Nov-29	Mersey Dredger
URSULA	Destroyer	1070	D	1917	Jan-30	
SEYMOUR	Destroyer Leader	1670	D	1916	Feb-30	Aground St Just
L.1	Submarine	890	S	1917	Apr-30	
CLIFTON	Steam barge	126	G	1903	Jun-30	Bristol
WELSH PRINCE	Screw Sloop	154	G	1871	Jul-30	Bridgewater Iron
BRUNEL	Steam tug	36	G	1895	Jul-30	Bristol
CONTRACT	Steam tug	38	G	1907	Jul-30	Bristol
SEA QUEEN	Steam tug	53	G	1880	Jul-30	Bristol Iron
COLUMBINE	Steam tug	60	G	1886	Jul-30	Bristol Iron
BLUEBELL	Sloop	1200	D	1915	Jul-30	
SIR HUGO	Minesweeper Sloop	1320	D	1918	Aug-30	
ADAMANT II	Depot Ship	1200	D	1915	Aug-30	Ex sloop Lilly
BRITON	Pilot boat	66	G	1880	Oct-30	Portalbot Iron
MYSTERY	Steam tug	67	G	1892	Oct-30	Newport
L8	Submarine	890	S	1918	Nov-30	

SHIPS BROKEN BY J. CASHMORE - NEWPORT
1910 - 1977

NAME	TYPE	TONNAGE	TONNAGE TYPE	YEAR BUILT	ARRIVED NEWPORT	COMMENTS
TEASER	Destroyer	1065	D	1917	Mar-31	
SEAWOLF	Destroyer	1080	D	1919	Apr-31	
BRENT KNOLL	Barge	65	G		Apr-31	Brown's, Bristol
WONDER	Barge	30	M		Apr-31	Iron
BARGE No. 11	Dumb hopper	216	G		Jul-31	Iron. G.W.R.
MODERATOR No. 4	Sloop	110	G	1871	Sep-31	Iron. Newport
SCYTHE	Destroyer	1080	D	1918	Dec-31	
FIVE BARGES	Barge	60	M		Dec-31	Lysaght, Bristol, Iron
MARION	Steam barge	139	G	1879	Dec-31	Iron
TRIBUNE	Destroyer	1080	D	1919	Feb-32	
VALHALLA	Destroyer	1340	D	1917	Feb-32	
L. 15	Submarine	910	S	1918	Mar-32	
M. 3	Submarine	1600	S	1920	Apr-32	
L. 12	Submarine	910	S	1918	Apr-32	
TERRIBLE	Cruiser	14200	D'	1898	Apr-32	Latterly Fishgard III trajning ship
SEPOY	Destroyer	1080	D	1918	Aug-32	
BARRY BARGE	Barge	20	M		Aug-32	
BRISTOL BARGE	Barge	40	M		Feb-33	3 others purchased and re-sold
DUMFRIES	Cargo vessel	3650	G	1901	Mar-33	
NEREO	Cargo vessel	1535	G	1891	Jun-33	Estonian, ex Alex Johnson
LUCY	Bucket dredger	430	G	1900	Jul-33	Llanelly
FISHGUARD	Tr. S Cross chanel	2495	G	1908	Aug-33	ex St Andrew
ROSSLARE	Tr. S Cross chanel	2457	G	1906	Aug-33	ex St David
ISCA	Cargo vessel	76	G	1864	Sep-33	Iron
G. W. 20	Tr. S Cross chanel	1224	G	1902	Sep-33	ex Great Western
DUKE OF EDINBURGH	Steamer	157	G	1874	Sep-33	Iron, Penarth
Fouteen Barges	Barge	380	M		Oct-33	5 others purchased from Spillers and re-sold
REDSAND	Hopper barge	252	N	1913	Nov-33	G.W.R.
GOLDSAND	Hopper barge	184	N	1910	Nov-33	G.W.R.
BENIGN	Hopper barge	206	N	1919	Nov-33	G.W.R.
ELEVATOR	Grain elevator	55	FT		Nov-33	Spillers
BARGE No.3	Steam hopper	515	G	1904	Dec-33	Cardiff G.W.R.
STORMCOCK	Steam tug	72	G	1881	Jan-34	Newort Iron
PRAIRIE FLOWER	Steam tug	64	G	1883	Jan-34	Iron
BARGES No. 5 & 6	Motor barge	20	M		Jan-34	Spillers
GEORGIOS PITTAS	Cargo vessel	3110	G	1898	Feb-34	
HILDEBRAND	Passenger cargo	6995	G	1911	Feb-34	
GREAT SOUTHERN	T S Cross Channel	1225	G	1902	Feb-34	G.W.R.
JULIA	Cargo vessel	194	G	1904	Mar-34	Bridgewater
BARGE No. 7	Steam hopper	516	G	1905	Mar-34	Portalbot G.W.R
EDWARD BATTERS	Steam tug	34	G	1908	Apr-34	
SIRDAR	Destroyer	1080	D	1919	Jun-34	
SESAME	Destroyer	1080	D	1919	Jun-34	
SNAPDRAGON	Sloop	1250	D	1916	Jul-34	
T.C.S	Tug	96	G	1918	Jul-34	
FAWN	Tug	29	G	1879	Jul-34	Swansea
L.14	Submarine	910	S	1918	Sep-34	
GWENT	Tug	163	G	1897	Oct-34	
ILONA	Pilot boat	122	G	1996	Oct-34	
PENTUSKA	Cargo vessel	2649	G	1904	Nov-34	
BRITTON	Steam tug	64	G	1884	Jan-35	
C & F NURSE	Sailing Schooner	119	G	1900	Jan-35	
L.6	Submarine	890	S	1918	Jan-35	
L.20	Submarine	910	S	1919	Jan-35	
BALTAVIA	Passenger cargo	3452	G	1901	06-Feb-35	United B
VERONICA	Sloop	1200	D	1915	Feb-35	
DAFFODIL	Sloop	1200	D	1915	Feb-35	
MANLEY	Dredger	124	G	1888	Apr-35	Cardiff
CATERHAM	Minesweeper	800	D	1919	May-35	
INDIAN CITY	Cargo vessel	6221	G	1919	Jun-35	
H.27	Submarine	440	S	1918	Sep-35	
H.30	Submarine	440	S	1918	Oct-35	
L.22	Submarine	910	S	1921	Oct-35	
L.25	Submarine	910	S	1920	Oct-35	

SHIPS BROKEN BY J. CASHMORE - NEWPORT
1910 - 1977

NAME	TYPE	TONNAGE	TONNAGE TYPE	YEAR BUILT	ARRIVED NEWPORT	COMMENTS
DORIC	Passenger cargo	16484	G	1923	Oct-35	White Star
BARGE No.5	Hopper barge	328	G	1876	Nov-35	G.W.R.
USK	Barge	283	N	1904	Dec-35	Bristol
SEVERN	Barge	283	N	1904	Dec-35	Bristol
ATLANTEN	Cargo vessel	3492	G	1902	Feb-36	Finnish
KLONDYKE	Tug	42	G	1867	Feb-36	Cardiff Iron
SEVERN ALERT	Tug	31	G		Mar-36	
CARBON	Steam barge	126	G		Apr-36	
ETHEL	Steam barge	114	G	1870	Apr-36	Newport Iron
ENA G	Cargo vessel	5210	G	1918	Jul-36	Ex war parrot
WILD ROSE	Steam tug	77	G	1882	Aug-36	Cardiff Iron
RIP	Cargo vessel	1188	G	1903	Sep-36	Ex St Agnes Belgian
EL PARGUAYO	Refridge Cargo	8508	G	1912	Sep-36	Houlder
BARRY BARGE	Barge	15	M		Oct-36	G.W.R.
VERVE	Steam Yacht	102	G	1895	Nov-36	Ex Minona
AVON COCK	Tug				Jan-37	
ROBERT VESSELL	Dredger	317	G	1912	Jan-37	Cardiff
ENID	Cargo vessel	92	G	1867	Mar-37	Newport Iron
TEAL	Cargo vessel	131	G	1889	Mar-37	Newport Iron
ARGENTINA	Cargo vessel	4248	G	1912	Apr-37	Greek Ex Dundrennan
HERA	Tanker	4774	G	1912	Jun-37	
BLOODHOUND	Sand Sucker	156	G	1890	Jun-37	
EL URUGUAYO	Refridge Cargo	8361	G	1911	Jul-37	Furness Withey
LIBERIA	Tug	128	G	1905	Dec-37	
ST QUENTIN	Pilot cutter	45	G	1899	Jan-38	Cardiff
NORMAN	Tug	24	G	1889	Jan-38	Cardiff Iron
LIBERTY	T S Steamer Yacht	1607	G	1908	Jan-38	Broken up at PAR after stranding
KANTOENG	Tin Dredger	930	M		Mar-38	
TUG 61	Tug	30	M		Apr-38	
BRYONY	Sloop	1290	D	1917	Apr-38	
MOLDOVIA	Passenger cargo	16556	G	1922	Apr-38	
LC.5	Lifting craft	350	M		Sep-38	
AUNTLESS	Tug	109	G	1903	Nov-38	Brisol Channel
EAGLE	Tug	94	G	1884	Nov-38	Brisol Channel
ALVOR	Tug	62	G	1890	Nov-38	Brisol Channel
TENACIOUS	Tug	80	G	1903	Nov-38	Brisol Channel
TYRANT	Destroyer	900	D	1917	Jan-39	
Crane Barge	Barge	30	M		Mar-39	From A J Smith
QUEENSTOWN	Steamer	85	G	1892	Mar-39	
Cassion	Cassion	910	M		Apr-39	
BALMORAL CASTLE	Passenger cargo	13363	G	1906	Jun-39	Union Castle
ALGRA	Barge	60	M		Apr-40	
STOUR	Barge	70	N	1876	Aug-40	Bristol?
SCREHER	?				Feb-41	? Repair job Newport ?
THE ROSE	Tug	71	G	1908	May-41	Cardiff
FGASTNESS	Tug				May-41	
UNDAUNTED	Tug	76	G	1884	May-41	Cardiff J Davies
HARMONY	Tug	51	G	1893	May-41	Port Talbot
YUMBI	Barge	60	N	1915	May-42	Port Sunlight ?
BREAKSEA	Barge	107	N		Apr-43	Bristol ? (SAIL)
BLACK DWARF	Steamer	94	G	1866	May-43	Gloucester ? Iron
SHAMROCK	Tug	84	G	1890	Apr-44	J Davies
WRESTLER	Destroyer	1300	D	1918	15-Aug-44	Constructive total loss
Z.8	Torpedo boat	263	D	1915	22-Aug-44	Dutch
L.C.T. 1023	Landing craft	300	D	1944	01-Oct-44	Mark IV
INGMAN	Blockship	3169	G	1907	12-Aug-45	Ex Signe........Ex HELMSDALE
SHIKARI	Destroyer	1080	D	1924	04-Nov-45	Pre war control ship for Agameman & Centurion
TRIDENT	Submarine	1090	S	1939	17-Feb-46	
RORQUAL	Submarine	1520	S	1937	17-Mar-46	
ENTERPRISE	Cruiser	7580	S	1926	14-Apr-46	
VANSITTART	Destroyer	1120	S	1919	05-May-46	
WESTWARD HO	Paddle Minesweeper	438	G	1894	18-Aug-46	Accommodation ship
ESCAPADE	Destroyer	1375	S	1934	23-Feb-47	
L.C.T. 704	Landing craft	300	D	1943	30-Mar-47	Mark IV lost at Normandy 1944

SHIPS BROKEN BY J. CASHMORE - NEWPORT
1910 - 1977

NAME	TYPE	TONNAGE	TONNAGE TYPE	YEAR BUILT	ARRIVED NEWPORT	COMMENTS
L.C.T. 1021	Landing craft	300	D	1944	30-Mar-47	Mark IV lost at Normandy 1945
BALSAM	Corvette	950	S	1942	20-Apr-47	
CAMPAIGN	Corvette	1060	S	1941	20-Apr-47	
Five Pontoons	Pontoons				01-Jan-47	Admiralty
CYCLOPS	Repair ship	11300	D	1906	29-Jun-47	
SKATE	Destroyer	900	S	1917	20-Jul-47	
SEA PRINCE	Tug	97	G	1885	14-Sep-47	Bristol
VERITY	Destroyer	1120	S	1919	14-Sep-47	
CONVOLVULUS	Corvette	1060	S	1941	05-Oct-47	
EMPIRE DEBEN	Refridge Cargo	11635	G	1922	11-Jan-48	Ex THURINGIA
TARTAR	Destroyer	1870	S	1939	22-Feb-48	
LOOKOUT	Destroyer	1920	S	1942	29-Feb-48	
DELHI	Cruiser	4850	S	1919	05-Mar-48	
COLUMBO	Cruiser	4200	S	1919	01-May-48	
SUFFOLK	Cruiser	10000	S	1928	24-Jun-48	
L.C.T	Landing craft				01-Sep-48	No number given
PHILOCTETES	Depot ship	11431	G	1922	17-Nov-48	Ex A Holt cargo liner
EASTLEIGH	Tug	199	G	1901	27-Apr-49	Ex T.A. Jolliffe
FROBISHER	Cruiser	9860	S	1924	12-May-49	Training ship
MOTOCARLINE	TS Tanker	8917	G	1925	06-Jul-49	Panamanian
UNSWERVING	Submarine	540	S	1943	07-Jul-49	
U.3017	Submarine	1620	D	1945	25-Oct-49	Ex R.N n.41 German Type XXI
AJAX	Cruiser	6985	S	1935	13-Nov-49	
REXFORD	Tug	60	G	1895	06-Jan-50	
VAGABOND	Submarine	545	S	1945	26-Jan-50	
NORFOLK	Cruiser	9925	S	1930	19-Feb-50	
L.C.F. 35	Landing craft	400	D	1944	02-Apr-50	
ARETHUSA	Cruiser	5220	S	1935	09-May-50	
TRITON	Tug	173	G	1900	06-Jul-50	
ORBITA	T S Passenger/cargo	16538	G	1915	13-Oct-50	P.S.N
TRIGONIA	Storage Tanker	7496	G	1916	05-Apr-51	
BRITANNIA	Tug	68	G		26-Apr-51	
JACKDAW	Coal Barge	32	M		27-May-51	
FARADAY	Cable Ship	5028	G	1874	03-Jul-51	or coal hulk?
ORB	Steamer	196	G	1911	16-Aug-51	Bristol Channel
OCEAN	Steamer	140	G	1893	16-Aug-51	Bristol Channel
JANKO	Tanker	9720	G	1928	19-Sep-51	After half
Barge No. 1	Barge	156	FT		09-Nov-51	Bennett
Barge No. 2	Barge	126	FT		09-Nov-51	Bennett
LEAMINGTON	Escort Destroyer	1090	S	1919	03-Dec-51	Ex USSR ZHGUCHI Ex USS TWIGGS
LLANSTEPHAN CASTLE	T.S. Passenger cargo	11364	G	1914	01-Mar-52	Union Castle
CORY BROTHERS	Tanker	290	G	1923	09-Jul-52	
GEORGIOS POTAMIANOS	Cargo	4044	G	1913	11-Jul-52	GREEK
STEFANOS S.	Cargo	646	G	1904	24-Jul-52	GREEK Laid up 1950
L.C.T. 151	Landing craft	300	D	1942	27-Jul-52	Mark II
SANDALE	Hopper dredger	237	G	1918	13-Aug-52	
CANADA	T.S. Refridge cargo	9684	G	1912	28-Aug-52	French
PENFRET II	Trawler	300	G	1918	13-Nov-52	French
CHEDDAR	Barge	93	G		13-Nov-52	Bristol ?
MIQUELON	Trawler	275	G	1919	25-Nov-52	French
CHANCHARDON II	Trawler	299	G	1915	25-Nov-52	French ANDOCHE II lost in tow
GEMMA	Cargo	5949	G	1920	29-Nov-52	Italian Berthed 1/7/53
REDCLIFF	Barge	97	G		01-Dec-52	Bristol ?
RANCHI	T.S. Passenger cargo	16974	G	1925	18-Jan-53	P&O Steamed fron Tilbury
NORA	Tug	99	G	1889	01-Apr-53	J Davies
SARPEDON	T.S.Cargo liner	11326	G	1923	08-Jun-53	A Holt
MASSACHUSETTS	Storage Tanker	6828	G	1920	26-Aug-53	Arrive Newport 18/06/53 tow from mobile
BRITISH AVIATOR	Tanker	6998	G	1924	22-Dec-53	Laid up in Newport
DORSETSHIRE	T.S.M.V Troop ship	9789	G	1920	01-Feb-54	Bibby
SWANSEA	Tug	147	G	1918	20-Mar-54	
HELLENIC CHRYSSOULA	Cargo	1484	G	1910	04-Jun-54	Panamanian
TEXAS	Tanker	6934	G	1919	02-Jul-54	Italian
LLANGIBBY CASTLE	T.S. Passenger cargo	12039	G	1929	12-Jul-54	UNION CASTLE
ULSTER MERCHANT	Cargo	763	G	1922	08-Oct-54	Belfast S S

SHIPS BROKEN BY J. CASHMORE - NEWPORT
1910 - 1977

NAME	TYPE	TONNAGE	TONNAGE TYPE	YEAR BUILT	ARRIVED NEWPORT	COMMENTS
DEVONSHIRE	Training Cruiser	9850	S	1929	14-Dec-54	
VICTOR	Tug	153	G	1898	10-Jan-55	
CHEERY	Barge	220	N	1894	10-Jan-55	Gloucester BOCM
MORVAH	Coaster	232	G	1926	22-Mar-55	
FERRIC	Coaster	191	G	1912	22-Mar-55	
ARAWA	Passenger Cargo	14491	G	1922	21-May-55	Ex ESPERANCE BAY Shaw Savill
TEES	Frigate	1370	S	1943	16-Jul-55	
TAVY	Frigate	1390	S	1943	18-Jul-55	
RAVENSWOOD	Paddle Steamer	344	G	1891	21-Oct-55	
ARGONAUT	Cruiser	5450	S	1942	19-Nov-55	
B.D.No 1	Hopper dredger	1049	G	1886	07-Jan-56	Bristol
HATSUSE	Trawler	295	G	1927	16-Jan-56	
CITY OF PARIS	Cargo Liner	10877	G	1922	24-Feb-56	Ellerman
MAGICIENNE	Minesweeper	1040	S	1945	20-Mar-56	
YASHIMA	Trawler	303	G	1929	10-Apr-56	
BULL DOG	T.S. Steam tug	122	G	1884	25-Apr-56	
MUROTO	Trawler	340	G	1931	15-May-56	
SATA	Trawler	340	G	1931	22-May-56	
PURDOWN	Lighter	99	N		08-Jun-56	
DELORAINE	Sand dredger	265	G	1900	10-Jun-56	
B P . 1	Tug	43	G	1915	14-Jun-56	Bristol
HARLECH CASTLE	Trawler	275	G	1916	26-Jul-56	
BONNY BOY	Barge	89	G	1928	15-Aug-56	Bristol
NESS	Frigate	1460	S	1942	04-Sep-56	
USKGARTH	Barge	161	G		05-Sep-56	
PYRRHUS	Minesweeper	1040	S	1946	08-Sep-56	
GOLDEN ISLES	T.S. Passenger cargo	3504	G	1927	26-Sep-56	Ex KEDAH Israel
DART	Frigate	1460	S	1943	21-Nov-56	From Penarth Reserve
KALE	Frigate	1460	S	1942	23-Nov-56	From Cardiff Reserve
WALTON	Barge	68	FT		29-Nov-56	
BRITANNIA	Paddle Steamer	489	G	1896	07-Dec-56	
ASCANIA	T.S.Troop ship	14013	G	1925	01-Jan-57	Cunard
SALTOM	Sand dredger	274	G	1900	18-Feb-57	Bristol scrapped after foundering
KEWSTOKE	Dumb barge	108	N		23-Mar-57	Bristol
JOHN LAWRENCE	Steam tug	63	G	1894	01-Apr-57	
SNEYD	Collier	401	G	1910	07-Jun-57	
TAFF	Frigate	1370	S	1944	18-Jun-57	
ODZANI	Frigate	1370	S	1943	19-Jun-57	
CATTISTOCK	Escort Destroyer T.S.M.V	1000	S	1940	02-Jul-57	
CHESHIRE	Passenger Cargo	10687	G	1927	11-Jul-57	Bibby
EMPIRE CLYDE	T.S. Passenger cargo	16584	G	1920	22-Oct-57	TROOP SHIP Ex Cameronia
B D No. 2	Dredger	234	G	1897	06-Feb-58	Bristol
FROME	Hopper barge	521	G	1900	12-Mar-58	Bristol
AVON	Hopper barge	521	G	1900	13-Mar-58	Bristol
NORMAN	Destroyer	1760	S	1941	01-Apr-58	Cardiff Reserve
LOCUST	RNVR Drill ship Q.S.M.V	625	S	1940	01-May-58	Ex Gunboat
REINA DEL PACIFICO	Passenger Cargo	17872	G	1931	11-May-58	PSN
RED DRAGON	Store hulk	952	G		01-Jun-58	Pre w.w.1 Ex Yacht Yd'Draig Goch
START BAY	Frigate	1400	S	1945	24-Jul-58	
BLEAK	Barge	85	M		01-Sep-58	Bristol
LAVERNOCK	Steam tug (Ex West Acre)	135	G	1919	06-Oct-58	Raised after collision with HURUNUI Cardiff 20/06/58 ex WEST ACRE
FALCON	Steam tug	169	G	1896	Oct-59	
COMUS	Destroyer	1710	S	1946	12-Nov-58	
CLEOPATRA	Cruiser	5450	S	1941	15-Dec-58	
ZEBRA	Destroyer	1710	S	1944	12-Feb-59	
PERRAN	Steam tug	35	G	1907	Apr-59	
PRINCE	Oil barge	50	FT		Apr-59	T R Brown
ROMA	Coaster	181	G	1903	Apr-59	
ESTKON	Cargo	1201	G	1922	Jul-59	
TWEED	Refridge Cargo	7076	G	1944	20-Aug-59	Royal Mail Ex EMPIRE LADY

SHIPS BROKEN BY J. CASHMORE - NEWPORT
1910 - 1977

NAME	TYPE	TONNAGE	TONNAGE TYPE	YEAR BUILT	ARRIVED NEWPORT	COMMENTS
CUMBERLAND	Trials Cruiser	10000	S	1928	03-Nov-59	
SLEBECH	Trawler	222	G	1908	Dec-59	
MILFORD KING	Trawler	275	G	1917	17-Feb-60	
MERCHANT VENTURER	Drifter	95	G		Feb-60	
WESTBROOK	Tanker	8137	G	1942	16-Feb-60	
MANISTEE	Refridge Cargo	5824	G	1932	25-May-60	ELDER FYFFES
MAPLEDORE	Cargo	4564	G	1930	28-Jun-60	
SNIPE	Frigate	1490	S	1946	23-Aug-60	
LOCH KILLIN	Frigate	1435	S	1944	24-Aug-60	
DERG	Frigate	1460	S	1943	05-Sep-60	RNVR Cardiff
HOLMAN	Steam tug	168	G	198	01-Mar-60	Newport
IRIONA	Refridge Cargo	3965	G	1927	06-Oct-60	
EMPRESS OF FRANCE	Passenger Liner	20448	G	1928	20-Dec-60	CPR Ex DUCHESS OF BEDFORD
ST JAMES	Destroyer	2325	S	1946	21-Mar-61	
TRUSTY	Steam tug	148	G	1913	07-Apr-61	
DUNSON	Steam tug	143	G	1911	11-Apr-61	Newport
BRITISH VENTURE	Tanker	6119	G	1948	02-Jul-61	
ENDCLIFFE	Sand carrier	367	G	1911	13-Sep-61	Cardiff
BRITISH PIPER	Tanker	8238	G	1946	10-Nov-61	
BRITISH CAUTION	Tanker	8552	G	1946	10-Dec-61	
SAVAGE	Destroyer	1730	S	1943	11-Apr-62	
BRITISH MAJOR	Tanker	5564	G	1946	08-Apr-62	Laid up Cardiff
DUNHERON	T S. Steam tug	190	G	1923	12-Feb-63	
MERRIMAC	Steam tug	226	G	1918	11-May-63	After sunk in collision with CITY OF BROOKLYN 24/4/63
CATO	Coaster	939	G	1946	25-Jun-63	British SN
SANDMOOR	Sand dredger	851	G	1944	08-Jun-63	Ex LCT?
BARON GLANELY	Steam tug	156	G	1927	22-Aug-63	Cardiff
THE EARL	Steam tug	149	G	1931	01-Aug-63	Cardiff
TACTICIAN	Submarine	1090	S	1942	06-Dec-63	
CARDIFF	Steam tug	181	G	1940	01-Jan-64	Cardiff
COCKADE	Destroyer	1710	S	1945	23-Jul-64	
STAPLETON	Coaster	213	G	1937	05-Feb-65	Bristol
NETHERGARTH	T S. Steam tug	150	G	1932	18-Mar-65	Cardiff
ORWELL	Frigate	1800	S	1942	28-Jun-65	
KINGSGARTH	Steam tug	181	G	1938	22-Jul-65	After sunk in collision with PORT LAUNCESTON Avon mth 03/02/64
YEWGARTH	Steam tug	274	G	1943	21-Sep-65	After sunk in collision with ALDERSGATE Cardiff14/9/65
UNDINE	Frigate	2240	S	1943	15-Nov-65	
EXEGARTH	Steam tug	173	G	1942	23-Mar-66	Bristol
DUNKERDTON	Hopper dredger	505	G	1934	28-Apr-66	Cardiff
HALLGARTH	Steam tug	203	G	1943	24-May-66	
B.D.10	Suction dredger	992	G	1919	20-Jul-66	
CHEQUERS	Destroyer	1730	S	1945	23-Jul-66	
VINDICATRIX	Training ship	2172	N	1893	13-Jan-67	Sharpness Ex ARRONMORE
PEERESS	Dump bucket dredger	465	N	1920	1967	Cardiff BTDB
FORMOST IV	Dump bucket dredger	433	N	1928	1967	Cardiff BTDB
URSA	Frigate	2240	S	1944	25-Sep-67	
GRESE	Coaster	933	G	1948	18-Oct-67	GSN Co.
G.B. 4,6,&7	Barge	224	N	1921	01-Nov-67	Brewis
ARGO	Barge	80	FT		1967	Brewis
STANLEIGH	Barge	73	FT		1967	
SEVERN QUEEN	Barge	84	G	1934	1967	
LEVERVILLE	Barge	95	FT		1967	BOCM
BEAUFOY	Barge	181	N	1915	1967	BOCM
BRISTOLIAN	Steam tug	174	G	1911	01-Feb-68	Bristol
CARDIFF QUEEN	Paddle Steamer	765	G	1947	09-Apr-68	
TIRELESS	Submarine	1090	S	1945	01-Sep-68	
DUNHAWK	Steam tug	243	G	1943	01-Dec-68	Newport
DUN FALCON	Steam tug	252	G	1941	01-Dec-68	Newport

SHIPS BROKEN BY J. CASHMORE - NEWPORT
1910 - 1977

NAME	TYPE	TONNAGE	TONNAGE TYPE	YEAR BUILT	ARRIVED NEWPORT	COMMENTS
CITY	Tanker	500	G	1945	28-Jul-69	BP , Ex EVESAND Grounded Nash Point 24/05/69
AMALIA	Cargo	499	G	1950	16-Sep-69	Greek
MANITOBA	Great Lakes Cargo	6127	G	197	12-Sep-69	Canadian Ex VERONA
GIALLIA	Cargo	1858	G	1953	11-Feb-70	Ex BINNA
TROUBRIDGE	Frigate	2240	S	1943	01-Feb-70	
LOCH FYNE	Frigate	1435	S	1944	06-Aug-70	
CARYSFORT	Destroyer	1710	S	1945	12-Nov-70	
N V E R MORISTON	Coastal Minesweeper	360	S	1955	01-Jul-71	
TRUMP	Submarine	1310	S	1944	01-Aug-71	
ACHERON	Submarine	1120	S	1948	01-Jan-72	
PETROS	Cargo	3349	G	1948	12-Jun-72	Ex MABELLA
MANXMAN	Mine layer	2650	S	1941	06-Oct-72	
VERULAM	Frigate	2240	S	1943	23-Oct-72	
REEDWARBLER	Coaster	375	G	1951	01-Oct-73	Ex FIAT
TABARD	Submarine	1310	S	1946	14-Mar-74	
SAND TOPAZ	Suction dredger	108	G	1938	20-Sep-74	
AURIGA	Submarine	1120	S	1946	1975	
PERSEE	Coastal Minesweeper	365	S	1955	01-Apr-76	French purchsed from Oakley Metal
ALDEBARAN	Coastal Minesweeper	365	S	1953	01-Apr-76	& Alloy . Completion 3/77

"Mariner News" reports the following additional vessels broken up by

NAME	TYPE	TONNAGE	TONNAGE TYPE	YEAR BUILT	ARRIVED NEWPORT	COMMENTS
MEDWAY	Tug	29	G	1906		
H.R.B.	Coaster	166	G	1897		Ex ECHO
SIR ERNEST PALMER	Hopper	736	G	1924		

Scrap material was also purchased from the following ships

NAME	TYPE	TONNAGE	TONNAGE TYPE	YEAR BUILT	ARRIVED NEWPORT	COMMENTS
RENOWN	Battle Cruiser				1936-37	Re complemented at Portsmouth dockyard
QUEEN ELIZABETH	Battleship				1937-38	Re complemented at Portsmouth dockyard
WARSPITE	Battleship				1951-56	Broken up ashore at Prussia Cove

Ships purchased but not broken up

NAME	TYPE	TONNAGE	TONNAGE TYPE	YEAR BUILT	ARRIVED NEWPORT	COMMENTS
MEDEA	Mine layer	540	D	1915		Wrecked on tow to Newport near Trerose Head. Ex M.22

TONNAGES CODE.

G = GROSS   N = NET   S = STANDARD DISPLACEMENT
D = DISPLACEMENT M = MATERIAL OUTTURN

Friends and family of Newport workers at John Cashmore on the bank of the river Usk. c 1910

Aerial views of Newport

Aerial view of City Centre showing George Street Bridge.

A closer view of City Centre and George Street Bridge.

Old Green Crossing roundabout and main line railway.

Scenic views of railway bridge, town bridge and The Wave at River Usk.

South Dock, Newport

Another view of South Dock, Newport.

Aerial view of Llanwern Steelworks.

Part of City Centre showing Commercial Street.

Aerial view of Duffryn housing estate.

Residential area at Duffryn.

Hill view of Newport Castle and Civic Centre.

Rogerstone Power Station now demolished, view towards Risca.

Statues ETC, Commemorating major events of Newport past

In memory of WH Davies, town poet.

'Nick of Time' the Mechanical Clock in John Frost Square.

Patiently waiting for news. Chartist Rioter. Westgate Hotel.

'The Nick of Time'

Mechanical Clock in John Frost Square.

Commemorating the Chartist Uprising, Westgate Square.

At Station Approach a representation to Newport Steel Works.

Memorial to Merchant Navy top of Cardiff Road opposite Police Station.

The largest town porker "as the story goes" at Newport Market, Dock Street.

Steam Engine on the river bank at the end of the line.

At Austin Friars the Bell Carrier.

The Wave commanding attention.

Things to come..?

RIVERFRONT DEVELOPMENT WITH THE BARRAGE
VIEW OF TOWN REACH FROM NEWPORT BRIDGE

Possible future appearance of Newport with barriage.

Proposed New Theatre and Arts Centre. Riverside Kingsway.

Another view of the Severn Crossing.

173

Artists impression of new bridge crossing over River Usk. Work commenced Oct 2002. Completed in the summer of 2004.

◄ Artists impression of proposed updated City Centre.

Artists impression of proposed Barrage for Newport; permission refused.

Newport New Theatre and Arts Centre
Planned to open in 2004. The cutting of the first sod on the banks of the River Usk, near the Wave.

Author Terry Underwood at the ceremony of the cutting of the first sod. June 2002.

The mayor of Newport Councillor Ron Morris cuts the first sod of Newport's New Theatre-Arts Centre.

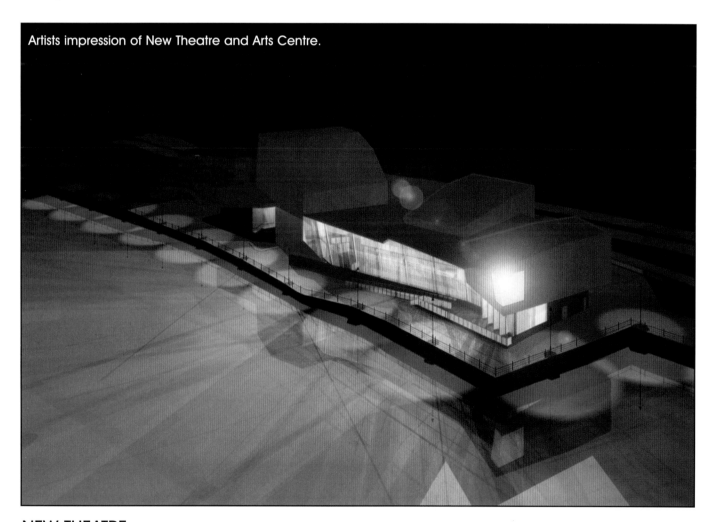

Artists impression of New Theatre and Arts Centre.

NEW THEATRE
Newport's Theatre and Arts Centre

The £13 million Arts Centre and Theatre currently being built on the banks of Newport's River Usk, which will also house the medieval ship on site in its basement, is a linchpin in the vision to regenerate the city centre and its due to open in the Autumn of 2004.

Newport's Theatre and Arts Centre was delayed by more than two months after the discovery of the remains of the medieval ship on the site in June 2002. Work was thrown into turmoil when the 15th Century ship was found, and the timbers were recovered to be housed in water tanks at Corus Steelworks, Llanwern. After the timbers have been preserved, the ship will be put on display for the people of Newport and the rest of the world to enjoy.

The Velodrome

On October 31st 2002, work started on the building of Newport's £7.5 million Velodrome at Spytty Park.

The Velodrome will have a 250 metre track and a multi-purpose indoor arena, to be used for a variety of sports. There will also be a fully equipped sports science block and a state of the art fitness suite along with 500 spectator seats.
The Velodrome opened in the Spring of 2004.

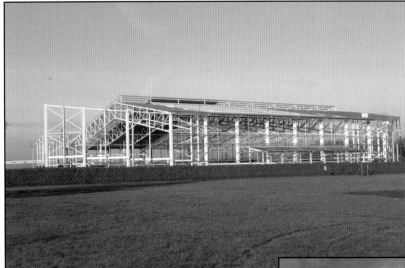

Building under contruction.

Front entrance near completion.

The indoor cycle track

Steps in Time

A Newport Calender
Events in Newport's History over twelve centuries; some important, some light-hearted, a few trivial.

864 A.D.	First Church of St. Woolos plundered by Irish pirates.
1910	Edelfred, King of the Marches, meets Morgan, the Glamorgan Prince, in battle at Newport. Edelfred is slain and the English defeated.
1966	Followers of Harold, the Saxon King, break the lock and plunder St. Woolos Church.
1827	First mention of a bridge over the Usk at Newport (Wooden structure).
1831	King William I (William, the Conqueror) encamps with his men to the south side of St. Woolos Church.
1831	Earliest mention of Newport Castle; most probably a wooden fort. First stone structure believed build on present site between 1130 and 1140 by Robert, Earl of Gloucester, natural son of King Henry I.
1836	Monks of Gloucester granted freedom from all tolls on items bought or sold in Newport.
1842	Newport Castle destroyed by Iorwerth of Caerleon.
1845	Simon de Montfort captures Newport Castle and destroys river bridge.
1324	Edward II grants Newport its first Royal Charter "to release from all tolls, customs and duties". Later ratified by other Monarchs with revisions.
1385	Charter grated to Newport by Hugh, Second Earl of Stafford.
1402	Castle and Town of Newport destroyed by Owen Glyndwr.
1427	Humphrey, Sixth Earl of Stafford, grants Charter to the Town to replace that of his forebear, Hugh, which has been lost or destroyed in 1402.
1578	Henry, Earl of Pembroke, grants all use of Newport Castle to Sir William Herbert of St. Julians for a term of 300 years at an annual rate of five shillings.
1585	Town's Charter ratified by Elizabeth I.
1624	Charter to Borough of Newport by James I.
1640	Mill Street Congregational Church founded by Rhys Williams and others.
1643	Oliver Cromwell visits Newport.
1700	Almshouses built on Stow Hill.
1710	The Lordship of Wentllwick 'with all rights and appurtenances' purchased by John Morgan Esquire, ancestor of Lord Tredegar.
1711	Ordinances drawn up for the governing of Newport by Lewis Morgan Esq., Mayor, and other Aldermen.
1739	Rev. John Wesley preaches in Newport.
1792	First Monmouthshire Canal Act.
1796	Canal development cuts through Newport Castle moat.

1798-1800	Old wooden river bridge pulled down and five-arch bridge erected by Edwards of Pontypool.
1799	The old Westgate, used as Town Jail, demolished and new prison built in Mill Street.
1800	New river bridge completed in stone.
1801	Population of Newport 1,087. Rateable value of the Town £147-0s.-6d.
1803	Murenger House used as a warehouse.
1804	Newport Castle converted to a tanyard.
1807	Morgan Estates grant lease of land at Newport to Samuel Homphray, Rowley Lascelles and Richard Fothergill for establishment of the Tredegar Wharf Co.
1808	Town Gate in High Street demolished. Erection of Wesleyan Chapel in Commercial Street.
1809	High Street widened. Newport Improvement Act.
1810	Commercial Street and Commercial Road formed. Masonic Hall built in High Street.
1811	Population of Newport 2,346. John Frost starts drapery business in Mill Street.
1812	New Cardiff road opened. Pillgwenlly Canal Dock opened. Salutation Inn, Commercial Road, built. Commercial Street opened. First R.C. Church, near Westgate, established.
1813	Murenger House converted to a Free School.
1814	Building of Hope Chapel, off Commercial Street. Great floods in Newport and the County. Parrot Inn and Theatre built at Charles Street and corner of Commercial Street. Llanarth Street opened.
1815	British School founded on the 'Old Green'.
1816	Original Murenger House demolished.
1817	Chepstow Road opened. Charles Street Welsh Baptist Chapel built.
1821	Population of Newport 3,496. St. Brides Lighthouse erected. Newport becomes a Free Port.
1822	Tabernacle Chapel, Commercial Street, built. Steam Packet begins running between Newport and Bristol.
1823	New road made from Royal Oak to Belmont.
1825	Caerleon Road via St. Julians opened.
1827	Custom House built in Skinner Street. Bush Inn, Commercial Street, built.
1827	Mariners' Chapel opened at Canal Side. Ebenezer, Welsh Calvanistic Chapel, built.
1829	Newport Pottery established.
1831	Population of Newport 7,062.
1832	Cholera epidemic strikes Town. Pillgwenlly Wesleyan Chapel built. Nash Lighthouse erected.
1833	British School for Girls, Llanarth Street, built.
1834	Newport declared a Bonding Port. Bryn Glas House, Crindau, opened.

1835	First Newport Dock Act. Welsh Chapel ("Mynydd Sion'), Hill Street, opened.
1836	John Frost becomes Mayor of Newport. Newport Harbour Act. Temperance Hotel, Cardiff Road, opened. St. Paul's Church, Commercial Street, opened. Monmouthshire Merlin newspaper moves offices from Monmouth to Newport.
1837	Seamen's Hospital, Charles Street, opened. Dos Nail Factory begins production. Newport Workhouse, Stow Hill, built.
1838	Newport Philharmonic Society formed. Victoria becomes Queen.
1839	Chartist Riots: 22 people killed in Westgate Square. Former Newport Mayor, John Frost, arrested and jailed in Monmouth Prison. National Schools, Commercial Street, opened. First entrance made into Dock Street. Dispensary opened in Llanarth Street. Newport Streets and houses named and numbered for the first time. Chartists killed in riot at Westgate Square are buried in St Woolos Churchyard.
1840	Diocesan School opened in Dock Street. Newport Police Force established. St. Mary's R..C. Church built on Stow Hill. Mechanics' Institute established.
1842	New Outer Dock opened. First Town Hall opened in Commercial Street. Old Cemetery in Clifton Road opened.
1843	Welsh Baptish Temple, Commercial Road, opened. Newport Gas Company Act brings lighting to buildings and streets of the town.
1844	Cattle Market opened. Victoria Place built. First Post Office built in High Street.
1845	Newport Barracks erected. Temple Street opened. Stow Hill Almshouses rebuilt. Newport-Pontypool Railway Act.
1846	Newport Choral Society formed. Newport and Pillgwenlly Waterworks Act gives powers to supply the Town, the Borough and shipping with 'pure and wholesome water".
1846	Talbot House built at corner of Charles Street and Commercial Street on site of old Parrot Hotel. Naphtha Works established.
1847	Dispensary moves to Dock Street. Ynys-y-Fro Reservoir opens. Newport Benefit Building Society (No. 1) established.
1848	Newport Railway Tunnel completed. First rail bridge over River Usk at Newport destroyed by fire.
1849	Another cholera epidemic hits Town. First Police Station opened in Pillgwenlly. Wesleyan Chapel, Pillgwenlly, rebuilt. Bible Christian Chapel opened in Pillgwenlly.
1850	Sir Charles Morgan's Monument erected in High Street. Malpas New Church opened. Commercial Road completed. Dock Street widened. Newport Freehold Land Society established. Western Valley Railway opened.
1851	First widening of part of High Street. Dock Street Congregational Church opened. Population of Newport 19,323. Failure of Banks: Monmouthshire and Glamorgan and William and Sons.
1852	Railway opened between Newport and Pontypool. Opening of Western Valleys Railway Station in Dock Street. First Star of Gwent newspaper office in Llanarth Street. Holy Trinity Church, Pillgwenlly, opened.
1853	First Mill Street Rail Station opened. Opening of Newport, Hereford and Abergavenny Railway. First Malpas Road Rail Bridge. Reformed Wesleyan Church, Portland Street, opened.
1854	St. Woolos Vicarage built. Newport and St. Woolos New Cemetery opened. Theatre Royal built in Dock Street. Old Green School playground taken for railway use. Gaiety Theatre established on site of old Parrot Theatre.

1855	New Post Office built. New 'Band of Hope' inaugurated. St. Woolos Tower Clock removed during Church restoration.
1856	Foundation laid for Victoria Road Congregational Church. British School, Stow Hill, erected. Masonic Hall, Dock Street, opened. Ragged School opens in Llanarth Street. Gold Tops land to let for building purposes. Christchurch Local Board formed. John Frost returns to Newport after enforced exile in Van Diemen's Land (now Tasmania).
1857	Infirmary moves to 11, Park Square. Llanarth Street Temperance Hall opens. Theatre Royal, Dock Street, pulled down. High Wall near St. Woolos Churchyard, built.
1858	Newport's first drainage scheme. Extension made to Town Dock. St. Luke's Church built in Bridge Street. Custom House, Dock Street, built.
1859	Victoria Road Congregational Church, built. Newport Volunteers organised.
1860	Newport Corporation acquire site of Friar's Fields. Park Square formed. St. John the Evangelist Church opened in Maindee. Sir Charles Morgan's Statue moved to Park Square from High Street. Opening of first Newport Hospital, Stow Hill.
1861	Co-operative Stores established in Baneswell. Bristol Channel Pilots Act.
1862	Severn Valley Railway opened. Grand Review of Newport Volunteers staged on Newport Marshes. Stow Hill Parapet Wall built.
1863	Bridge Street opened. Victoria Assembly Rooms erected in Bridge Street. Queen's Hotel, Bridge Street, opened. Stow Hill Baptish Church built.
1864	Havelock Street Presbyterian Church built. Slaughter Houses opened in Wyndham Street. New Ragged Schools opened in Dock Street. Second railway station opened in Mill Street.
1865	Alexandra Dock Act. Sirhowy Railway opened. Third Newport Indoor Market opened by Duke of Beaufort.
1866	Newport Bridge widened in improvement programme. Summerhill Baptist Church, Maindee, opened. St. Woolos Churchyard railed in and closed to further burials.
1867	Opening of first ward in Newport Infirmary. First Drill Hall, Dock Street, erected. First Newport Regatta held.
1868	First sod of Alexandra Dock cut. Sailors' Home opened in Dock Street.
1869	Monmouthshire and South Wales Permanent Benefit Building Society established. Closing of chapel burial grounds.
1870	Establishment of Free Library. Newport Licensed Victuallers' Association established. Formation of Newport School Board under Education Act. Newport Chamber of Commerce formed.
1871	Population of Newport 26,957. Jewish Synagogue opened in Francis Street. First Free Library opened in Dock Street.
1872	Severn Terrace erected. New Dry Dock opened.
1873	Second Newport Improvement Act. Tredegar Wharf Schools opened. St. Woolos Schools opened in St. Mary Street.
1874	Opening of St. Mark's Church, Gold Tops. Holy Cross R.C. Schools opened in Emlyn Street. Newport Athletic Club organised. Association Football Team formed to play for N.A.C.
1875	Opening of Alexandra Dock. Death of Lord Tredegar. Drill Hall (Royal Albert Hall), Stow Hill, opened.
1876	Newport Athletic Club Association Football Team switch to Rugby Football.

Sailors' Home, Dock Street, closed. Borough Extension Act.
Thomas Street Level Crossing walled up.

1877
John Frost dies, aged 93. Athletic Grounds at Rodney Parade officially opened.
Thomas Street-Mill Street Subway opened.

1878
Opening of new Corn Exchange in High Street. Pant-yr-eos Reservoir completed.
Wesleyan Chapel, Marshes Road, opened. Duckpool Road Baptist Church opened.
First ever U.K. rugby match under floodlights played against Cardiff at Rodney Parade :
known as the 'Electric Light Match'.

1879
Newport Turnpike Gates at Clarence Place, Stow Hill, Cardiff Road and Shaftesbury Street
abolished. High Street widened.

1880
Monmouthshire and Great Western Railways amalgamate. Mill Street and Dock Street
railway stations closed. Marshes Road Board Schools opened. Allt-yr-yn Board Schools opened.
First G.P.O. Telephone "Exchange opened. Temple Street/Lime Street Railway Footbridge
erected.

1881
Population of Newport 35,313. Primitive Methodist Church, Station Street, opened.
Prince of Wales Theatre opened on site of old Gaiety Theatre (formerly Parrot Theatre).

1882
New Free Library building opened in Dock Street. Alexandra Road Board School opened.
Board of Trade Offices built. Pill Harriers Rugby Football Club formed.

1883
St. Andrew's Church, Liswerry, opened. Commercial Street, Wesleyan Church closed.
Barnardtown Board Schools opened. New Railway Bridge, Dock Street, opened.

1884
Amalgamation of Newport Town Dock and Alexandra Dock. Newport Fire Brigade
established. Stow Hill Wesleyan Church built. St. Stephen's Church, Pillgwenlly, opened.
Formation of Newport Chamber of Commerce.

1885
Crindau Gas Works opened. Bolt Street Board Schools opened. Smaller-sized Talbot Hotel
re-built on same site. Wesleyan Mission Chapel, Price Street, opened.
Entrance made to Railway Station from Devon Place.

1886
Crindau Glass Works opened. Enlargement of Post Office in High Street.
Newport Coal and Iron Exchange opened. Work begins on Severn Railway Tunnel.
Third Westgate Hotel opened on site of those previous.

1887
Enlargement of Stow Hill Infirmary. Old Hope Chapel pulled down. Corporation Road
opened. New Co-operative Stores, Dock Street, opened. New St. Michael's R.C. Church,
Pillgwenlly, opened. Seamen's Church and Institute opened in Temple Street.
Slipway, Dry Dock and Wharf, Liswerry, opened. Newport Indoor Market being rebuilt for
fourth time.

1888
Bath and West Show held in Newport. Eveswell Board Schools opened.
Newport Corporation take over Waterworks at purchase price of £287,000.
Opening of Severn Rail Tunnel. Museum and Art Gallery opened in Dock Street.
St. John's Church, Rogerstone, opened. Stone Railway Bridge over the Usk constructed.
Extension of Newport Infirmary. The New Theatre opens in Charles Street on site of the old
Gaiety Theatre. P. & A. Campbell begin their Bristol Channel and South Wales Paddles Steamer
trips.

1889
Temperance Hall, Dock Street, opened. St. Mark's New Sunday Schools, Queen's Hill,
opened. Borough boundaries extended to include Maindee and parts of Nash and St.
Woolos. Newport Indoor Market opened (4th such). Christchurch Local Board dissolved.

1890
New Harbour Act. Corporation Baths, Stow Hill, opened. Clarence Place Ropeworks
established. Rodney Parade Gymnasium opened. Messrs. Mordey and Carney's Dry Dock
opened. Model Lodgings Houses, Dock Street, opened.

1891	Population of Newport 54,707. St. Julian's Church opened. Spring Gardens Board Schools opened. East Usk Road Baptist Chapel opened. County of Gloucester Bank opens in High Street. Newport constituted a County Borough. Explosion on petroleum steamer in Dry Dock: five people killed.
1892	National and Provincial Bank opened. Congregational Church, London Street, built. Bridge Hotel (formerly the "Heathcock'), demolished. Church of St. Matthew, Barnardtown, opened. Bible Christian Mission Hall opened in Hereford Street. First edition of South Wales Argus published on 30th May 1892. Associated Chambers of Commerce (U.K.) at Newport.
1893	Newport Bridge has its "Townside dip" removed. New Wesleyan Church, Victoria Avenue, opened. New East Usk Lighthouse erected.
1894	Belle Vue Park opened. Opening of Durham Road Board Schools. Newport Medical Association formed. Tabernacle Chapel, Commercial Street, rebuilt. Newport People's Bank (pioneer in the U.K.) established.
1895	Electricity Works opened in Llanarth Street.Harry Street, off Cambrian Road, opened. Tredegar Hall and Constitutional Club opened on Stow Hill. New United Methodist Free Church, Hill Street, opened. Completion of Newport Town Hall extensions. Cambrian Road opened.
1896	Newport High School built on Queen's Hill. Fire Brigade Station, Dock Street, opened. Victoria Hall, Bridge Street, destroyed by fire. Caerleon Road Presbyterian Church opened. Liberal Institute, Hill Street, opened. Infectious Diseases Hospital opened at Allt-yr-yn. Intermediate and Technical Schools open at Queen's Hill.
1897	Lysaghts Galvanised Sheet Works commences operation. Welsh National Eisteddfod held at Belle Vue Park. Fields Park Road opened. Celebrations on Queen Victoria's Diamond Jubilee. Tredegar Pier, Pillgwenlly, erected. London City and Midland Bank, on corner of Stow Hill and Bridge Street, opened. New Offices for South Wales Argus open in High Street, opposite Station Approach.
1898	Municipal Buildings, Maindee, opened. Opening of Maindee Branch Library. 'All Saints' Church, Crindau, built. New Catholic Schools, Pillgwenlly, opened. Caerleon and Marshes Road Tramways, opened. Local School Board Offices in Charles Street opened by Lord Tredegar.
1899	St. Mary's 'Iron' Church, Corporation Road, opened. West Park Post Office opened on Stow Hill. Sunday funerals abolished by Newport Corporation. Cardiff Pure Ice and Cold Storage opened on Marches Road. Empire Palace Theatre opened on site of New Theatre in Charles Street. '100 foot arcade', between High Street and Cambrian Road, opened.
1900	Beechwood Park opens. King's Head Inn in High Street destroyed by fire. Newport Union Offices at Queen's Hill inaugurated. St. John's Baptist Church, Risca Road, opened. St. Mary's Catholic Schools, Queen's Hill, opened.
1901	Population of Newport 67,270. Horse-drawn tramways taken over by Newport Corporation. Newport and Monmouthshire Hospital (later Royal Gwent) opened by Right Hon. Viscount Tredegar. Clytha Board Schools, Risca Road, opened. Corporation Road Forward Movement Hall opened. Death of Queen Victoria: Representatives of Church and State at St. Woolos.
1902	Coronation of Edward VII: Newport celebrates. National Telephone Company's Exchange in Dock Street, opened. Tredegar Dry Dock opened. Wesleyan Church, St. Julian's Avenue, opened. County Borough of Newport divided into ten wards. Monmouthshire Council Offices, Queen's Hill, opened (County Hall). 4th Battalion South Wales Borderers' Drill Hall opened in Dock Street.
1903	Electric Tram-cars replace horse-drawn variety. Corporation Road Board Schools opened. Queen Victoria Memorial Almshouses opened on Stow Hill. West Park Laundry opened. New Newport Workhouse, Stow Hill, completed. Extensions to Allt-yr-yn Infectious Diseases Hospital. Power Station, Corporation Road, built. With 4 trains carrying 700 men and 500

horses, Buffalo Bill (Col. William Cody) arrives to present his Wild West Show at Shaftesbury Park.

1904   Tidal Wave submerges land at Newport and Caerleon. Bridge Street Railway Bridge opened. New Church of St. Luke's opened in Bridge Street. Baptist Church, Llanthewy Road, opened. Newly-rebuilt King's Head Inn opened as King's Head Hotel. Lord Tredegar opens Newport Daily Exchange. Newport School Board dissolved. Electric trams commence running on Stow Hill route.

1905   Houdini plays Lyceum Theatre: Escapes from Newport Police cells. New Corporation Waterworks opens with reservoir at Wentwood: cost of £380,000. St. Woolos Board Schools, Stow Hill, opened. Pillgwenlly Police Station opened. St. Mary's New Presbytery built on Stow Hill. Seamen's New Institute, Ruperra Street, opened. Education Authority take over Tredegar Wharf Schools.

1906   Durham Road School built. Transporter Bridge opened. Newport Asylum, Caerleon, opened. Opening of Great Central Hall, Commercial Street. Work on deep water entrance to Newport Dock commences. Carnegie Free Library, Corporation Road, opens

1907   Prince of Wales, later King Edward VIII, visits Bath and West Show in Newport. G.W.R. trains collide at Ebbw Junction: Train driver killed and passengers injured.

1909   South Dock Extension disaster: 33 men killed. Boy hero Tom (Toya) Lewis presented with Albert Medal for bravery in Dock disaster. Alderman John Moses receives Freedom of Newport. Godfrey Charles Morgan, Viscount Tredegar, received Freedom of Newport.

1910   Newport Technical Institute, costing £40,000, is opened in Clarence Place. More bodies recovered from the South Dock disaster of 1909. Plaza Cinema opened in Commercial Road.

1911   Population of Newport 83,691.

1912   Dr Garrod Thomas of the Monmouthshire and Newport Hospital, a prime mover of the Newport Hospital Services, received Knighthood. 45th Annual Conference of the Trades Union Congress held at Newport. Newport County Association Football Team formed.

1913   Viscount Tredegar dies. Extension of Newport General Post Office. Gem Cinema in Commercial Road opened by Mayor. Newport boxer, Johnny Basham, knocks out Harry Price of Liverpool. Price later dies and Basham is arrested but ultimately acquitted. Houdini plays Newport again. Leaps from Tower Bridge in shackles to make underwater escape. Newport and Monmouthshire Hospital becomes Royal Gwent.

1914   New lock at Alexandra Dock opened by H.R.H. Prince Albert of Connaught. War declared on Germany. German liner "Belgia" boarded by Newport Police in Channel and brought into Newport Docks as a 'prize of war'. Torpedo fired in error at Alexandra Dock. Misses an Italian vessel and damages river bank.

1915   Newport residents told to black-out windows to reduce possibility of German air attacks. Newportonian, Mr J.H. (Jimmy) Thomas, M.P., attends a recruiting rally at Great Central Hall.

1916   Johnny Basham wins Lonsdale Belt outright after defeating Eddie Beattie in Welterweight Title bout. Newport Tramways introduces conductresses due to shortage of male labour. Sir John Beynon presents a manor house to Health Authority for use as a maternity hospital in memory of his wife, Lydia Beynon.

1917   Peacocks at Beechwood Park transferred to Belle Vue Park Electric Trams Service extended to Newport Dock Entrance at bottom of Alexandra Road.

1918   Royal Gwent Hospital debt paid off by a Newport industrial company. World War I ends. Food rationing relaxed. Prisoners of War return home.

1919   Whitehead Iron and Steel Co. to build factory in Mendalgief Road. Fete in aid of Royal Gwent Hospital to be held in Friars' Fields, later part of the hospital complex. Racial riots in George Street: Property damaged and over 30 people arrested. Reported losses of £76,000 on Transporter Bridge since its opening in 1906. Newport County reformed and elected to First Division of Southern League. 'Grant of Arms' to Royal Gwent Hospital.

1920	Newport tram workers' strike. Newport County in Football League: First Division Southern League becomes Third Division of Football League.
1921	Price of Wales (later King Edwards VIII) visits Newport Docks. Newport Rugby Club field All-International side. Every man capped by either Wales or one of the Home Countries. Population of Newport 92,358.
1922	Whitehead Iron and Steel Co. begin operation of new works at Mendalgief Road. Many old warships bought by John Cashmore Ltd. for breaking at Newport. Albert Augustus Newman receives Freedom of Newport.
1923	Cenotaph erected in Clarence Place. Famous Newport poet, W.H. Davies, presents valuable works to Town Museum and Art Gallery.
1924	Rt. Hon. James Henry (Jimmy) Thomas made Freeman of Newport.
1925	Spittles Cambrian Foundry near Town Dock, destroyed by fire.
1926	Isle of Wight death announced of Rev. Father Hill; 20 years in charge of St. Michael's. Route to cemetery thronged with mourners.
1927	Pavilion Cinema opens. John Cashmore Ltd. dismantling British submarines K2,K6 and H21. Alderman Thomas Parry receives Freedom of Newport.
1928	Lysaght's Institute, Corporation Road, opened.
1929	Lyceum Theatre converts to Cinema. Olympia Cinema in Skinner Street acquired by A.B.C. (Associated British Cinemas). James Walker elected as Labour's first M.P. for Newport.
1930	Father Hill R.C. Memorial School opens in Oswald Road.
1931	Death announced of Sir Garrod Thomas. St. Woolos Church becomes the Cathedral of the new Diocese of Monmouth. Population of Newport 89,203.
1932	John Cashmore dies, aged 92: Founder of John Cashmore Ltd. the Newport shipbreakers. Greyhound track to open at Somerton Park. Hundreds of unemployed men clean up old Tyne Engine Works, Mill Parade, preparatory to its use as unemployment centre.
1933	Peacocks at Belle Vue Park sold for £3 each. St. Julian's House, one-time home of the Firbank family (Railway Contractors) is demolished preparatory to building of Merlin Crescent.
1934	Horace Sampson Lyne received Freedom of Newport. New Bowling Green opened at Belle Vue Park. New Tredegar Wharf School opened; had been rebuilt on same site. New Synagogue to open on Queen's Hill. Old Synagogue in Francis Street closes.
1935	Foundation stone of new Holy Cross School laid. Newport Playgoers Society take over the old St. James' Church, Dock Street, henceforth to be known at The Little Theatre. Cunard White Star Liner 'Doric' arrives at John Cashmores for breaking. King George V and Queen Mary Jubilee celebrations in May. Alderman John Moxon receives Freedom of Newport.
1936	Newport mourns death of King George V. Clearance of site for Civic Centre commences. Newly-constructed Kingsway By-Pass, between Town Bridge and Cardiff Road, opened. Williamd Royce Lysaght, Alderman Frederick Phillips and Alderman Dr. John Lloyd Davies are made Freemen of Newport in triple ceremony unique in Town's history.
1937	First production of Little Theatre in Dock Street; the play 'And So To Bed' directed by Edward Granger. King George VI and His Queen, Elizabeth, arrive to cut first sod on site of new Civic Centre. Councillor, Mrs. Mary Hart, becomes Newport's first Lady Mayor. Last electric tram runs in September.

1938	Maindee Swimming Pools, Victoria Avenue, opened. Savoy Hotel buildings, on corner of Station Approach, demolished to make way for new G.P.O. Odeon Cinema, Clarence Place, opens showing 'Young and Innocent' with Nova Pilbeam. First communal air raid shelter built at Anchorage Yard, Brunel Street. Mr and Mrs W.H. Davies accompanied by John Masefield, Poet Laureate, and Mrs Masefield attend unveiling of commemorative plaque to W.H. Davies at his birthplace, Church House in Portland Street.
1939	Air-raid sirens tested. Liner 'Balmoral Castle' arrives at Cashmores for breaking. Maindee Super Cinema opens showing 'If I Were King' starring Ronald Coleman. Barrage balloons fly over Newport. Newport County win promotion to Second Division of Football League. Work commences on site of new Royal Ordnance Factory at Clark's Fields, off Corporation Road. Standard Telephone & Cables take over site in 1946. Royal Gwent Hospital celebrates Centenary. Anderson Shelters erected widely. War Declared on Germany.
1940	Police Administrative Department transferred from Town Hall to new Civic Centre. First bomb damage; direct hit on Cleveland Oil Depot, Corporation Road. Royal Ordnance Factory, off Corporation Road, opens. Poet, W.H. Davies, dies. Gas masks and stirrup pumps distributed throughout Town. Bomb falls on Dock Street; 3 year old boy buried but discovered unharmed. Bomb falls in Dewstow Street: Houses badly damaged. Enemy plane fouls Barrage Balloon and crashes on house in Stow Park Avenue, killing two children. Alexandra Dock Hotel badly damaged in raid: 3 killed.
1941	St. Julian's High School opened. Heroic P.C. Charles Cook, receives George Medal for his valour in Alexandra Hotel bombing. Rationing of clothes, boots and shoes commences. Bombs fall over wide area of Newport including Fields Park Avenue, Ridgeway Avenue and Glasllwch Crescent: 6 people killed and 41 injured. Parachute mines dropped on Eveswell Street area, Beechwood Road, Kensington Place and Archibald Street: 37 people killed, 42 seriously injured.
1942	Newport houses lose their metal gates and railings in aid of war scrap effort. World War I tank at junction of Livingstone Place and Chepstow Road also taken for scrap. Newport Empire Variety Theatre destroyed in fire. Mr Ernest Bevin, M.P. (Minister of Labour and National Service), opens Merchant Navy Club in Commercial Road. Spitfire is named "Pride of Newport" after being purchased by local contributions.
1943	United States troop camp established at Malpas.
1944	Blackout restrictions lifted. Joe Louis, World Heavyweight Boxing Champion, in exhibition fight in Allied Services Boxing Tournament at Athletic Grounds, Rodney Parade.
1945	Bonfires in the streets as Newport celebrates the end of the War in Europe (V.E. Day) and Victory over Japan (V.J. Day). Alway Estate built. Whitehead Iron and Steel Co. reveal that they produced most of the steel bars for Mulberry Harbour and the armoured plate for 'Pluto' (Pipe Line Under the Ocean). Both contributed to success of the Normandy Invasion. Field Marshall Bernard Law Montgomery ("Monty" of Alamein) arrives at Newport to receive Freedom of the Town.
1946	Royal Ordnance Factory becomes Standard Telephones and Cables Ltd. Transporter Bridge Tolls finally abolished. World War II Victory Parade through Newport.
1947	Pill Harriers Rugby Club ends after more than 60 years. Newport Cinemas to open on Sundays. Newport boxer, Johnny Basham, dies. South Wales Borderers (24th/41st Foot) received Freedom of Newport. Pavilion Cinema becomes Variety Theatre.
1948	Monmouthshire and Newport Executive Council offices open in Caerau Road for administration under new National Health Service of Chemists, Opticians, Dentists and Family Practitioners. 39,000 rats killed in Newport under Ministry of Food Scheme.
1949	Death of Rt. Hon. J.H. (Jimmy) Thomas. St. John's Church, Maindee, gutted by fire. Factory of Monsanto Chemicals opens. Blaen-y-pant home for Senior Citizens opened by Captain Geoffrey Crawshay, Chairman of the Welsh Board of Health. School of porpoises seen frolicking in Usk near Old Town Bridge.
1950	Last meeting of Newport Council at Town Hall prior to taking residence at Civic Centre. After reverting to films in late 1949, the Pavilion Theatre finally closes.

1951	Festival of Britain celebrations take place in streets and factories across Newport. Employees of Newport Hosiery Co., Portland Street, strike. Population of Newport 105,547.
1952	Church House, Portland Street, birthplace of Newport poet W.H.Davies, is listed as of outstanding historical and architectural interest.
1953	Atlantic Shipbuilding Co. opens in Alexandra Dock. Queen Elizabeth II visits Newport.
1954	Gem Cinema in Commercial Road closes. First Mosque in Monmouthshire opens at rear of boarding house in Ruperra Street. Mrs Mary Hart, Newport's first Lady Mayor, receives Freedom of Newport.
1955	St. John the Baptist Church, Risca Road, gutted by fire.
1956	P. & A. Campbell Pleasure Steamers announce end of sailings from Newport.
1957	Plaza Cinema closes. Redevelopment of Pillgwenlly commences. First Compulsory Purchase Order under 1957 Housing Act covers Frederick and Portland Streets.
1958	Newport Transporter Bridge to be used in making of the film "Tiger Bay". Hartridge Comprehensive School opened. Clayton Moore, T.V.'s masked Lone Ranger, visits the Childrens' Ward at Royal Gwent Hospital.
1959	Construction commences of Spencer Steelworks at Llanwern: hundreds of shale lorries pass through Town every day. Two Newport men charged with murder of Dock Street Newsagent, Augustus (Gus) Roberts.
1960	Work begins on the building of Lodge Farm Housing Estate, Caerleon. Dick Richardson of Newport becomes European Heavyweight Boxing Champion. Great Central Hall closes after 54 years.
1961	Lyceum Theatre, Bridge Street, finally closes its doors in February after the Annual Pantomime, 'Little Miss Muffet' starring Sandy Powell. Population of Newport 108,123.
1962	Completion of Spencer Steelworks, Llanwern. Work begins on George Street River Bridge. Commercial Road Baptist Church closes.
1963	Newport Rugby Club are only team to beat Wilson Whineray's 'All Blacks' during their tour.
1964	George Street Bridge opened. Olympia Cinema closes.
1965	H.M. Tax Office, Clarence Place, built. British Glues and Chemicals, off Corporation Road, demolished. Work begins on the A.B.C. Cinema, Bridge Street (Site of old Lyceum).
1966	Newport By-pass Section of M4 opened. Severn Bridge opened by H.M. Queen Elizabeth II. Duffryn Comprehensive School opened.
1967	Prime Minister, Mr Harold Wilson, opens new timber terminal at Newport Docks.
1968	Lower Dock Street largely disappears with new Town development. Sovereign Arcade, Kingsway Centre, built. Dolman Theatre, Kingsway Centre, built. New Library and Museum built in John Frost Square. Chartist Tower Block built.
1969	Clock Tower added to Civic Centre. Royal Regiment of Wales receives Freedom of Newport. New A.B.C. Cinema Complex opens on site of old Lyceum Theatre. Commences with Tommy Steel in film 'Half a Sixpence'.
1970	Fire Brigade Station, Dock Street, demolished. Capitol Cinema, Dock Street, demolished. British Statistics Office, Cardiff Road, built. Old Newport High School building in Queen's Hill taken over for Queen's Comprehensive School. St. Joseph's High School, Duffryn, opened.
1971	Christchurch School demolished. Population of Newport 136,847.

1972	Wales Gas Headquarters, Mill Street, demolished. John Frost Square built.
1973	Corn Exchange, High Street, demolished. Clarence House, Clarence Place, built. Old Green Development begins. Bettws School built. First tenants move into Gaer Vale. Pillgwenlly Redevelopment Scheme starts.
1974	Caerleon integrated with Newport Borough. Monmouthshire becomes Gwent. Alexandra Dock Hotel, previously rebuilt after 1940's bombing, now finally demolished.
1975	British Tubes (formerly Stewart and Lloyds), Corporation Road, demolished. Old Green Roundabout and Underpass opened. Holy Trinity Church, Potter Street, closes after 123 years. Newport Borough begins renovation of recently acquired Tredegar House and Country Park.
1976	Pedestrianisation of Commercial Street begins. John Cashmore close their shipbreaking operation after nearly 60 years. Alma Street Baptist Church demolished.
1977	Construction of Queensway. Demolition of old Anchor Brewery, Cardiff Road: Site earmarked for new Police Headquarters.
1978	Pill Labour R.F.C. combine with Hibernians R.F.C. to form New Pill Harriers. Price Street Methodist Church closes prior to demolition. 104th Air Defence Regiment of Royal Artillery receive Freedom of Newport.
1979	Proposals to move Cenotaph to new site at Civic Centre.
1980	Newport Power Station, Corporation Road, demolished. Newport Nail Factory, Somerton, demolished. Canal Restoration started. Steel Strikers march on Civic Centre. Temple Street Police Station, closed in 1905, finally demolished.
1981	Inmos, on Cardiff Road, built. Corporation Road Railway Bridge demolished. Odeon Cinema, Clarence Place, closes. Pillgwenlly Community Centre opens. Population of Newport 130,799.
1982	Cold Store, Shaftesbury Street, demolished. Celtic Manor Hotel opens on site of former Lydia Beynon Maternity Hospital. Bolt Street Enterprise Park built. Royal Oak Inn, Chepstow Road, demolished. New Royal Oak to be built on same site. Ebenezer Welsh Church, Commercial Road, closes.
1983	Newport Indoor Market redevelopment begins. Newport's David Pearce becomes British Heavyweight Boxing Champion.
1984	St. John's School, Risca Road, demolished. Sainsbury's Supermarket, Malpas Road, built. Bolt Street School closes.
1985	Compton and Webb Factory demolished. Extension built to Maindee Police Station. Labour Leader, Neil Kinnock, M.P., opens the Newport Centre on June 29th. Transporter Bridge ceases operation.
1986	Pedestrianisation of Commercial Street completed. New Public Conveniences, Cardiff Road, opened. Aneurin Bevan Court, apartments for aged, opened at Duffryn. G.J. Lovell's new factory built at Queen's Meadow. General Post Office moves to Bridge Street.
1987	Studio 1 and 2 Cinema (formerly Coliseum) in Clarence Place, closed,
1988	Newport County, in financial difficulties, are 'wound up'. Welsh National Eisteddfod held in Tredegar House and Country Park. Plans for River Usk Barrage are unveiled.
1989	Newport A.F.C. (The Exiles) formed. More street off Newport Town Centre to be pedestrianised. New Docksway Industrial Road constructed between the Newport Centre and Docks Gates.
1990	Paul Bothwell Kincaid's controversial statue of W.H. Davies, Newport's 'Tramp' Poet, unveiled in Commercial Street.

1991
Queen's Comprehensive School, housed since 1970 in former building of Newport High School, closes doors for last time. Work commences on Celtic Lakes Business Park, Duffryn. Victoria Walk Shopping Precinct, formerly Y.M.C.A. Building in Commercial Street, opened and closed. Statuary commemorating Chartist Riots of 1839 unveiled on 28th January in Westgate Square. Merchant Navy Commemorative Memorial unveiled at junction of Kingsway and Cardiff Road (Gilligan's Island). 'The Wave', a giant steel sculpture by Peter Fink, unveiled at Town Reach, near Newport River Bridge, by Duke of Kent. Application for Newport to become a city is turned down. New Law Courts at front of Civic Centre opened. Transporter Bridge to re-open. Financial support from C.A.D.W.
Population of Newport 133,318.

1992
Statue of Sir Charles Morgan moved from Park Square to new site in Bridge Street, near Westgate Square. 'Octopus' Bridge in Lower Dock Street, demolished. South Wales Argus celebrates Centenary. Work starts on second Severn Bridge near Caldicot. Original buildings of Royal Gwent Hospital demolished, revealing new development at rear. Major face-lift at '100 foot arcade' between High Street and Cambrian Road commences. 'In The Nick of Time' Clock which was designed by Andy Plant and Ali Wood for the Ebbw Vale Garden Festival is resited in John Frost Square.

1993
Newport Police leave Civic Centre for new Divisional Police H.Q. which opens on Cardiff Road. Work commences on new Bus Station in Kingsway. Private Bill to be presented to Parliament for proposed River Usk Barrage Scheme. Proposals announced for M4 By-pass to the south of Newport Shaftesbury Street and Malpas Road developments of by-pass for Malpas Tunnels at an advanced stage.

1994
Public Enquiry into Usk Barrage Scheme opens at old Law Courts in Newport's Civic Centre. 'Big Brother' arrives. Council install C.C.T.V. cameras in Newport Town Centre to increase security. Newport Association Football Club, 'The Exiles', return to play in Newport after exile in Gloucester. Davies Bros. (Deebees) taken over by Robert Price (Builders' Merchants) Ltd. of Swansea. Newport Celebrations in Westgate Square to mark anniversary of Chartist Riots of 1839. The event to become a regular feature.
Newport Technical College closes down. Joe Sheppard, maintenance engineer for Newport Transporter Bridge died and was cremated. His ashes were taken to the top of the Bridge and scattered into the River Usk at his request.

1995
The renovated Transporter Bridge was officially opened by Clare Short M.P. on Friday 15th December. The route for the M4 relief road announced, wildlife groups speak out against scheme.

1996
L.G. formerly Lucky Goldstar to build near Newport. Korean firm to spend £1.7 billion on two factories. Celtic Manor Golf Course given green light. Green Group slam tarmac madness, proposed relief road to by-pass the M4 is to go ahead.

1997
Work on L.G. Factory begins. Footbridge built over the A48 road at Coedkernew to act as gateway to factory sites. Alan Howarth selected as M.P. candidate for Newport.
Virgin Cinema opens at Leeway Retail Park.

1998
Legend Court Theme Park could create 6,500 jobs. L.G. future of plant still in doubt. Council gives go-ahead for redevelopment of Westgate.
£100 million upgrade for Celtic Manor Hotel.

1999
The Labour Club on Stow Hill converted into homes. Roman remains found on Celtic Manor Golf Course. Newport's bid to become Millennium City. Major Film Studio planned for Penhow. Theme Park objections from Wildlife and Environmental Group.

2000	In celebration of the new Millennium, floodlighting was switched on and a grand fireworks display took place at the Transporter Bridge. Transporter Bridge Visitor Centre opened by Mayor Graham Dally who presented a plaque to Bridge Chairman Terry Underwood. Theme Park Project is dead. Celtic Springs Business Park planned. Morrison developments given outline planning permission to develop Business Park in Newport. Westgate Hotel to be transformed into Shopping Centre. New road plan would mean moving Cenotaph from Clarence Place. Chapel Park, Charles Street, Park opens on site of demolished Church.
2001	Council drops plan to move memorial. Riverside Walkways near completion.
2002	Newport granted City status. Her Majesty Queen Elizabeth and Prince Phillip visits Newport, reception held at Newport Centre. First sod cut on River Usk Bank for a new Theatre. Remains of a medieval ship unearthed on the site of the New Theatre. Medieval ship site opened to the public, campaigners unite to save the ship. Welsh Assembly grant Newport £3.5 million to save the ship.
2003	£100 million new City Centre Scheme announced. Velodrome near completion. Wetlands at Nash opened to the public. Timbers from medieval ship rehouses at Maesglas in water tanks. South Distribution Road Bridge over the River Usk near completion. Newport Technical College to be turned into flats. New Hospital planned for Newport, to be built on the Corus site, formerly Whiteheads Iron and Steel Co. Newport in Bloom wins the competition for the whole of Wales for the fifth year in succession. Odeon Cinema, Clarence Place, reopens as Newport Live Arena.
2004	The Velodrome indoor arena at Spytty Park now open. The Southern Distribution Bridge and road due to open in the summer of 2004. Newports' New Theatre and Arts Centre on the River Usk bank due to open in the autumn of 2004. The Riverefront Theatre and Arts Centre, although unfinished, opened its doors to a selected group of city councillors and A.M. members of the public who had contributed in some way or another on May 24th 2004.

The foregoing is not intended to be comprehensive – for this, many books would be required – but as an informative and nostalgic ramble through time.

Murals in progress at the Civic Centre

Roger Smith's artist impression of murals currently being painted at the Civic Centre ground floor by him. The Westgate Square Commercual Street.

Montage of historic Newport by Roger Smith, one of the new murals he is painting at the Civic Centre, Newport.

191

Mural of Newport Rugby Football Club.

New Murals to be displayed on the Ground Floor at Newport Civic Centre by artist Roger Smith.

Mural of Newport Centre Swimmimg pool.

192

QUEEN IN NEWPORT – JUNE 13TH 2002

The Queen visited Newport on June 13th 2002 as part of her Golden Jubilee Tour of Wales. The news was welcomed by Newport's Mayor Mr Ron Morris who said "We are delighted that the Queen is visiting Newport as part of her Tour of Wales, the visit is an honour for Newport and everyone who lives and works here".

And those campaigning for Newport to receive city status also welcomed the Royal visit.

Sir Harry Jones, Leader of Newport Council, said "No announcement about city status has been made yet, we believe that Newport has a strong case to be honoured as the Golden Jubilee City. Newport already acts and feels like a city, and if granted the honour, we are ready to ensure that the benefits of city status will be felt across Wales".

Newport was granted city status on the 14th March 2002.

Her Majesty The Queen visits the City of Newport, June 13th 2002 as part of her Golden Jubilee tour of Wales.

Greetings from Her Majesty Queen Elizabeth 2nd arriving at Newport Station.

Her Majesty The Queen and Prince Phillip Duke of Edingborough are welcomed to the new City.

A Toast
to the Toastmaster

Harry Poloway B.E.M.

Harry Poloway born on December 20th 1915, as a lad had no idea what exciting days lay ahead of him.

Articled pupil at Newport Corporations Electrical Department with whom he remained until his retirement in 1975 - following 42 years of service.

During a luncheon attended by members of the Royal Family on a visit to Wales they noted the strong voice, upright presence, and charming smile of Cardiff Cities Toastmaster, young Harry Poloway regularly received many accolades from diners, officials and certainly from these Royal guests.

At the outbreak of war, Harry joined the RAF voluntary reserves soon seeing active service in Egypt, South Africa and Italy.

Returning to Wales from his war time activities Harry returned to his previous employment and his clutches as Toast Master finding himself once more in great demand.

His father who was a Tailor in Clarence Place, encouraged Harry by making him his first red tailcoat. Soon to be worn at a City Hall Function in Cardiff following an invite from the Lord Mayor's Secretary to M.C. the function as official Toastmaster, a title he has held for nearly 50 years, a national record.

When her majesty the Queen and H.R.H. Prince Phillip went on a state visit to Washington DC, it was necessary to take them with them a British Toastmaster. Harry Poloway B.E.M. was duly elected.

A Commander of the order of St. John, Honourary Banker of the Variety Club of Great Britain, and a stalwart of his local synagogue, a Past National President of the Institute of Toastmasters. An Honourary member of the Institute of Public Relations, a royal favourite, whereby almost every charitable organisation in South Wales has called upon the services of "Harry the Gavel".

When Harry received his British Empire Medal his dear wife Vicki, a Yorkshire lass, to whom he has been married for 60 years, together with his friends (and there must have been thousands), were delighted and proud to share in his success. The county's living legend is still in royal demand.

In 2002 Newport became a city and was visited by her Majesty the Queen and Prince Phillip on 13th June, and who was invited to be toastmaster at the important event? HARRY POLOWAY B.E.M.

'Truly our master of ceremonies'.

Harry shows off his British Empire Medal.

Harry receives the Toastmaster Award.

Harry Poloway B.E.M.,
Newports own Toast Master.

Harry Poloway on board the Brittania
The countrys living legend still in Royal
demand.

Be upstanding for...? Me? No it's him, the one sitting down.

PAUL FLYNN M.P. FOR NEWPORT WEST

Paul FLYNN Labour - Majority: 9,304 (26.5%)
House of Commons, London SW1A OAA.

Paul Flynn was elected to Parliament in 1987. Born 9 February 1935, he was educated at, Cardiff and University College of Wales, Cardiff. An industrialist in the Llanwern Steel Works from 1955 to 1982, he worked briefly as a local broadcaster before becoming a researcher for Llew Smith, then MEP for South Wales in 1984. He was a member of Newport Borough Council 1972-81, and Deputy Mayor of the Council, 1980. He also served as a Gwent County Councillor 1974-83, having previously contested Denbigh for Labour at the October 1974 general election.

Paul Flynn was appointed a frontbench spokesperson on Welsh Affairs in 1988 before becoming an Opposition spokesperson on Social Security, 1988-90. He also served on Transport Select Committee, 1992-7. Winner of the Campaign for Freedom of Information Award in 1991, he was also joint winner of The Spectator Backbencher of the Year in 1996. A fluent Welsh-speaker, he was elected to the Gorsedd of the Bards in 1991. His book, Commons Knowledge: How to be a Backbencher was published in July 2000, he was awarded The New Statesman Elected Representative, where he first published his account of Welsh Labour's leadership elections. Married with three children, his political interests include relaxation of soft drugs, animal welfare, constitutional reform, pensions, social security and the Welsh language.

Wards

Constituency comprises the following electoral wards:

Allt-yr-yn, Bettws, Caerleon, Gaer, Graig, Malpas, Marshfield, Pillgwenlly, Rogerstone, Shaftesbury, Stow Hill, Tredegar Park.

2001 General Election Result

Electorate: 59,345   Turnout: 59.1%

Party Votes Cast
% Change 97-01

FLYNN, Paul
Lab   18,489
52.7 -7.8%
MORGAN, Bill
Con 9,185
26.2 +1.8%
WATKINS, Veronica
Lib D 4,095
11.7 +2.0%
XXXXWELD, Anthoney
PC 2,510
7.2 +5.5%
MOELWYN HUGHES, Hugh
UKIP 506
1.4 +0.6%
XXILL, Terrance
BNP 278
0.8

Newport West was captured by the Conservatives at the first general election following division of the borough in 1983. Mark Robinson, a Junior Welsh Office Minister, tried to defend his tiny majority in 1987 however, allowing Labour to regain control. With the 1992 and 1997 elections Labour substantially increased its majority. The National Assembly elections in 1999 also recorded a Labour victory in Newport West, also saw a five-fold increase in the support for Plaid Cymru. The sitting MP, Paul Flynn was untroubled by a similar surge to Plaid Cymru in June 2001 and was returned substantial, if slightly reduced, majority.

Although almost wholly English-speaking town, Newport has hosted the National Eisteddfod to great acclaim, and a new Welsh-medium primary school is flourishing. Newport has also played an important part in the renaissance of Welsh pop music, coupled with major inward investment projects in electronics and other hi-tech plants. The creation of the Celtic Manor Resort Hotel by local multi-millionaire Terry Matthews, prior to Newport becoming the venue for the 2010 Ryder Cup golf competition. A renaissance is underway at Rodney Parade, the home of Newport Rugby Club. A new era of professional rugby union has seen an influx of some of the world's greatest players in an effort to restore the standing of the famous Monmouthshire club.

ROSEMARY BUTLER
AM for Newport West

Majority: 4,710

Rosemary Butler is a former member of Newport County Council and represented Caerleon for 26 years before relinquishing her post to stand for the National Assembly. She served as the town's Mayor and as Chair of Leisure Services. Brought up in the Rhymney Valley, she was educated at St Julian's High School in Newport. She is former member of the Broadcasting Council for Wales and the Sports Council for Wales. She has also served as a Museums and Galleries Commissioner and was a Director of Tourism South & West Wales Ltd.

Rosemary Butler was appointed Secretary for Pre-16 Education in the first Assembly Cabinet. She returned to the backbenchers in the reshuffle following the formation of the coalition with the Liberal Democrats. She was also subsequently defeated in the election to become Deputy Presiding Officer of the National Assembly. She has subsequently been appointed the National Assembly representative on the European Union Committee of the Regions. Rosemary Butler is a member of the Culture Committee, the European Affairs Committee, the Legislation Committee and a member of the South East Wales Regional Committee. A founder member of Newport Women's Aid, she is also a school governor. She is married with two children and one grandchild.

Register of Members' Interests (July 2001)

Membership/Chair of bodies in receipt of Assembly funds - Governor, University of Wales College, Newport (Resigned as of 7.12.99)

1999 Assembly Election Result

Electorate: 57,243

Turnout: 42.3%

	Party	Votes Cast	%
BUTLER, Rosemary	Lab	11,538	47.6
GRAHAM, William	Con	6,828	28.2
VICKERY Bob	PC	3,053	12.6
WATKINS, Veronica	Lib D	2,820	11.6

Roy Hughes now Lord Islwyn

Former M.P. to become a Lord. Hughes, Roy b. 1925; addys. Y.R. Pontllanfraith, G.S., Ruskin Coll. Oxon. Former Administrative Officer. El for Newport (later Newport East) 1966-97. Elevated to the House of Lords as Lord Islwyn of Casnewydd. Lord Islwyn passed away in December 2003.

Lord Islwyn on one of his many walk-abouts

Councillor Noel Trigg with his wife Valerie.

Friends of Noel and Valerie from Korea.

Boxer Noel Trigg.

Noel on bike.

Noel Trigg

Noel, a renowned Welsh champion boxer of the 1950s, has continued to enjoy a busy lifestyle since retiring from the sports shop business that he ran some 25 years ago.

He went from the world of sport into the licensed trade as landlord of the Coach and Horses, Caerwent, before returning from three-and-a-half years living in Gibraltar to build the Gladiator pub at Malpas.

The Gladiator became one of Newport's most successful and thriving pubs, and it was certainly a sad day for the locals when Noel decided to call time some seven years later.

During this time, Noel and fellow Korean War Veterans were invited to Seoul, where he was presented with a Peace Medal, on behalf of the Korean government, followed by a memorable week's sightseeing, when their hosts were the Satbyul Lioness Club and its chairwoman Kim So Sik and treasurer Kim Jae Wha.

Noel still retained an involvement with boxing, managing local light-heavyweight Roger Wilson and opening a gymnasium over the old Harlequin pub in Shaftesbury.

But local government was to take an increasing role in Noel's life, and after moving to Bettws Lane, he was elected to Newport Borough Council as a Labour candidate, serving the Bettws constituency. This soon became akin to a full time job as Noel worked relentlessly to improve Bettws' image. A major initiative was the formation of Bettws in Bloom, an organisation still going strong that is known nationwide and was last year nominated for an award in the prestigious Britain in Bloom competition.

Council work continues to play a central role in Noel's life, together with his family of wife Valerie, daughters Louise, who is married to the Press Association's rugby union correspondent Andrew Baldock, Melanie, her partner Lee, four grandchildren - Kirsty, Gabrielle, Luke and Chloe - together with great-grandchild Elise.

Nine-year-old Luke is showing great promise as a talented sportsman, particularly as a footballer, cross-country runner and tennis player. A chip off the old block!

Through Noel's council work, he has made many new friends and renewed acquaintances with a lot of old school pals.

He is still fighting fit, even though twelve rounds might be a little beyond him these days.

Bettws in Bloom

Flowers in your garden,
Flowers at your feet,
Bettws flowers blooming,
Waiting to compete.

Nodding when the wind blows,
Smiling when there's sun,
Every flower a winner,
Well done Bettws, well done.

Terry Underwood

ARTHUR MACHEN
Author and Journalist

Writer Arthur Machen, was born in Caerleon in High Street on 3rd March 1863. He wrote many books that contained impeccable English and with a complete understanding of human nature reached the hearts and minds of those who took the trouble to read them.

Machen was profoundly Celtic and it was the landscape which surrounded Caerleon that first awakened the creative urge in him.

The following is how Machen describes the moments that inspired him to write books:
"I believe it was in November of that autumn of 1880 that i set out one morning to walk to Newport for no particular reason that I can remember, probably there had been a slight frost during the night. The day was shining and there was a crispness in the air which made me want to step it out. I had climbed up the long hill from Llantarnam and was on my way towards Malpas when I saw Twym Barlwm on the heights above Pontypool, it appeared dressed in radiant blue under a paler blue sky, the sun shone on the little white houses and farm cottages on the mountainside which made the whitewashed walls stand out gloriously as if they were marble. I experienced an indescribable emotion, and I always attribute that moment and that emotion my impulse towards literature."

Author Arthur Machen.

In the garden.

The birthplace of Caerleon author Arthur Machen in High Street.

Commemorative plaques where Authur Machen was born.

That day was the commencement of his career as an author. Later Arthur Machen moved from Caerleon to find work in London, he worked in theatre playing small parts in Shakespearian plays, he also worked for a number of London newspapers as a journalist. Often talking about Caerleon the town of his birth, where his daydreams became reality on his frequent visits back home.

He remembers the Summer Sun of some fifty years ago shining beautifully on a little white town in a dream, with a white road coming down the hill from Newport, through St. Julians Wood and so to the level river meadows, then winding in a curve and coming to the town over the bridge … my town, Caerleon.
He wrote once:

"I shall always esteem it as the greatest piece of fortune that has fallen on me, that I was born in that noble fallen Caerleon-On-Usk in the heart of Gwent, my greatest fortune, I mean, from the point of view which I now more especially have in mind, the career of letters. For the older I grow the more firmly am I convinced that anything I may have accomplished in literature is due to the fact that when my eyes were first opened in earliest childhood they had before them the vision of an enchanted land, as soon as I saw anything I saw Twym-Barlwm, the mystic tumulus, the memorial of peoples that dwelt in this region before the Celts left the land 9f Summer."

During his lifetime Arthur Machen wrote thirty books and thousands of newspaper articles.
His books include…

The Anatomy of Tobacco	1884
The Chronicle of Clemedy	1888
The Great God Pan	1894
The Three Impostors	1895
Hieroglyphics	1906
The House of Souls	1906
Dr. Stiggins - His Views and Principles	1906
The Hill of Dreams	1907
The Bowmen and other Legend of the War	1915
The Great Return	1915
The Terror	1917
War and the Christian Faith	1918
The Secret Glory	1922
Far Off Things	1922
Things Near and Far	1923
Strange Roads and with The Gods in Spring	1923
Ornaments in Jade	1924
Dog and Duck	1924
The London Adventure	1924
The Glorious Mystery	1924
The Shining Pyramid	1925
The Canning Wonder	1925
Dreads and Dolls	1926
Notes and Queries	1926
The Green Round	1933
The Cosy Room	1936
The Children of the Pool	1936

His book 'The Bowmen and other Legends of the War' written in 1915 took the nation by storm with his account of the vision that appeared in the sky over Flanders during the First World War. The story became known as "The Angel of Mons", when British troops were faced with thousands of German soldiers attacking their trenches, all seemed lost, when Bowmen appeared in the sky as Angels firing arrows, the German troops went into full retreat, many were left dead. The story was so well written that Machen's readers believed it to be true.

Since then the years have passed and the little boy who wandered over the hills of Gwent became an old man, more than forty years of writing brought him little monetary gain, he said in the preface of one of books, "if I had not been practiced in letters, I am at least past master in the lodge of disappointment." However in spite of this Machen had his reward, he had worked with all the world peering from time to time into places of dense darkness and above all voyaging into the unknown, perpetually climbing the steep white track that vanishes over the hill.

Arthur Machen, born at 33 High Street in Caerleon in 1863, novelist and journalist was married with two children. He died in 1947 at the age of 84. A plaque has been erected on the house where his life began to commemorate "A life well lived"…

Alexander Cordell
Author of 'Rape of the Fair Country'.

Alexander Cordell's first novel, 'A Thought of Honour' was published in 1954 but it was with the publication of 'Rape of the Fair Country' in 1959 that his reputation was made and since, the novels have steadily flowed.

If it were possible for Welshmen to confer their nationality on those who could not legitimately claim it, Alexander Cordell would be top of their list. For Mr. Cordell, many will be surprised to know, is not a Welshman by birth, although the beat of his heart would dictate otherwise. He has, however, lived and worked in Wales for more than half his lifetime and the respect and friendship of the Welsh for this man is unquestionable. Likewise, he has great affinity with the people of the 'Valleys' and a very special relationship with the people of Newport.

Many of his novels are wrought around the history of Wales in the early nineteenth century and the iron and coal industries of that time. The depth of his research is impressive, embracing industrial, political and sociological aspects of the period and he admits that his discoveries have both excited and saddened him. He has devoted himself to revealing the injustices and horrors of working-class life during the period - with truth, with accuracy and, of course, like the fine novelist he is, in a compelling and readable manner. His great novel 'Rape of the Fair Country' and its companion volumes "The Hosts of Rebecca' and 'Song of the Earth' comprises his Welsh Trilogy and between them shed more light on the history of their times than a library of historical tomes.

But it must not be thought that Alexander Cordell is a one-subject writer. Born in Ceylon (today Sri Lanka) and educated at the Marist Brothers College in Tientsin, North China, he is widely travelled and has produced some splendid novels with a backdrop of China and the Far East. Other subjects range from the Irish 'Troubles' to a most enjoyable biography of the Cardiff boxer, James Driscoll, 'Peerless Jim'.

Above all, he is interested in putting the record of history straight. Historians, he believes, lie by omission and he refuses to be led down this road. The pages of his books fairly explode with life and peopled with characters so real that they hurt. One becomes involved in their loves, tears, laughter and tragedies and, with so readable an author, it is impossible not to be swept along by the impetus of their lives.

Wales has no finer chronicler than Alexander Cordell and his love of the Welsh, inherent in his work, is reciprocated by the Welsh.

Alex was born George Alexander Graber on 9th September 1914 in Sri Lanka.

Throughout his working life he lived at Abergavenny, Tidenham Chase near Chepstow, Bangor, and Wrexham, North Wales.

He paid many visits to Newport Library researching information for many of his novels, which included the following:

A Thought of Honour; Rape of the Fair Country; The White Cockade; To Slay the Dreamer; The Hosts of Rebecca; Song of the Earth; Race of the Tiger; The Sinews of Love; The Bright Cantoress; The Healing Blade; The Fire People; The Dream and the Destiny; If You Believe the Soldiers; Land of my Fathers; Peerless Jim; The Sweet and Bitter Earth; Requiem for a Patriot; Tales from Tiger Bay; Moll; Beloved Exile; Dreams of Fair Women; The Love That God Forgot and many others.

Terry Underwood and Alexander Cordell at 'The Hill' Abergavenny in June 1997.

Leslie Thomas OBE

Author of "The Virgin Soldiers"

Few people in Newport have not heard of Leslie Thomas, One of their own. For a Newportonian he most certainly is, born in the Town and, as a child, living successively in Milner Street, Maple Avenue and Maesglas. Millions of copies of his novels and other writings sell every year and some, such as "The Virgin Soldiers" have been made into successful films.

Newport is truly proud of him but it would be understandable if his own feelings were somewhat cooler, for his early traumatic experiences here would have embittered a lesser man: Not so Leslie Thomas. His affection for Newport is genuine, with a view that Fate has decreed his start in life. He recognises that in some perverse way his whole future was charted in these inauspicious beginnings and of which he so movingly tells in an autobiography of his early life, 'This Time Next Week'.

During the 1930's and early 40's he had enjoyed the carefree life of most young lads - playing marbles, conkers and involving himself in the escapades common to most adolescents. True, his father was at sea more often than not and true, his mother was left with very little money to do her best for Leslie and his younger brother, Roy, but such details mean nothing to eager youngsters who can't wait to go out and play.

It all ended in 1943 when, within a few short months, the loss at sea of his father was followed by the death of his mother from cancer. Life changed for him overnight. He was placed in Barnardo Homes, firstly in Devon and then in Kingston-Upon-Thames.

For almost 40 years Leslie Thomas has been one of Britain's most popular novelists, a best-seller with thirty titles to his name and international sales figures exceeding fourteen million.

He was born of a seafaring family in Newport. Gwent, South Wales, on March 22nd, 1931. His grandfather was one of the old Cape-Horners, who voyaged on sailing ships around the dreaded Horn. He is said to have left the sea because he objected to his shipmates' bad language. Thomas's father was drowned when his ship was torpedoed in 1943, and his mother died six months later. He and his younger brother, Roy, found themselves in a Dr. Barnardo's Home, and experience evoked years later in his first book 'This Time Next Week' (Constable 1964). This book remains in print and is used as a set of books for schools. He is now a Vice - President of Barnardo's.

Experience as a National Serviceman resulted in his first novel, the best-selling 'The Virgin Soldiers' which has been published all over the world and was made into a successful film produced by Carl Foreman. (Thomas' entry in 'Who's Who' encapsulates his army career: "1949-51. Rose to Lance Corporal.")

Thomas was a widely-travelled newspaperman, covering Royal tours, the trial of Adolf Eichmann, the funeral of Sir Winston Churchill and many other notable events. After the publication of 'The Virgin Soldiers' he became a full-time writer and has now produced twenty-five novels and three travel books - Some Lovely Islands', My World of Islands' and 'The Hidden Places of Britain' He has also written a second volume of autobiography, 'In My Wildest Dreams'. His latest novels include 'Chloe's Song', 'Dangerous Davies and the Lonely Heart and most recently 'Other Times' published by Heinemann.

Thomas made his first broadcast thirty-seven years ago, and since then has made many more. On television he appeared in documentaries and talk-shows. Among these have been 'Parkinson', 'This is Your Life', 'Wogan' and 'Through The Keyhole'.

He continues to travel widely. His interests are classical music, non-fiction reading, antiques, cricket, stamp collecting, photography and islands.

Leslie Thomas has received an Honourary MA Degree from the University of Wales and an Honourary Doctorate of Literature from the University of Nottingham.

Thomas has three grown-up children from his first marriage and one - a son Matthew - from his second. His wife Diana Thomas is his business manager. They live in Captain's Row. Lymington.

Cricket is Leslie's great love and he is a member of the M.C.C. and an enthusiastic supporter of The Lords Taverners. Frequently he can be seen on 'the box' in chat and game shows. Leslie Thomas loves life and embraces it fully, if only to confront it with the lifeforce it once tried to reject.
"His writing is unaffected, atmospheric, truthful, funny, often poignant" Larousse Dictionary of Writers.

Author Leslie Thomas receives award from university

DESMOND LLEWELYN

The Newport-born actor Desmond Llewelyn, who placed the gadget man Q in the James Bond series of films became a patron of the Friends of Newport Transporter Bridge just a few months before he died in December 1999.

The 85 year-old actor who lived in Bexhill died from injuries he received in a car crash on December the 19th. Just two days before the crash, Desmond performed a book signing session at the Newport store of W H Smith in Commercial Street. The book was his own life story called 'Q the Biography of Desmond Llewelyn'.

Born in Blaen-y-Pant House at Bettws, Malpas on the 12th of September 1914, Desmond spent his childhood in awe of the Newport Transporter Bridge and he spent many hours riding across the River Usk on its Gondola. At a University of the Third Age Meeting, held at Shaftesbury Street Methodist Church in June 1999, Desmond talked about his life in Newport and mentioned several times the love and interest he had for the Bridge. It was then I asked him if he would consider becoming a Patron of the Friends of the Transporter Bridge. With a twinkle in his eye and a broad smile, he readily agreed.

On Friday the 17th December 1999, Desmond finally realised his dream when he was invited to drive the gondola on the Transporter Bridge across the River Usk and back again. A dream that he held for most of his lifetime came true.

The following list of James Bond films that Desmond Llewelyn appeared in as Q.

1963   From Russia With Love – with Sean Connery as 007.
1964   Goldfinger – with Sean Connery
1965   Thunderball – with Sean Connery
1967   You Only Live Twice – with Sean Connery
1969   On Her Majesty's Secret Service – with George Lazen as 007
1971   Diamonds are Forever – with Sean Connery
1973   Live and Let Die – with Roger Moore as 007
1974   The Man with a Golden Gun – with Roger Moore
1977   The Spy Who Loved Me – with Roger Moore
1979   Moonraker – with Roger Moore
1981   For Your Eyes Only – with Roger Moore
1983   Octopussy – with Roger Moore
1985   A View to Kill – with Roger Moore
1987   The Living Daylights – with Timothy Dalton as 007
1989   Licence to Kill – with Timothy Dalton
1995   Goldeneye – with Pierce Brosnan as 007
1997   Tomorrow Never Dies – with Pierce Brosnan
1999   The World is Not Enough – with Pierce Brosnan

Desmond Llewellyn.

Steve Taylor
Newscaster and announcer for HTV

At 47 Steve Taylor became a well known face on television screens in Wales, exuding warmth, charm and authority. The authority has been an integral part of his career as a journalist and a broadcaster. Educated at St. Julian's Grammer School, he began his career in journalism with the South Wales Argus in his native Newport, moving onto the Western Mail in Cardiff before joining the BBC where he worked in Wales and in London as a news reporter, presenter, and producer in both Radio and Television, working for BBC Radio Wales, BBC World Service and BBC 1 Six o'clock and Nine o'clock news.
In 1993 Steve joined HTV and has worked as a sports presenter and anchorman for the flagship HTV News programme.
He has reported on events in a variety of locations around the world including South Africa, the Middle East and most recently, Kosovo.

Steve on location.

Steve Taylor
Commentator and News Presenter for HTV
On Screen in the newsroom at the studio in Cardiff.

ON SCREEN: Presenter Steve Taylor, left, in the HTV newsroom

209

Tony Wright
Radio Presenter for
Capital Gold

Tony Wright on stage,
radio presenter going live.

Tony with Tony Blackburn

On interview. Caring for kids.

Tony Wright

As many will know Tony Wright has become one of Wales' most popular radio presenters, he started in the industry in 1987 and has gone on from strength to strength. His radio career has enabled him to travel extensively and has broadcast live his radio programmes from the USA and from Europe. He has also had the opportunity to meet through his work some of the biggest names in showbusiness including Cliff Richard, Tom Jones, and Henry Mancini just to name a few.

Raised in Pill and Maesglas Newport by his grandparents, Tony remembers with affection his childhood attending Maesglas Infant and Junior School. He says 'our house backed onto the school play yard so at play time I would call over the wall to my Nan who would be washing the clothes with the single tub and mangle in the garden (as the darn thing leaked so much) for an apple, then when she would throw one over there would be about 15 of us kids waiting to catch it'.

When he left school he found various jobs in Newport but could never stay very long in one place, as it was not really what 'he wanted to do'. Eventually Tony trained as an actor (something he longed to do since school). He did several TV parts including appearances on Casualty, House of Elliot, The Old Devils and She Wolf in London for Universal Pictures. After the three months in work and nine months out of work experience that many actors have to face, Tony decided that another course of action was needed. So after reading that there was a one-year placement going at BBC Radio Gwent in Cwmbran, he applied, got the post and became a fieldworker. Gathering information about local issues and broadcasting them on the station. Just before the year placement was up he saw another advert this time in the Guardian and again decided that he would try his hand at being a traffic & travel reporter for (what was then) Red Dragon Radio. He got the job and worked alongside the News Team collating the traffic and travel reports for South Wales, and broadcasting them live on the breakfast and drive time shows. Because he put a bit more 'personality' into these reports the management at the time agreed that he should be given a few over night shows to do, to see if he could crack it as a presenter. He did and eventually did every day part of the show until he reached what he had really wanted to do. The Breakfast Show - the most listened to show on the radio.

So having found his forte Tony decided that this radio lark suited him and as a result of his dedication he has been nominated for several national awards over the years, has had many other offers of work and gained a loyal fan base. He says 'I have been tempted now and again to move away and take other offers', 'but the grass is not always greener on the other side and besides I love this town I was born in, and where I still live.'

When asked what his proudest moments are Tony thinks long and hard and says 'I can honestly say I have done so many things and met so many people I have admired in showbusiness, that I still can't believe I am that kid from a council estate in Newport'.' But it is me despite the odds and I suppose that's what I am proud of and I am immensely proud of my grandparents who brought me up and moulded me into the person that I became.'

In 2003 Tony became Welsh Radio Presenter of the year. Well done Tony.

Mike Buckingham

South Wales Argus Feature Writer

Mike Buckingham was born at Wokingham, Berkshire in 1944, the son of a Royal Canadian Air Force officer. After a private education in the South of England he joined the Royal Air Force, serving in Britain and the Middle East until 1964 when he joined his first newspaper, the Bicester Advertiser, as a reporter.

For several years he worked on local and regional newspapers including the Bucks Herald, the Southern Evening Echo, the Evening Gazette, the Middlesbrough-based Evening Gazette and the Scottish Daily News before reading for a history degree at the University of Wales, Aberystwyth. During his university vacations he worked for the Daily Mail In Glasgow.

After university he worked as a government information officer for a short while before resuming a career in mainstream journalism. He came to Gwent in 1985 and through Richard Frame, with whom he was to collaborate on two books The Haunted Holy Ground (1990) and Through The Century's Eye (1995) a pictorial history of Newport, met Alexander Cordell, the Anglo-Welsh writer.

Buckingham, Frame and Cordell formed a close friendship and when the author died in 1997 Buckingham and Frame collaborated his biography which was published the following year by the University of Wales Press. The Cordell biography was published the same month as Buckingham's first humourous novel, Cwmikaze, published by Victor Gollancz.

Despite working in a mainly left-wing milieu Buckingham has remained sceptical as to the benefits of socialism and maintained outright, hostility to government attempts at social engineering, especially in the field of race relations. His column in the South Wales Argus/Argus, 'Buckingham on Wednesday' is a crusade against those whom he considers to be morally bereft but a sounding-board for eccentrics, a threatened breed. His interest in art led to his writing an art column for the South Wales Argus at the same time as writing for the Western Mail under the nom de plume Phil Cook. Both in his Argus column and feature articles Buckingham has supported literary and artistic

endeavours in the town including Newport County Borough Council's public statuary programme and its plans for a new theatre and arts centre.

Mike Buckingham's hobbies are military history and aviation. He is a pilot member of Cardiff Wales Flying Club.

Mike Buckingham,
South Wales Argus Reporter

Mike with Alaxander Cordell out on location

NIGEL JARRETT

Nigel Jarrett was described by the legendary Welsh musician and choir conductor Glynne Jones as being "one of the most sympathetic and intelligent journalists writing on music in the British provincial Press". Since the late 1980's, he has been music critic of the South Wales Argus and throughout his career has combined newspaper writing with literary work.

He retired from the Argus in December 2002 after 32 years but continues as its music critic and occasional feature-writer and columnist. Mr Jarrett was a protégé of Kenneth Loveland, the distinguished Argus editor and music critic, whose early recognition and support of such talents as Dame Gwyneth Jones, Dame Margaret Price and Sir Geraint Evans were important in their subsequent development.

He 'shadowed' Loveland for over ten years in the 1970's and 1980's while his mentor had ceased to edit the paper was continuing as its freelance music critic. Loveland died in 1998.

Mr Jarrett has reviewed symphony concerts and recitals throughout South Wales, attended over 200 performances of Welsh National Opera, taken a hand in the formation of the Welsh Jazz Society and encouraged amateur and young people's performance everywhere. His always fair but honest notices of local amateur operatic societies helped them to improve their production values.

In the 1990's, Nigel Jarrett began to see his poetry and short fiction, hitherto written only out of personal interest, appear in some of Britain's most respected literal journals, and in 1995 he won the Rhys Davies Memorial Prize for contemporary short-story writing. His winning entry 'Mrs Kuroda on Penyfan', described by the literary critic David Callard as "a perfect realisation of expatriate longing and anxiety", has twice been broadcast by the BBC.

All the while his career at the Argus was changing. He was in charge of monitoring the paper's editorial content as part of the news desk team for much of the 1990's and devised techniques which were taken up by other newspapers in the group, combining the role with that of edition manager for Newport, leading a team of reporters in the paper's busiest area. In 2001, he became business editor, taking sole charge of the Business Argus and acting as the paper's representative among the business community in South Wales.

He had begun his career on the Pontypool Free Press and for four years reported on Welsh rugby for the national Sunday papers. His contributions to the Sunday Mirror were described by its correspondent Tudor James as "among the best sports reports arriving here from any part of the British Isles".

Mr Jarrett's stories began to appear in London Magazine, for many Britain's foremost literary periodical, which in the 19th-century published Hazlitt and Leigh Hunt. One of his stories, 'The Lister Building', appeared in the LM anthology 'Signals-2'. His poetry has appeared in New Welsh Review, Poetry Wales, Poetry Ireland, Poetry Salzburg and many others. He is also the co-editor with his old school pal, Godfrey Brangham, of 'The Day's Portion', a collection of the miscellaneous writings of Caerleon-born mystic and author Arthur Machen, a book much praised in America, where Machen admirers are legion.

Nigel Jarrett was born in Pontnewydd and educated at West Mon Grammar School, Pontypool, and the University of Wales. He now lives with his wife, Ann, in Llanvaches. He has two children and two grandchildren. He describes himself as 'a disappointed artist' and is insanely devoted to music, especially Jazz. He thinks there is nowhere as agreeable as the Gwent countryside, with the possible exceptions of the Lake District, Stratford-upon-Avon (when the Royal Shakespeare Company is there, Provence and Tuscany. He also likes London when it is free of what he calls "a peculiarly English species of menace", though as a writer he has nothing against menace as such. Among his faults he lists impatience, suffering fools gladly, manic self-criticism and something he calls "sel(fish)-sufficiency".

Nigel Jarrett, South Wales Argus Columnist.

The Welsh Fusiliers
gain the Freedom of Newport

The band of the Royal Welsh Fusiliers marching through Newport.

The Mayor of Newport, Councillor Ron Morris outside Newport's Civic Centre.

The Royal Welsh Fusiliers leaving the Civic Centre with flags flying.

Newport Schools

Somerton Infants School c1933 and of course in the front row with a bandage on his knee, author to be , Terry Underwood.

Alway Primary School, Headteacher:- Mr. A. Croker.

Pillgwenlly Primary School and Nursery.

Pillgwenlly Primary School, Headteacher:- Jill Richards.

Year six, St. Julians Junior School with Teacher/Deputy Headmaster Mr. Patrick Drewett.

Gaer Primary School.

Alway Primary School, Ken Powell, Chairman of School Governors.

218

St. Julians Junior School accompanied by Mayor of Newport, Mr. Frederick Sweeting with Sir Harry Jones. Planting of time capsuales. at the foundations of the Beaufort Centre, St. Julians.

St Woolas Primary School, Stow Hill, Headteacher:- Heather Vaughan.

Stan Stennett M.B.E.

Stan Stennett began his working life as a lorry driver with British Road Services based in Crawford Street, Newport 1941. When called to do his National Service he found himself still in Newport doing his service at Newport Barracks. Following the war he rejoined the staff at Crawford St. Garage driving now for British Road Services.

In 1947, Stan entered a talent contest at Newport's Royal Gwent Hospital and he won the competition, that was the commencement of his professional career in theatre.

The phrase: 'All round entertainer' is one which these days is misused. However, it really can be said to describe Wales' Premiere Entertainer, Stan Stennett.

Stan has been in the business for more years than he cares to remember, having been a semi-pro during the war, before joining the Army. On his demob, he formed a comedy musical trio and toured with such greats as Max Miller in the late 1940's and had summer season in Ayr on the bill with a young Lionel Blair!

The 1950's were a boom time for Stan, by then a solo comedian and musician (he is an accomplished guitarist and also plays trumpet). He appeared in Theatres all over Britain with some of the biggest American Stars of the day: Billy Daniels, Johnny Ray, The Deep River Boys, James Cagney and Chico Marx, as well as all the British Household names. He was a regular on BBC Radio, was featured in 'The Showband Show', 'Welsh Rarebit' and topped the bill in Pantomimes and Summer Shows with Morecambe and Wise, Ken Dodd, Jimmy Young, Jon Pertwee etc etc!

In the early 1960's he joined 'The Black & White Minstrel Show' and was to stay with them as principal comic for seven years, helping them win the 'Golden Rose of Montreaux' TV. Festival. It was without doubt the finest show of its kind, and Stan worked with such 'greats' as George Chisholm, John Boulter and Leslie Crowther.
The last thirty years has seen Stan concentrate on working in Wales, on TV, Radio and Stage. He holds the record of five consecutive years in Panto at Cardiff's New Theatre, has formed his own production company to stage Pantos and Summer Seasons in Porthcawl, Colwyn Bay, Southport as well as on tour. He has, together with his wife Elizabeth, and sons Roger and Ceri, administered Theatres and cinemas in Tewkesbury, Hereford, Porthcawl and Caerphilly. Together they have produced a children's video entitled 'Grandpa Stan and the Three Pigs' in association with Central TV, as well as working on other TV comedy and drama ideas.

Stan became known to millions in the 1980's as 'Sid Hooper' from TV's 'Crossroads', a character he portrayed for seven years. He also had a stint in 'Coronation Street'. He has turned his hand to Opera, playing the part of 'Frosch' in 'Die Fledermaus' at St.David's Hall in Cardiff. Last Christmas, he was appearing in his touring panto, 'Mother Goose', around South Wales, an event which has become very much part of children's lives over the years. Recently he has appeared on the small screen in 'Heartbeat' and 'Doctors' and the big screen in 'Twin Town', 'Oh Little Town of Bethlehem' for which he was shortlisted for a BAFTA award and 'Plots with a View' with Christopher Walken. To round it all off he became a regular on the BBC Radio Wales soap opera, 'Station Road'.

He holds a Private Pilot's license, loves golf, was awarded the MBE by Her Majesty The Queen in 1979, for his services to Theatre and Charity, has been the subject of 'This is Your Life'. and is a Fellow of the Welsh College of Music & Drama.

In December 2001 he performed at the Dolman Theatre, Newport the pantomime, 'Mother Goose', taking the role of Billy with Bonzo his dog to capacity audiences.

Young Stan Stennett, in his army days.

Stan Stennett, well loved Welsh
stage and TV performer.

Stan Stennett as a driver for British
Road Services, Crawford Street,
Newport.

Stan with the Rythemacs.

Top of the bill, Stan Stennett.

Stan with Tommy Cooper and friends.

Stan leads out with Des O'Connor.

Stan with Ken Dodd.

Stan Stennett and Windsor Davies.

Tommy Cooper and Stan Stennett.

Black and White Minstrel Show with Stan Stennett.

Stan on a wing and a prayer.

What do you mean don't jump.
I've got my umbrella.

I don't know what this is
but it could be the joystick.

Stan with wife Betty,
outside their home in Cardiff.

Stan receives his M.B.E. with wife Betty and sons
Roger and Cerrie.

Dave Willetts, Westend Star

Dave Willetts whilst working as a Trainee Engineer for Girling's Cwmbran, joined the Newport Group of Amateur players in 1976. The group 'The New Venture Players' were at the time casting the musical 'The King and I', Dave walked in, auditioned for the part of the King and scored tremendously with the Dolman Theatre audiences.
Dave remained with the NVP for eight years playing the leading roles in 'Uncle Gilbert', 'No No Nannette', 'Half a Sixpence', 'My Fair Lady', 'South Pacific', 'The Card', 'Kiss Me Kate', 'Brigadoon', and 'The Pyjama Game', before going professional.

In 1985 Dave played the leading role of Jean Val Jean in the Royal Shakespeare Company's production of "Les Miserables", directed by Trevor Nunn, at the Palace Theatre, in London's West End.
He then went on to play the role of the Phantom in Andrew Lloyd Webber's "Phantom of the Opera", directed by Hal Prince, at Her Majesty's Theatre, London, thus becoming the first person in the world to play the leading roles in both these coveted musicals. He also played The Phantom, at the Opera House, Manchester, for which he won the Evening News award for best performance.

Dave created the role of Major Lee, opposite Petula Clark in "Someone Like You" at the Strand Theatre, London. He also created the role of Zero Janvier in the British premiere of Tim Rice's "Tycoon", at the Sydmonton Festival, and the role of Torn in Trish Ward's "Lonely Hearts", directed by Stephen Rayne.

He received great critical acclaim when he sang the role of Jesus in Andrew Lloyd Webber and Tim Rice's "Jesus Christ Superstar" at the Barbican Center in London, and then went on to perform the same role in the 1993 European tour.

Dave has many international concert appearances to his name, including such venues as the Ahoy Stadium, Rotterdam, the concert halls of Monterey and Mexico City and the Royal Albert Hall - London, as well as numerous sell out concert tours of the UK. In 1992, he was invited to be the only British performer for a concert in Los Angeles on behalf of the American Cinema Awards Foundation, to honor James Steward and Lauren Bacall.
In 1995 he starred in a gala concert in Munich, to honour the achievements of director Hal Prince,

As well as his own concerts, Dave has starred in numerous highly successful staged concert tours. These include "The Magical World of the Musicals" (1995) - "Something Wonderful", a celebration of the music of Rogers and Hammerstein (1996) "A Lot of Living ", celebrating the work of American composer Charles Strouse (1997) and more recently, a national tour of" The Magic of the Musicals" (1999).

Dave worked closely with the great American composer, John Kander, for a special concert broadcast by the BBC, and subsequently released on CD. He is also closely connected with the work of Stephen Sondheim, having played the role of Ben, in the Irish premiere of "FOLLIES" in Dublin (1996). His portrayal of Sweeney Todd, in another Sondheim classic "SWEENEY TODD" (1996), was described by the critics as "…the definitive performance…", and more recently, he played George in the regional premiere of Sondheim's "Sunday In The Park With George" (1999).

In 1996 Dave created the role of Dr Jekyll and Mr Hyde in the World premiere of "Jeckyll", at the Churchill Theatre - Bromley. His varied musical abilities were shown to great effect when he appeared at London's famous Pizza On The Park, receiving great critical acclaim for his "Jazz' N ' Chat" style of "dinner shows".

He has presented his own radio shows on National BBC radio , and has guested on most TV shows and was delighted when he was surprised by Michael Aspel , to be the subject of "This Is Your Life".

Dave has a very successful recording career, with three solo albums , and numerous show albums to his name. In 1997 Dave re-created his portrayal of Jean Val Jean for the 10th anniversary production of " LES MISERABLES ", at the Theatre Royal in Sydney - Australia.

In 1999 / 2000, he took on the role of Captain Hook in J .M Barrie's" Peter Pan" at the Marlow Theatre.
2000 also saw another National tour of" Something Wonderful" and the highly successful "Magic of The Musicals".

Current Projects

- Currently readjusting "Charles & Algernon" written by (Charles Strausse - "Annie").
- "Jekyll" the revised 1996 production currently in negotiation.
- Concert work around Europe, and Mediterannean cruise concert.

Dave Willetts,
Westend Star of London
Musicals

Dave as the Phantom of the Opera.

Dave with Mickey Rooney in America.

Dave in Les Miserables.

Dave in Concert.

226

James Johnston

James, known as Jimmy, had his first stage role whilst at Hartridge High School where he played the Artful Dodger in 'Oliver'.

It was obvious to me when I watched Jimmy in that school production that he was destined for stardom. He then joined us at the New Venture Players Operatic Society where he thrilled the Newport audiences at the Dolman Theatre.

He left New Venture to attend stage school at Italia Conti graduating with flying colours. He went on to perform as principal dancer in Aladdin at Weston Super Mare. Then on to the British Premier of 'Seven Brides for Seven Brothers' at the Theatre Royal, York; 'Barnum' of Michael Crawford fame at the Operatic House in Manchester and Victoria Palace in London; 'Cats' at New Theatre London where Jimmy is the only actor worldwide to have played all the male roles in the show; 'Les Miserables' at the Palace Theatre London, when he played 'Thermador' Master of the House; on to the British Premier of Sherlock Holmes with Ron Moody at Cambridge Theatre London; in 1990 he was in the original cast of Miss Saigon at Theatre Royal Drury Lane.

James Johnston of Newport, West End actor/dancer.

Following which he took a years break from the West End spending 7 months cruising around the caribbean. In 1992 he was back in the West End joining in the original production of 'A Tribute to the Blues Brothers',

another world premier followed with James playing Hindley opposite Cliff Richard in 'Heathciffe' at the Hammersmith London. Jimmy played 'Will Parker' in "Oklahoma" opposite Maureen Lipman at the National Theatre, London. From this performance he was nominated for a Lawrence Olivier Award, another accolade in a successful career.

James with Cameron McKintosh and James's mother Maureen.

Performing to numerous members of the Royal family. James has done three Royal performances.

Off stage Jimmy with his long term friend Kevin Healy has a soul band namely "The Soul Police' entertaining at many conferences. He is a keen golfer, and ex school boy boxing champion of Wales and still plays weekly competitive football and tennis at least once a week. He is married to Phyllidia, herself a professional dancer with one son, Harley, aged four years.

I'm sure there is one mother in Newport having such a talented son whom she, and Newport, are well proud of.

Jimmy with Michael Crawford meets Princess Anne at the West End production of Barham.

Jimmy and cast of Oklahoma meet Prince Charles.

Jimmy and cast of Oklahoma meet Her Majesty the Queen.

James with Hollywood actor
Martin Sheen.

Proud daddy with son Harley.

Just born, Harley with daddy
James and mummy Phillipa.

Shirlie with Suzi Quatro.

In Cinderella.

Teddy the "Bear" facts.

Shirley's Handsome Troupe.

Shirlie Roden

Shirlie Roden hails from Newport, South Wales, and graduated from Warwick University with a BA(Hons) in English and European Literature.

She is co-writer on the highly-successful ROY ORBISON STORY (nominated for Best Musical in the 1995 Olivier Award). Her Joan of Arc musical JEANNE was the first rock opera to be performed at Sadlers Wells Theatre, London, and she co-wrote TALLULAH WHO? with Willie Rushton and Suzi Quatro, which sold out at the Queen's Theatre, Hornchurch; plus the Old Testament musical AD/BC with RSC writer/actor John Kane, which premiered in Easton, Pennsylvania, USA. She has also written original music and lyrics for Sue Townsend's BAZAAR AND RUMMAGE. Her children's operetta PADDINGTON BEAR'S MAGICAL MUSICAL toured England successfully for a year and her specially commissioned version of BEAUTY AND THE BEAST received great reviews at Liverpool Playhouse. Next in production is her musical adaptation of Richard Llewellyns' famous Welsh novel HOW GREEN WAS MY VALLEY, for which she has written book, music and lyrics, and she is currently working on an original idea for a musical entitled COUNTERPOINT.

Shirlie is a performer in her own right, with four albums of her own material to her credit: SKYDANCER, THE PATH OF DARING, THE CHILD I KNEW and her tribute to Slovenia, THE VANISHING LAKE; plus two albums of traditional songs SHIRLIE SINGS and SONGSTERS OF THE GROVE. She has worked extensively as a solo artist in England and Europe (she is particularly successful in Slovenia) and has received wide acclaim in the press for her music, singing and her Sound Workshops where she teaches the use of the voice as a healing instrument. She is a frequent presenter at Mind, Body & Spirit Festivals and has just completed her first book called SOUND HEALING, plus a CD for healing with Suzi Quatro entitled FREE THE BUTTERFLY.

Her acting credits include Fruma Sarah with Topoi in FIDDLER ON THE ROOF at Manchester Opera House; Musetta in LA BOHEME at the Kammer Opera in Vienna; the Narrator in the touring production of JOSEPH AND THE AMAZING TECHNICOLOR DREAMCOAT; and Prison Officer Meg Jackson in the stage version of cult Australian drama PRISONER CELL BLOCK H. Most recently, she appeared with Jeremy Irons and John Wells in POETRY IN MOTION at the Richmond Theatre. Shirlie has also worked widely in rock music with such artists as Ray Davies and the Kinks, Mike Oldfield, Ultravox, David Gilmour, Ian Gillan, Suzi Quatro and Hot Chocolate, and has featured as both singer and voice-over artist on radio and television commercials.

Memories of Newport

We lived in Enville Road, off Ridgeway - what was called 'the posh part of town - but in fact the road was 'unadopted' which was a source of constant aggravation to my mother and great delight to us growing children. I remember endless hours of fun building mud pies and splashing through reservoirs of puddles in winter, and riding my bike over smooth dusty craters in the summer. The opposite side of the road was fondly called 'the dump' - a large wilderness of waste land full of nettles, blackberry bushes and weeds, with a hilly section we called 'the land slide', which ruined many a pair of white cotton knickers as we gleefully slid from top to bottom amid the stones. 'The dump' was a great source of entertainment as we grew up, with dens among the undergrowth and huge holes as, with the optimism which belongs only to children, we tried to dig our way through to Australia and anywhere else our fancy took us.

As I grew older, I ventured further afield, exploring Ridgeway and the surrounding countryside with my best friend Barbara, who lived next door. There was an old deserted stone quarry where we hunted for newts, and the remains of the Newport Canal which we fell into many times as we reached for frog spawn or fished for minnows to put in jam jars. Then there were the locks, old, rotting and dangerous, and the dares we made to ride our bicycles over the wooden planks still suspended high above them. There were the bluebell woods, May blossom that my mother would superstitiously not have in the house, Easter pilgrimages to the distant Twm Barlwm with packs of sandwiches and blistered, aching feet, conkers and blackberries in autumn season and snow drifts up to our knees in winter with wild tobogganing down nearby hills. And best of all, Bonfire night with a huge communal fire on the dump and neighbours with home-made parkin and burned baked potatoes and Ridgeway pulsing with crowds of people, smoke, fireworks, bangers and police telling us all to go home. As if we would. And all year round, the endless rain sweeping in from the mountains. It was a world of fun, innocence and adventure, but never boredom, with a great outdoors always to be explored and investigated, whatever the weather.

As we grew older, Barbara and I moved further afield in search of our one big passion - ponies. We hadn't yet discovered boys, so we made friends with local farmers in an endeavour to ride their horses. Mr. Attwell, who lived on his tiny smallholding just over Ridgeway called Cwrtymynws Farm was a constant source of entertainment in his corrugated iron house with oil lamps. Many winter evenings we sat around his open fire while he taught us how to make owl calls or imitate cock pheasants. Then there were Tom and Marian Stephens at Ynysyfro Farm next to the Reservoir in the picture postcard Little Switzerland view from Ridgeway. Barbara and I became almost like their adopted daughters as we spent more and more time there, feeding the pet lambs, learning how to put the milking machines on the cows, separating the milk into cream and bottling it, feeding the hens, helping with the haymaking - and of course, riding the old steeplechaser Henry. The Stephens also walked foxhound puppies for the Tredegar Farmers' Hunt and took the old dogs back again when their hunting days were over, so the farm was full of shaggy haired welsh hounds with magical names like Ganamede and Graceful, Tanker and Tailor, General and Marshall, as well as the usual sheepdogs and farm cats. There were many hungry doggy mouths to feed and I always remember they kept the dog meat in boxes up in a tree! I suppose it was too smelly to keep in the house.

Newport Market Day was the social and business stronghold of the farming men - young girls were not allowed to attend - but gymkhanas and point to point races were a great social occasion, as we climbed into the shooting brake with the Stephens, everyone dressed in their best. There was also a very different attitude to fox hunting then from now. Tom Stephens was a cattle and sheep farmer and often complained the foxes killed more lambs and hens than they needed to eat. He had neither the time nor the expertise as a gunman to shoot accurately, so he always welcomed the Tredegar Farmers Hunt at Ynysyfro. I rode with them on a number of occasions on a wild Welsh mountain pony from another farm who was far too spirited for me. More often than not, I fell off ignominiously and on the one and only occasion I ever saw a kill, I was 'blooded' by the huntsman, only to be yelled at by my father as a 'barbarian' when I got home and ordered to wash my bloodstained cheeks immediately.

But I loved the countryside. It simultaneously uplifted and calmed me. My meditation was to sit beneath an oak tree and gaze upon the distant Twm Barlwm, and I ran barefoot across those fields where now the M4 Motorway cuts its roaring swathe. My childhood haven Ynysyfro Farm has now been turned into a golf course and every time I go back home, more housing estates erode the beautiful soft countryside that gave me so much and nurtured my heart and spirit. If I write of a past that sounds just too idyllic, then it is perhaps because for me, it was. Those memories of Newport I hold are some of the happiest in my life, and at fourteen years old, when my schoolfriends were attending High School dances on a Saturday night wearing high heels and hot lipstick, you would still find me in the safe haven of the cowsheds, wellies on, up to my knees in mud. I instinctively knew there was a long life ahead of me with plenty of time for all that sophistication, and I just didn't want to grow up too fast.

But there was something else that began to pull me, apart from the beauty of the Welsh countryside - music! My first classical piano teacher at the age of five had scared me, so my father sent me to Bunty Jones in Woodville Close where I learned all the easy-play versions of the musicals. I sometimes think this early influence developed my ability to write for theatre as I thumped away at 'The King and I' and 'Oklahoma'. I had started school at Clytha where we were greatly encouraged to write diaries every day- in fact, I still have mine and they must have afforded my teachers a great deal of amusement with the candid descriptions of just about everything that was taking place in our household, from pregnancies to mice nests and the sad demise of a cat who refused to be housetrained! But at the age of ten, a new school opened locally and I was moved to Glasllwch School in Melbourne Way. It was here that my singing career really began, with the encouragement of primary teacher Ethel Thomas. A few of us were put into the top class early and were often given the responsibility of creating the daily prayer services ourselves. I suddenly found myself in demand as a soloist and thereby began my ritual which continues to this day of standing at the side of the stage and praying for help before I go on. As a child, it was to qualm the myriad butterflies dancing inside me whereas now it is to create inspiration and harmony. Recently I returned to Glasllwch School to reminisce and strangely, it still all looked exactly the same - even the school hall and the stage where I made my first wobbly appearances as that little girl who just wanted to sing.

From Glasllwch I moved to Newport High School. for Girls where I encountered the dreaded discipline of the compulsory School Hat and Hat Detention for not wearing it. As back-combing and bouffon hairstyles grew in popularity, so did the hats move farther and farther to the back of our heads, secured at the most precarious angles with hat pins. Funny to think of it now, but there were even Deportment Stripes awarded to girls who walked well and 'lines' given for bad behaviour. Mainly my friends and I spent a great deal of time in rebellion about the usual female parameters of short skirts, hair colour and patterned stockings and I am afraid to report I was on a number of occasions sent to the Headmaster Mr. Parry Michael for disciplining because of insolence in the-classroom! Our school motto was 'Ni da ni gelli gwel' (Nothing is good where better is possible). But I seemed to excel at being cheeky!

The school was split into four 'houses', St. Andrews, St. David's, St. George and St. Patricks and each year we had an inter-house Eisteddfod. By now I was becoming more ambitious with my singing and my target was to win the Girls Vocal Solo every year, which on a couple of occasions I achieved. I still remember the Eisteddfod as a very exciting occasion, as your house captain came round and tried to persuade you to enter as many categories as possible, from art to recitation to poetry writing and piano duets. It was always a thrill to me when the all the competition topics went up on the notice board and I would stand there with a growing feeling of excitement, reading them all. Although at that time I had no wish to become an actress, I think it was the creative and theatrical side of the whole event plus the team spirit that inspired me. As well of course of the chance of winning and being on that stage again! The piano lessons stopped at sixteen and I had vocal training for a year from Gabriel Capus of the Welsh National Opera who lived opposite in Enville Road. My voice began to grow, as did my confidence.

Meanwhile, I was gradually developing into a teenager in every way and a very different kind of music was exploding around me at home. From the age often, with two older brothers discovering rock and roll, I had been exposed to American imports such as Chuck Berry, Bo Diddly, Jimmy Reed, Big Bill Broonzy and Howling Wolf - not to mention of course Elvis Presley, Bill Haley, Buddy Holly, Eddy Cochran, and the Everly Brothers. Brother Martin (at St. Julains High School) played bass while Robin (at Newport High School for Boys) played guitar, piano and sang lead vocal. For a while they were in the same group, the Forefathers, and then they split to form separate bands. Our front room in Enville Road became a hive of activity as rehearsals took place, and I was not allowed in. I was fascinated - not only by my elder brothers' male friends, but by the exciting new sound of the music. They were rehearsing in the room kept for special occasions with the best carpet and furniture, so my mother insisted the boys took their shoes off to go in. In protest one day at being excluded from something so interesting I tied all their shoe laces together and hung the shoes from the banisters, as well as turning coats inside out. The boys were furious! But I was allowed in for a couple of rehearsals and sat enthralled at what I heard and saw.

School dances were becoming the big thing, and my brother Robin with his group The Avengers was right at the front of it. The two Newport High Schools were then still segregated with the width of the boys' school drive dividing it from the girls, and the only sight of the opposite sex was during break time when everyone stood at the edge of the drive, trying to check out the talent from a distance. I was constantly plagued for spare tickets as the rock and roll dances quickly sold out, and suddenly became aware that my brother was becoming very popular with the girls.

St. Woolos Church Hall opposite the Cathedral was a regular venue and it was there that I first stood on a real stage and sang with Robin's band - although it took a great deal of persuading and pleading before he allowed me on to do my version of a bluesy 'Summertime' from Porgy and Bess, and Little Richard's 'Send Me Some Loving'. Walking back home along Risca Road in the cool summer night air afterwards, pointed stiletto shoes off and stockinged feet on the pavement, I was hooked. Forget the classical stuff, forget the musicals and the Eisteddfod - I wanted to sing this new modern music. The Rolling Stones broke on to the scene with an impact that was like pure rebellion, and I was even more desperate to sing. I went to see them in Cardiff and laughed all the way through their act as the entire female audience around me screamed. I was laughing at the energy, the gut feeling, the pure excitement of rock music - even if they were doing cover versions of the American greats.

My best friend Barbara and I began to dress in denim jeans and collarless blue grandfather' style shirts, and my father bought me my first acoustic guitar. I think it cost a cool fifteen pounds. We spent school break trying to write songs, and some members of our class even collected enough money to buy a reel of tape for us. There were no Adats then, Walkmans or digital recordings. Not even a cassette player. But a friend's father had an old Grundig tape recorder and we begged to borrow it. Looking back, it seems funny to remember the dreams and frustration running in tandem as we attempted to record a demo tape - me singing, Barbara pounding the piano. Whatever we recorded, when we played it back on the Grundig, it all came out in gibberish backwards! We needed money to make a demo, and there were Talent Competitions at the Working Men's Clubs in the valleys advertised in the Argus each week with cash prizes, so we plastered on the makeup to look more grown up, and sneaked off to audition as a dubious duo entitled 'Shirlie and Babs', intent on gaining experience so I could get a recording contract - magical words which both haunted and inspired us. Amazingly, some club bookings followed until our parents found out what we were doing. My father was Technical Director of the Crescent Toy Company in Cwmcarn, and was well-respected in the valleys around Cross Keys, so he wasn't too keen on his teenage daughter becoming a club act!

School holidays found me in London singing in the folk clubs to get experience. I even got on to cult tv programme 'Ready Steady Go' imitating Marianne Faithfull and oh what a feeling when I walked into Newport High School assembly the following Monday - for the first time in my life, I felt like a star! Still at school studying A Levels, I got a weekend job at Mount St. Albans Country Club near Caerleon, singing with a dance band. We had an old bass player from the valleys called Sid - such a sweet old man, he would never come to the front door to pick me up, but knocked on the back door cap in hand, in deference to my father's managerial position. 'There's something in your voice makes a man want to cry', Sid often told me. I didn't understand his words at the time, but I often think of them today when I focus on using my voice for my healing work. At Mount St. Albans I learned more about how to present and perform a song professionally, as well as a few other things - such as how to escape being chased around the building by the piano player and club manager simultaneously!

I left the High School with the obligatory three A levels and eleven O levels. It was in those days a good school with a high standard of achievement and some inspiring teachers whose words remain with me even today. But I had no interest in going on to further education at university or to train at drama school. In fact, I'd avoided all the school productions and Newport Playgoers Society. All I wanted to do was sing and record, and nobody seemed to be able to tell me how I could achieve my dream. The next few months were a dark hole as I trained in Cardiff to learn shorthand and typing. 'At least do that', said my father. 'You can always fall back on it'.

I left Newport in 1968 to work at University College in London as junior junior junior (yes really, number three!) secretary to the Provost, Lord Annan, and it was he who persuaded me to go to university. When I graduated from Warwick in 1971, 1 was signed to EMI Records with a group of students in the aptly-named band Children. We didn't last that long, but I had placed one foot on the road and have been singing ever since - from rock concept musicals touring America with The Kinks, to backing vocals with Erroll Brown and Hot Chocolate on their anniversary tour, to studio sessions with David Gilmore from the Floyd and Mike Oldfield. I also made it into musical theatre playing Frumah Sarah opposite Chaim Topol in Fiddler on the Roof at Manchester Opera House, Musette in 'La Boheme' at the Kammer Opera in Vienna, the Narrator in 'Joseph and the Amazing Technicolor Dreamcoat' and Prisoner Officer Meg Jackson in 'Prisoner Cell Block H' on tour. I've recorded three albums of my own songs and my first book 'Sound Healing' was published this year.

My mother was born in Mountain Ash, daughter of a coalminer, and I have taken my Welsh background and the spirit of the mountains with me wherever I have gone in the world. We weren't taught Welsh at Newport High School, but I have since learned to sing in the national language. Whatever people may say about Newport now, whatever kind of a city it has become, for me it was the greatest place to be brought up in. When I return there, every street corner where I lived still holds a memory for me, of friends, of feelings, of conversations, laughter and tears, of people long since dead but never forgotten. But most of all, it is the mountains and the countryside that were my inspiration and hope, my calm when there was turmoil and argument with in me, and in the house around me. The view of Ynysyfro Farm and Twm Barlwm from Ridgeway sits on my piano today to remind me of who I am and the gifts I received as I grew, and to inspire the music afresh within me. This then is my memory of Newport and for this, I am eternally grateful.

"My love reaches you".

THE TROUPERS - Music Hall company based in Newport

The Ad Hoc Theatre Company based in Newport was formed in 1993 which included the now popular and well-known and talented music hall company called 'Troupers'.

The company disbanded in 2002 after giving over 170 performances in Newport and the South Wales area and raised £30,000 for various charities.

Trouper's Music Hall
1993 - 2002

170 Performences
over £30,000 raised for various charities.

Back - Brian Wilson, John Davies, Don Smith, John Samuel,
David Leyshon Williams, Haydn Gabb, Bruce Campbell, Derek Richards.

Middle - Derek Smith, Pat Willson, Olive Samuel, Eira Richards, Mary Gabb.

Seated Front - Nesta Leyshon Williams, Anne Price-Jones,
Jeannette Massocchi, Sue Morgan, Sharon Davies.

Rhys George

A Newport born youth dancing his way to success.

Rhys George was born in Newport in 1985 and began dancing at a very early age. When only eight years old in 1993 he danced and acted his way through several pages of script in a New Venture Players Production of "Dodger 'The Artful One'", at the Dolman Theatre, Newport, followed by a dancing role in "The King and I" in 1994.

Later he attended various dance schools and academies. In 2002 when just 17 years old Rhys achieved an ambition by winning the top award when dancing an the Gillian Lynne Choreographic Awards of 2002.

Although still in training Rhys has yet another ambition to fulfil, that of performing in the musical "Chicago", and so the list goes on for this unstoppable young man. He has been studying for the past six years at the Elmhurst School of Dance and Performing Arts.

Rhys George's Timeline:

Oct	93	Dodger
March	94	King And I
Aug	94	Tuition scholarship to Urdang Academy Summer School, Covent Garden, London.
May	95	Black Cat in "A Tale of Sleeping Beauty" Sadlers Well in London.
Aug	95	Royal Ballet School - Summer School
Aug	96	In Bugsy Malone at The Edingburgh Festival with National Youth Music Theatre.
Sept	96	Gained an aided place via Music & Ballet scheme to study full time at Elmhurst School for Dance and Performing Arts, Camberly, Surrey.
Aug	98	Won the David Rymer Scholarship at the Yorkshire Ballet Seminars, Ilkley.
Aug	98-99-2000	Won places for 3 consecutive Summer Schools with Birmingham Royal Ballet, Junior and Senior levels.
Feb	2000	Won Beatrice Sparks Prize for men plus achievement in "Dance & Academics:.
July	2001	Won Elmhurst Prize for drama together with 9 GCSE's A-C grade, and a National Dance award to fund continual training in Jazz and Commercial Theatre.
Aug	2001	Performed at New Theatre, Cardiff under guidance of the Dance Company "Diversions".
Feb 15	2002	Won the Gillian Lynne Choreographic Award.

Whew! Well done Rhys, Chicago here we come!!!

Performing in the 1996 production of 'Bugsey Malone'.

Rhys with Kevin O'Hare on the left principal - Birmingham Royal Ballet and on the right David Rymer who gives the scholaship for the Yorkshire Ballet Summer School.

Rhys (on the right) perfoming at the Diversion Summer School.

Pat Wells - West, New Venture Player and Newport Playgoers

Pat joined N.V.P. in 1976 and was Secretary for 21 years, having also served as Ticket Manager and Publicity. She has played many character roles, her favourite being Meg Brockie in "Brigadoon" and Lady Thiang in the "King and I".

She has also been a member of of Playgoers for 26 years. In 1986, she and Ron Bailey and three other "Thespians" organised and produced the first gala, combining other societies and soloists, to be held at the Dolman Theatre in aid of St. David's Foundation - with the added thrill of having Sir Anthony Hopkins as guest of honour. A truly magic and memorable evening. They produced two more such galas in 1988 and 1990.
She has always enjoyed singing - in the Adams Jeremiah Singers and now concerts. She has filmed in the "Time Bandits" and also on HTV in the programme "All Kinds of Everything".

A member of Trinity Methodists Church, Pat has written and produced pantomimes and shows for them and performed in the Newport area in religious musicals with the combined churches.

She produced a one-night in November 1995 at Newport Centre of Terry Underwood's "Sunday Boys" for the Chartist celebrations, which combined seven school choirs and Newport Philharmonic Choir. An exciting evening for all present!

Pat is now production and publicity officer for Newport Playgoers Society and involved in the successful studio monthly afternoon entertainments. In 1997 she and Ron Bailey formed Patron Productions to continue producing concerts and entertainment to raise funds for various charities who have benefited by many thousands of pounds from their partnership.

Pat Wells-West, Newport actress. For the New Venture Player
and Newport Playgoers.

Caroline Sheen

Caroline Sheen, who has been starring in West End musicals over the last four years, was educated at Caerleon Comprehensive School from 1987 to 1994.

Coming from a family steeped in the local amateur musical tradition, Caroline made her early theatrical appearances with Cwmbran Operatic Society at the Dolman Theatre. She played juvenile and principal parts in productions such as South Pacific, The Sound of Music, The Mikado, Charlie Girl and Fiddler on the Roof

She developed her acting skills at Gwent Young Peoples Theatre in Abergavenny under the careful eyes of Gary Meredith and Julia Davies. For three years in succession she was chosen to participate in the prestigious National Youth Theatre of Wales (1992-1994) performing in Brecht's Caucasian Chalk Circle and singing the part of the Balladeer in Stephen Sondheim's Assassins.

Caroline, daughter of John Sheen a well known actor of Cwmbran Operatic Society, and cousin of Michael Sheen a rising young actor/singer who recently starred in a Royal Shakespearean Production, is now treading the West Ends boards herself. Over the last few years, Caroline has established herself well and truly in Theatreland.

Caroline Sheen, West End actress.

It was as a seven year old that she began her career by appearing in a Cwmbran Operatic Society Production with her father John at the Dolman Theatre.

Caroline graduated from Guildford School of Acting in 1998 with a 1st Class B.A. Honours degree and she was plucked from college to make her professional and West End debut in no less a show than Grease!

Before graduating from the Guildford School of Acting. Since then Caroline has played many principal roles, appearing in Stephen Sondheim's "Into the Woods", also with the legendary 'Abba', playing Sophie in 'Mamma Mia' in the West End. She then started in a role in the musical 'The Witches of Eastwick'.

In June 2000 Caroline created the part of Jennifer in Cameron Macintosh's spectacular production of The Witches of Eastwick at the Theatre Royal, Drury Lane.

She has recently made television appearances on the Mike Doyle Show and singing alongside Aled Jones in a St. David's Day special.

In addition to all this she has appeared on television acting, singing and dancing her way through life. There's an old saying, 'if you go for an audition and twinkle a little you'll become a star', and Caroline Sheen is proof of that.

Caroline maintains her strong links with Newport and its environs, being a regular audience member at local productions and an avid fan of Newport Rugby team.

James Rhys Lawrence

James began studying with vocal tutor, Irene Livingstone six years ago, and his voice developed into a fine boy soprano. His first public singing appearances were at St Woolos Cathedral.

His love of singing progressed into a love of the stage, when he was invited to sing in the childrens' chorus of 'Oliver' with the Newport Operatic Society in November 2000.

During 2001, James was invited to sing in a performance of 'Carousel' by the Lyric Musical Society. Later that year he sange a duet, 'Pie Jesu', with Standard and Pirelli in their Christmas Review.

James was involved in a production in the Dolman Theatre in Newport called 'Born to Perform' (celebrating the Centenary of the Royal Gwent Hospital), with an all children cast. He has a lead role singing songs from 'Oliver'.

James ended the year performing solos in Carol services and also at St Woolos Cathedral.

James Rhys Lawrence.

2002 turned out to be incredibly busy. Having now joined the Lyric Musical Society, James took part in 'H.M.S. Pinafore' and 'Oklahoma' and culminated in getting the lead role in 'Oliver' at Abertillery Amateur Drama and Music Society.

'There were some notable performances in the production. None more so than James Lawrence in the title role. His clear soprano voice thrilled the large audience'.
Derek Gradditch, NODA Society News, Spring 2003

James was then invited to join the Newport Playgoers and play a small part in 'Our Town'; first performed in the Dolman Theatre, Newport and then taken down to the prestigious open-air theatre in Cornwall, The Minack.

Later that year, James, sang with Judy and Friends Concert Group for Children in Need which was televised. He also made his debut CD album of five tracks, recorded at Shabbey Road Studios in Caerphilly.

This year, apart from being a guest singer in several venues, James has concentrated on completing this album of nine tracks. Three of the songs are accompanied by a young choir of talented vocalists all pupils of the Rougemont School, and of vocal tutor, Irene Livingstone. Special thanks to all of them for giving up their time.

James with vocal tutor, Irene Livingstone.

Huge amounts of work and enthusiasm have gone into the musical production to achieve the highest vocal and orchestral standards. The musical orchestrations are all special arrangements.

The continued dedication of Irene, James and his family, has turned 'his beautiful voice' into 'La Belle Voce'.

A Celebration of songs about love and hope - the very things which have inspired them; and we hope, through this album, will inspire you.

NEWPORT MALE VOICE

The Newport Male Voice was established in 1943 as a means of relieving the tensions of the latter War years, also to help raise spirits and morale of the troops and civilians at that time. It started with a membership of twenty-five with rehearsals held in the front room of a house in Colne Street, Newport. This was the home of singing teacher Agnes White, who was the Choir's first Musical Director. This small but enthusiastic group of singers played a worthy part in the War effort giving concerts in aid of the Mayor's War Charities, and taking part in 'At Home' Concerts for the returning troops.

After the end of the War, membership increased by around a further twenty-five and the Choir made rapid progress, by fulfilling BBC radio engagements, competing at Eisteddfods and giving concerts to the general public. The Choir obtained their first Eisteddfod success at Mount Zion Chapel, Newport in 1946. Other successes followed with the Choir winning the Mansel Bowl at the Bath Music Festival at the Premier Male Voice Award at the Bournville Festival, Birmingham. The Choir was also chosen to represent Wales at the 'Four Countries' recording at the Reading Music Festival.

The Choir has made successful European Tours to Belgium, Holland, France, Germany and Denmark, and had the privilege to perform at the British Embassy in Paris and at Fredericksborg Castle, the residence of the Danish Royal Family. On several occasions, the Choir has performed at the Royal Albert Hall as part of the '1,000 Voice Choir' and performed during the UK visit of the Emperor of Japan at Cardiff Castle. They travelled extensively throughout Canada in 2002, receiving a tremendous welcome wherever they went.

In the year of 2003, Newport Male Voice Choir celebrated 60 years of its formation. The Choir has raised substantial amounts of money for its many deserving charities and established many firm friendships in countries all over the world.

"May you continue with this wonderful work for many years to come".

Newport Male Voice Choir performing in the Great Central Hall c1950.

The Choir on their Canadian Tour.

Newport Male Voice Choir. M.D. Sara Jones. Pianist, Barbara Davis.

NEWPORT MALE VOICE CHOIR

BARITONE

B Rodgers
A Lewis
D Dyer
F Stewart
G Meredith
L Pocock
G Strickland
R Booth
J Scott
C Coxall
D East
P Beard
D Williams
K Marshall
D McCarthy
TOTAL = 15

2ND TENOR

A Lewis
A Jones
R Elliott
R Hill
L Vincent
K Anstice
R Harvey
R O'Brien
G Suller
E Jones
S Porretta
D Penk
A Gettins
G Oakley

TOTAL = 14

MD – Sara Jones

Pianist – B Davis

1ST TENOR

J Ganner
M Price
K Cosslett
R Bell
K Fallon
G Cairns
D Sims
R Lewis
R Johns
D Lee
T Nicholls
E Starkey
J Blake
Martyn Price

TOTAL = 14

2ND BASS

L Smith
C Cadogan
M Cook
D Davies
A V Williams
B Hill
C Conner
T Jones
G Oakley

TOTAL = 9

Newport Male Voice Choir with President Mr Haydn Walters 4th from the left - front row.

Newport Male Voice Choir performing at St. Julians Methodist Church with Terry Underwood as compere.

The Great Central Hall, Commercial Street.

A large orchestra with a much larger choir with standing room only for the audience, well one anyway c1950's.

The Gwent Police Choir.

The Gwent Police Choir. 2002

Singer/actor Ian Frost with Terry Underwood, as compere, performing with The Gwent Police Choir 2002.

Risca Male Voice Choir

Risca Male Voice Choir with musical director Martin Hodson.

Risca Male Voice Choir in Action.

Risca Male Choir

Founded in 1970, Risca Male Choir has established an enviable reputation; the choir has not been afraid to experiment with and explore many musical styles. This diversity can be admired and enjoyed through its numerous recordings.

The choir's competition successes have included the title "Male Choir of the Year", winning the Welsh Choral Challenge shield, the National Eisteddfod and the Bronze Medal from the Malta International Choral competition. Most recently, Risca were the Male Choir Winners at the International Choir Festival of Jersey.

The repertoire of Risca Male Choir includes traditional material, operatic and music theatre items, and original compositions from the world of classical music. A highlight from the classical field was a much-acclaimed performance of Cherubini's Requiem in D minor for male voices and orchestra. The choir has given many premiére performances of works by contemporary welsh composers, including particularly music by Mervyn Burtch and Richard Roderick Jones. A performance of Beowulf and Grendel, a large work by Mervyn Burtch for male voices and brass band, resulted in the choir being given the 1997 WS Gwynn Williams Award, recognising its contribution to music making in the community, and also its continued promotion of new Welsh music. In November 2000, Risca Male Choir was invited to perform the cantata Owain ab Urien as part of a centenary celebration of works by the Welsh composer David Wynne.

The choir is also famous for its unique theme concerts, one of which was turned into a feature length television programme. Other television appearances have included The Magic of the Musicals, which feature Bryn Terfel, Peter Karrie and Catherine Zeta-Jones, an appearance on the National Lottery's first birthday broadcast , and in the summer of 1998 a performance on GMTV's Breakfast Show. In January 2000, Risca male Choir featured in the BBC Millennium Songs of Praise from the National Stadium in Cardiff. In May 2002 Risca Male Choir took part in the FA Cup Classics concert broadcast on BBC1 from Cardiff Arms Park. The choir also featured in the BBC Wales programme Can They Hack It?

In July 1999 Risca Male Choir took part in a recording with Bryn Terfel and the Orchestra of the Welsh National Opera. The CD called We"ll Keep a Welcome was released by Deutsche Grammaphon in October 2000, quickly reaching Gold status.

Risca Male Choir has taken many successful concert tours, including visits to France, Germany and the Czech Republic. Three highly acclaimed visits to California have been particularly memorable.

Martin Hodson MBE

Martin Hodson is now a freelance musician having retired from full time work in education where he has been, since 1981, Director of Music and Head of Performing Arts at the Crosskeys Campus of Coleg Gwent. Alongside this highly successful career in teaching, his name has become a byword for musical versatility.

As an accompanist he has been much in demand to work with choirs, as well as instrumental and vocal soloists. As a singer, Martin has performed in opera, oratorio and music theatre, broadcast a solo recital for BBC radio and takes particular pride in performances of the great song cycles of Schubert and Schumann. This experience, along with love of theatre, poetry and languages, has equipped Martin Hodson well for the task of vocal coach and choral director.

With Crosskeys College Choral Society he has conducted acclaimed performances of the great choral repertoire, including Elijah, Messiah, The Creation, Rossini's Stabat Mater and Petite Messe Solennelle, and Requiems by Mozart, Verdi and Fauré. In 1998 the choir gave the premiére performance of Seascapes by Richard Roderick Jones.

Martin has also worked in music theatre projects as vocal coach, repetiteur and director. Performances he has conducted include 42nd Street, Sondheim's Into the Woods, The Gondoliers, A Chorus Line, and Fame.

His association with Risca Male Choir is special and has been crucial in developing the choir's distinctive style and repertoire. His many arrangements for the choir are a crucial part of its repertoire and a number have now been published.

In June 1999 Martin Hodson was awarded the MBE in the Queen's birthday honours list in recognition of his services to education and music in the community.

OLYMPIA CINEMA – SUNDAY NIGHTS

VARIOUS BANDS APPEARING IN NEWPORT

Tickets Available from : DAVIES MUSIC STORES, BRIDGE STREET
FUSSELS SPORTS, HIGH STREET

Ralph Bright and his Broadcasting Band (Bristol)

Aneurin Thomas and his Collegians (with Howard Jones : Vocalist)

Joe Gregory's Accordion Band

Murray and his Band

Milton Mace and his Sweet and Swing Band

Jack Joseph and his Seabank Hotel Orchestra

Bill Berry's Rhythm Club Sextet

Rialto Accordion Band

Ken Lewis and his Radio Band

Joy Clarke and her Accordion Band

Waldini and his Gypsy Band

Keith Matthews and his Orchestra

Labour Hall, Stow Hill

St Mary's Hall, Stow Hill (now Zanzibar)

St John Bosco Hall, Cromwell Road

Orchard Street Hall

Railway Institute, Malpas Road

Ebbw Bridge Club, Cardiff Road

KINGS HEAD

Syd Clement's Ambassadors Dance Orchestra

Serenaders Dance Orchestra

Billy Rabbit and the Beachcombers Dance Orchestra

Allan Dale and his Mayfair Band

and the bands of

Jim Haley, Dennis Hooper, Henry Dougherty, Ronnie Allan

Appearing St John's Hall, Victoria Avenue

251

Newport Dance Bands

Anewrin Thomas
& His Collegians

The Georgians

Henry Dougherty's band

PRINCIPAL :
VANESSA CLARKE

The Vanessa Clarke School of Dance was established thirty-two years ago, also known as the Beechwood School of Dance, Vanessa has enjoyed working with her dancers at the Beechwood Church Studios on Chepstow Road, Newport.

Vanessa Clarke is a member of the BBO who has won awards for the Best Choreography at the Waterford Festival in Ireland and in 1997 she was Head of Choreography at a show staged in the London Palladium.

Her dancers have performed in many theatres in Newport and Cardiff. Every year, Vanessa choreographs a summer show and a pantomime for the Newport Pantomime and Musical Society. Twice a year, Vanessa's pupils perform in their own show at the Dolman Theatre and from these events over the years, the School has raised many thousands of pounds for national charities.

The most recent charity being for the Noah's Ark Appeal, Children's Hospital for Wales.

VANESSA CLARKE School of dance

The Stars in Their Eyes.

253

Vanessa's School of Dance in London.

More fun for the girls.

At rehearsals.
Vanessa, Front row (left).

PRINCIPAL : SHARON FITZGERALD

The Sharon Fitzgerald School of Dance was formed in 1991 at Somerton Community Centre, Newport. Apart from her own dance shows which she produces and performs at the Dolman Theatre, Sharon choreographs musicals for the Newport Operatic Society. Her dance routines are always electric and exciting to watch. Currently, Sharon is choreographing the annual pantomime for Stan Stennett Productions, with great success. She has also played many leading roles in musicals and pantomimes. In April 2003, Sharon played the leading part of Babe Williams in the American musical The Pajama Game performed by Newport Operatics.

Sharon Fitzgerald Dancers.

Sharon Fitzgerald (centre front row) with the troupe.

Senior group of dancers, 'all very elegant'.

Reaching for the stars.

Juniors shining bright.

THE LAWRENCE SCHOOL OF DANCE

PRINCIPAL – MARGARET LAWRENCE WATERS

The Lawrence School of Dance was formed in 1990 and is currently using the Church Hall at Bishpool Methodist Church, Newport.

Margaret started her dance training with the Margretta Spicer Little Academy of Dance and is now herself a registered teacher with the British Ballet Organisation.

Over the last thirteen years, Margaret has choreographed and provided dancers for The New Venture Players Musical Productions and Standard Music Society.

Margaret Lawrence Waters.

Beautiful babes.

Dancers at the bar.

Margaret Lawrence-Waters

Margaret started dancing at the age of 7 doing most of her training with Molly Spicer of the LITTLE ACADEMY OF DANCE. During this time Margaret fell in love with Ballet and after winning a scholarship with THE BRITISH BALLET ORGANIZATION aged 11 decided to make dance her career. When Margaret was 17 she was accepted for the famous BALLET RAMBERT SCHOOL where she continued to train.

Growing too tall for ballet Margaret decided to make her career in commercial dance and was very soon working on the prestigious cruise liner QE2. Margaret worked on the ship for two and a half years firstly, then having a short break to do pantomime in the Theatre Royal Bath with John Noakes, Peter Purves, Lesley Judd and Ben Warris. Margaret then returned to the ship as dance captain for a further two and a half years. During her time on the ship Margaret worked with many stars of the television and theatre but her favourite person she met has to be Sir Anthony Hopkins.

After leaving the ship Margaret continued her career with the comedy duo The Krankies becoming one of their four dancers Margaret continued to work for them for 5 years performing in all of their pantomines, summer seasons, and tours.

Margaret has worked with many of the top choreographers including Irving Davies, Dougie Squires, Peter Gordeno, and Alan Harding to name a few.

Since returning to Newport Margaret has got married, had two children, Adam and Rebecca, and opened her own own dancing school specialising in her first love. classical ballet and modern jazz.

Margaret is still very much involved with the theatre and has choreographed and performed with most Newport societies, and is at the moment working with The Standard Pirelli Operatic Society,

Following in your steps.

Pretty as a picture.

258

MARGRETTA SPICER (MOLLY)
THE LITTLE ACADEMY OF DANCING

Molly commenced dancing lessons at the age of four at a local school – and it's true to say she has been dancing ever since.

At the age of ten, Molly entered the Bristol School of Dancing and studied dance under the direction of Principal Muriel Carpenter. From the age of twelve performed professionally for many years as a solo dancer in Summer and Christmas seasons at theatres throughout the country, including productions with Western Theatre Ballet under the direction of Elizabeth West and Peter Darrell.

In 1960 Molly returned to Newport and opened her own school of dance under the name of The Little Academy of Dance and obtained teaching qualifications with the B.B.O. (British Ballet Organisation) and in more recent years was awarded a fellowship with I.S.T.D.

In 1985, Molly was invited to become an examiner for B.B.O. by Mr Edward Kelland-Espinosa and continues in this capacity to the present time.

Over the years, Molly Spicer has choreographed and provided dancers for many operatic and musical societies.

Molly Spicer and Vera Morcan.

Margrette Spicer at the age of? - well, very young.

Beautiful Ballet.

Siamese Dancers?
Not quite, but very good anyway.

STC MUSICAL SOCIETY

The STC Musical Society was formed in 1958 under the original name of Standard Telephones and Cables Operatic Society. Up until then, the theatre group only performed pantomimes and revues, at which we excelled. I say "we" because I was a major part of the society. One evening coming home by train from London's West End and after seeing a wonderful musical there, choreographer Gloria Harries, and myself (Terry Underwood) tried talking to our then producer, Fred Bayliss into trying our hand at staging musicals. Fred's reply was "don't be daft, we haven't got enough men". So his answer from Paddington to Newport Station was "No, no, no, we haven't got enough men". Walking over Newport Town Bridge around 3 o'clock in the morning, Gloria said "Fred, if we find you enough men, will you say 'yes'?". His reply was "Oh, I suppose so, but where are you going to get them from?". So I said "leave it to me, I'll go down to see Newport Male Voice, they may say yes". And they did. About twelve men came and joined STC Operatic and we performed our first musical in 1958 'Katinka'. Next came 'Oklahoma'. Fred said "where are we going to get male dancers from?", and I said "how about Malpas Gymnastics?", and those lads joined us and did a fine job.

STC MUSICAL SOCIETY
presents

MACK & MABEL

Book by
MICHAEL STEWART

Music & Lyrics by
JERRY HERMAN

At

THE DOLMAN THEATRE
NEWPORT

Theatre cast. Standard Telephones and Cables operatic Society

The full company of the STC
Musical 'Katinka' produced
in 1958.

Margaret Shead-Gwatkin with
Malcom Thorne in the Standard
Telephones and Cable production
of 'La Belle Helene' (Welsh Premiere)
in 1964.

Eric Lane
Tribute Event held for Modest "Grand Master" of Stage Management

On the evening of Sunday 14th January 2001, members and officers of Newport Operatic Society, Newport Playgoers and a number of other Amateur Theatrical Organisations will gather together with relatives, neighbours and friends of the late Eric J Lane, to celebrate, in words and music, his outstanding contribution to the Amateur Theatre. That celebration will warmly acknowledge his long and dedicated service as General Secretary of Newport Operatic Society and "Grand Master" of stage management at the Dolman Theatre.

Newport Operatic Society will particularly remember the year 2000 as being the year it said "Goodbye" to Eric Lane. In February, Eric retired from the position of General Secretary, having completed 31 years of dedicated service and, on 4th December, he died after loosing a painful battle with cancer, "Bringing down the curtain" on 46 years of involvement in amateur theatre.

Eric was born in Swindon in 1921 and at the age of 16 he commenced employment in the famous Swindon Railway Workshops. His career with the railways was interrupted in 1939, when he joined the RAF to do his duty

Eric Lane.

for king and country, including service in India as a radio reconnaissance officer. He resumed employment with the railways at the end of the War, joining the office staff and advanced his career to eventually become Regional Personnel Manager for British Rail in Cardiff, from which he retired in 1982 early to look after Enid in her fight against cancer.

He married his first wife, Enid in 1952 and together they moved work to various railway towns and cities including Dudley, Neath, Plymouth and Cardiff as Eric's career progressed. It was whilst living in the Midlands Enid, a mezzo soprano, joined Cradleigh Heath Operatic Society. She also persuaded Eric to join the Society and even got him on stage playing a small role. Whilst Eric was not keen on being in the spotlight, he enjoyed the ambience of the theatre and began on make-up and make-up props and a commitment to helping backstage. That commitment continued when he moved to Neath and his interest was nurtured through "hands on" stage management training with Neath Operatic Society, for whom he also became Secretary.

On being promoted to the Personnel Manager position in Cardiff, he and Enid joined Newport Operatic Society, with Eric becoming both Stage Manager and General Secretary in 1969. He continued in both these roles until last year, gaining particular recognition for his skill as a technical director. He was also Stage Director for Newport Playgoers for twelve years and continued to be actively involved in set design and management up until a few weeks before his death. He was a leading member of the organising committee of the Newport Festival of Musical Theatre, which attracted Operatic Societies from all over the UK to perform in competition at the Dolman Theatre in week long festivals during the period 1990 to 1993. With Lorraine he was in charge of props for a few years with Swansea Operatic Society at The Grange Theatre.

His first wife Enid died in early 1984 and he met his second wife, Lorraine, later that year. Lorraine is also a long standing member of Newport Operatic Society and Newport Playgoers, who has worked alongside Eric in stage management. Lorraine is justly proud of Eric's achievements in the amateur theatre, one of his hobbies. The other main hobby is running a market garden at home, his beloved Badgers Wood in Bassaleg where his ashes are now buried. Throughout his long involvement with the amateur theatre Eric was never less than modest, compassionate, generous, and dedicated in his approach to his work and life.

By D. Denzil Reed of Swansea

To look at and to review in a short period of time, a friendship which lasted from 1953 to the end of 2000 - is a task that I'm not sure how to start - or to carry out with the right degree of respect and accuracy - but I am sure that our greatly loved and dear late friend Eric William James Lane will find my efforts acceptable - he always allowed me a great deal of lea-way ever since we first worked with one another just over 47 years ago.

We first met when he had recently been appointed to a very Senior Officer's post in the Motive Power Dept of British Rail - we ran and looked after the hundreds of steam locomotives - and the appointment of this " thirty-four-some" - upstart with friends in high places at Swindon - didn't go down very well with many people in South Wales.. He was quite determined to prove them wrong -and how right he was - and how wrong they were!

He brought some new thinking into an antiquated system - and some of his quite revolutionary attitudes to some prehistoric causes - caused more than just "raised eyebrows" amongst some of the senior staff - which was much to the joy of people like myself who suffered from flat foreheads through continually banging them on our desks - on so many subjects for so long..

Another novel idea he brought to the job was the fact that he was prepared to listen to other peoples' opinions - and in no time at all, he was being admired - I would have said "loved" which would have been acceptable in the 50's but totally unacceptable in this new Millennium where the so many lovely words like "love" and "gay" have been hijacked and now mean something entirely something. Eric and I shared so many similar views - one I have just mentioned.

During those early years at Neath, we both worked backstage with the Melyncrythan Amateur Operatic Society - as many of the people working in the office were players and non-players in this then great Society - which was always playing the latest shows released for amateur Societies. I was also the Secretary of the Clydach Society and before long, we had a nice little arrangement - where our stage crew used to go to Neath - and we got a hugely experienced crew back for our own show at Clydach. Eric was the "Props" expert and nothing was too difficult to make - with his enthusiasm and ingenuity.
He was a great asset to us - as he was to you people in Newport for so many years.

At that time with the Railways being dismantled by Doctor Beeching, he was a great "borrower" of bits of wood and other items that could be changed from a Railway unit to an Operatic one - and he knew all the Foremen Fitters and Coppersmiths and Wagon Repair Carpenters - men who eventually used to run away from the Depots when they knew he was coming to see them. I well remember having been made responsible for the cranes and other lifting gear at Fishguard Harbour and he came down with me to Fishguard on my first visit and in a walk-about of their locomotive fining shop found the blacksmith cooking lobsters on the forge - a very profitable sideline to repairing locomotives - and in no time at all, we used to regularly meet the Boat Train from Fishguard to collect the fresh lobsters which used to be then put on the 5.30 express from Swansea to Paddington and were given to Enid at Swindon Station by the Driver. He was one of the best organizers I ever knew.

He and I also organised the first Senior Management Office Outing which meant we travelled by train on the Central Wales Line to Llandrindod Wells. We had a private coach for the 40 of us which included a guards van - the only one on the lonely - and lovely - Central Wales line with a built in bar. We were fortunate enough to have a next door neighbour to our Office, Evans and Bevans Brewery which proved to be an excellent arrangement at Christmas time and, of course, when we used to hold the Office Outings.

Another of our liquid holidays was when the Clydach Society played at the Waterford Festival - a land of great hilarity, wonderful music with people of a similar ilk to ourselves - to say nothing of the drama, tears and laughter depending on whether or not you were winning or not-winning the Waterford glass for your efforts. I remember him teasing Pauline and wanting to know who she had supported to win the Best Supporting Female performer rose bowl. I also have a vague recollection of he and I posing for a photograph each with a pint sized silver tankard of C.D.C.Gin and Tonic. So many happy days - now nearly 40 years ago and never to return.

Our paths moved apart for a while when he left Neath and he and Enid were both transferred to a new Office on the Bull Ring at Birmingham. They lived at Stourbridge and in no time at all, he was tearing the house about and, would you believe it, I was transferred to Birmingham for about six months and lived with them for a while. By then - Enid had joined the Cradley Heath Society and played the lead in Vagabond King, and then they both ventured into the world of G&S with the very excellent Stourbridge G&S Society. In no time, Eric was making props and humping Scenery and the lucky people in the Midlands took full advantage of them both.

By this time I had changed my job and was a technical Representative in the Shell-Mex and BP group of companies and in no time at all, all of Eric' cars, tractors and rotovators were running on BP lubrication oils.

They had now moved to Plymouth and bought a lovely bungalow at Yelverton - a stone throw from Dartmoor Prison which we visited occasionally - not for very long I assure you - and certainly not for overnight stays. No sooner had he moved in that he was on the phone about getting our Central Heating Engineers to call and get an oil fired heating system installed - which I was able to do through my colleagues in the company. By the time that was finished, he had grand ideas about extending the bungalow and had actually dug the footings by hand when they moved him again to Cardiff which was fine as we were able to meet more often.

It was not long after this that he bought Badgers Wood in Bassaleg and became a welcomed Stage Manager for the Newport Society and then their Secretary for over 30 years.

As he got very firmly entrenched at Newport, I was doing daft things at Clydach, I decided in 1977 to resign from the Amateur Theatre world and concentrate on the one-third of acre of wilderness the builders jokingly called a "Mature Garden"

Before I could really start on this new venture, I found myself Head-Hunted for the Swansea AOS and reluctantly agreed to help them out as Secretary for the next show. Twenty three shows later, I am still there but there is a chance I might be able to renew my retirement later this year although our Centenary celebrations are taking a great deal of my time. Both Eric and Lorraine joined us when he eventually retired and yet again, this peer of excellence was beside me yet again in my new Society with all the grand things that you get from playing in the Grand Theatre. Redundant equipment at the Grand soon found its way to the Dolman at Newport.

Also in the sixties, I was persuaded to become a Regional Representative for the National Operatic and Dramatic Association - or NODA if you prefer. If you wondered how Eric was so well-informed, you now know that I used to give him copies of the minutes of most of my meetings both locally and in other parts of the UK on a regular basis. I then became the Councillor for Wales which meant that I could attend your shows twice a year and was always most graciously received in Newport. In October 1994, I had the great honour to be installed as the National President of NODA at the Cardiff.

International Arena and guess who was there? No such an occasion would have been complete without him and Lorraine, of course.

Our paths have been close and parallel for way over 40 years and yet there is yet another fraternity in which Eric and I had a close relationship. We were both Freemasons and were both initiated in the early Seventies - he at Cardiff and me at Swansea. We visited each other's Lodges on many occasions and shared all the pleasures that true fraternal friendship brings. We both shared many honours in the Craft and as he held high office in two lodges in South Wales, his loss is being doubly felt. He gave outstanding service to his Lodges and was well loved and respected.. He became the Worshipful Master in both of them - a job he did in his usual manner - most excellent!

Enid - Eric's first wife passed on after a long and painful illness which upset him - and his close friends - tremendously. The pair of them had such a large circle of friends - which was as well as they had virtually no family on either side. His garden at Badgers Wood - with all the machinery still running quite happily on BP oils - became the centre of his life along with that of the Play Goers, the Operatic Society and his beloved Lodges.

His second marriage to Lorraine and the arrival of a ready-made family was yet another high spot in his life - and the last 16 years or so have been ones of what might be called his "Indian Summer". Despite back problems which plagued him for most of his adult life, he was totally immersed in his big garden and his new family and who can ask for anything more - as George Gershwin said?

He leaves each and every one of us with stories to tell - with some particular reminiscence that happened in such and such a show - and everyone will have amply sampled his often overwhelming generosity and hospitality.

I am sure there are many people here who could have more eloquently spoken about their friendship with Eric but nobody knew him better than I did - for as long as I did - or was so upset to see him so
ill at the end. His ashes are now being buried in the garden at his beloved Badgers Wood.

Whilst nobody would wish to end such a long friendship - I am glad he did not suffer for long and I am sure if there is such a thing as an Amateur Operatic Society wherever he is now, I am sure they will have roped him in to make their props by now.

I wondered how to close my talk about Eric and was reminded of the New Vicar making his first sermon to his inquisitive congregation at his first Service. He took much longer than normal and the natives were getting restless. When he said - "And what else can I tell you " a small voice in the back of the Church said "Amen"

And so - I say Amen with the ardent wish "May he rest in Peace".

Eric at the Dolman Theatre Workshop.

Eric on the set at the Dolman Theatre.

Eric puts the finishing touches to scenery.

NEWPORT PLAYGOERS

On 19th December 1924, members of seven Newport dramatic societies met in the Y.M.C.A. Commercial Street, to consider the future of many small dramatic, art and literature groups in the town.

There was considerable artistic and dramatic talent in Newport but it was the drive and vision of a Newport art shop and bookseller Ifan Kyrle Fletcher, that instigated a meeting of many small groups of talented actors etc. to come together and combine forces, thus establishing the now renowned group – The Newport Playgoers.

On 19th January 1925, thirty people attended the second meeting, chaired by Ifan Kyrle Fletcher, a committee was elected and subscriptions fixed at 2/6 for the remainder of the 1925 season.

The Chief Officers of the newly-formed Newport Playgoers Society were :-

President	-	Mr T J Webley
Vice President	-	Mr Ifan Kyrle Fletcher
Treasurer	-	Mr Harold Phillips
Joint Secretaries	-	Mr J E Howard
		Mr J Stanley Watkins

President, Hugh Moelwyn Hughes.

By the summer of 1925, an open-air production of 'As You Like It' was performed in the grounds of Brynglas Central School and in 1926, the society gave its first performance of 'Pygmalion' at the Lyceum Theatre.

The policy of producing public performances in the Lyceum continued until 1929 when 'The Skin Game' and 'the Mask and the Face' was produced. In all, seven plays were performed in the Lyceum. In 1933, the society moved to the Park hall in Hill Street, here began the plans for a permanent theatre and the building up of the finances to carry out the project. Buildings were examined, discussed and rejected, and eventually the society acquired their own building, then known as St James Church. This church was originally called Hope Chapel, which included John Frost as one of its members, and on August 11th 1839, over two hundred Chartists attended divine service there.

A Building Committee was formed and Arthur Dolman proposed the target collection of £4,000 to acquire Hope Chapel. Eighteen months of feverish work, planning, altering and equipping passed before The Little Theatre, as it was named, opened in January 1937 with a weeks production of 'So to Bed', directed by Ted Granger. Membership soared to an unbelievable figure of over 3,000 and there was a long waiting list. During the 1940's and the War years, thousands of troops were entertained, both by the Playgoers own concert party 'Flashlights' together with visiting British and American concert parties which kept the society intact and alive during a very difficult period.

In 1960, Sovereign Securities Limited arrived in Newport, these developers purchased a number of properties in the area to turn into shops and offices. They approached Playgoers to sell them The Little Theatre and the adjoining property. The result finally ended up with Newport Playgoers re-housed into a fine new building more central in the town and re-named The Dolman Theatre after a Newport solicitor Arthur Dolman. Although not a founder member of Playgoers, he represented, though his friendship with Ifan Kyrle Fletcher, a link with the original driving force of the society.

Since the opening of The Dolman in 1967, the society has mounted eight mainstream stage productions each season for its members which is a wonderful achievement and is helping in a big way by keeping performing arts alive in this city of ours.

Keep it going Dolman.

Newport Players at 'The Minack' open air theatre in Portcurno in Cornwall.

Newport Players at 'The Minack' in Cornwall.

Princess Margaret, greeted by Arthur Dolman at the Dolman Theatre in 1967

Arthur Dolman Meeting Princes Margaret in the Theatre that was named after the Newport Solicitor.

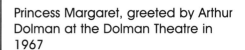

President Trevor Jones and Newport Playgoers meet Princess Margaret.

Jill James, Tony Wright and cast of 'The Deep Blue Sea'.

Passing stars of Newport Playgoers Society
Gone but not forgotten.

Trevor Jones passed away January 2001.

Eric Lane passed away December 2000.

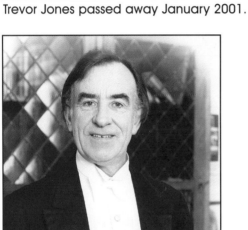

Harry Preece passed away January 2001.

Jill James passed away July 2002.

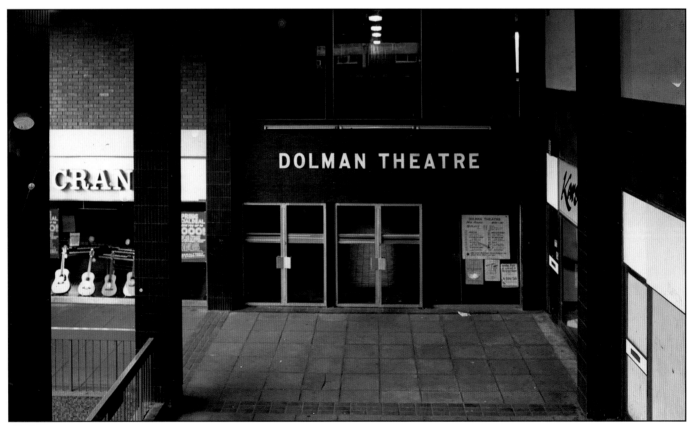

Entrance and exit. Newport Playgoers Dolman Theatre.

THE FORTUNAIRES

The Fortunaires Singing Quartet was formed in 1955 as part of a musical and variety group and worked together until 2001 when illness effected the group. The original group was formed by Newport author and playwright Terry Underwood for his production of Cinderella for the Standard Telephones and Cable Company.

The original group consisted of Harry Denham, Bob Pickard, Don Edwards and Dennis Jenkins who played the parts of Flunkys in Cinderella and their singing achieved rave reviews. After a very busy time in the late fifties around Newport and South Wales entertainment scene, they entered the first Vocal Group Championship of Great Britain (Amateur) Contest at the Soho Fair, London in 1958, sponsored by 'Disc' magazine and won First Prize.

Many TV and Radio dates followed including a spot on the famous '6-5 Special' Programme on BBC TV. By this time, Dennis Jenkins was forced to leave the group through work commitments and a young talented lady was found to fill his place for a short while. When Peggy left the Fortunaires, no way could they perform as the 'Threetunaires' so the very talented comedian and vocalist, Newport-born Peter Hourahine was more than happy to fill the vacant spot. Although a close harmony style group, they also shone with comedy numbers and this suited Peter, with superb talent for comedy.

After many years on the professional and semi-professional circuit, they have found time to raise thousands of pounds for many charities.

In 1994, the group completed a unique double by winning the Whitbread Senior Citizens UK Talent Competition at Southport.

The Fortunaires have appeared with such star names as Roy Castle, Tom Jones, Norman Vaughan, The Tanner Sisters, Arthur Worsley and a very youthful Cliff Richard, to name but a few.

For many years, Peter Hourahine was the driving force for the Fortunaires, when accompanist Rita Hildred joined the group in 1993. Rita and Peter played a large part in the continuing success of the group over the last few years, performing regularly at theatres in Newport and Cwmbran in revues and in their own show, 'the Fortunaires'.

Newport's famous singing group the Fortunaires and friends.

Rehearsing, The Fortunaires at the piano accompanied by Rita Hildred.

The young Fortunaires, Harry Denham, Don Edwards, Bob Pickard and Peter Hourahine.

Sing as we go.

We've won again!

Peter Hourahine

Peter first trod the boards 60 years ago when he appeared in the Army Cadet Production of "Sleeping Beauty" at St. Matthews Church Hall in Church Road.

In 1946 he appeared in the pantomime "Babes in the Woods" at the Drill Hall of the Army Cadets.
Peter then joined the army serving until the Royal Welsh Fusiliers and Durham Light Infantry between 1947 - 1949 when he made his acting debut on a demob course at the college of Rhine Army Gottingen Germany.
He began working for Standard Telephones & Cables Ltd. joining their drama group then onto pantomimes and revues. He met the singing group "The Fortunaires" in 1957 first appearing with them in a revue "Out of the Blue" written and directed by Terry Underwood.

The choir and some solo acts from that revue including Peter appeared and won The Carol Levis Talent contest at the Lyceum Theatre in Newport which gave them all the opportunity to take part in a show named "Top Town" which was televised from Manchester in 1958.

Between the years 1958 - 59, Peter did lots of work appearing on 6-5 Special, ITV, BBC and Radio Luxemborg. Following which he turned professional with a resident group at Butlins Pwllelli where he played alongside such artists as Cliff Richard, Roy Hudd and Roy Castle.

On returning to Newport he rejoined the STC Operatic Society and is still with them today (2005). His first musical performance as as Mr. Snow in "Carousel" at the Lyceum in 1960, going on to play in a further 80 musicals and achieving the following awards, in "Fiddler on the Roof" he gained a Best Male Performer award in 1973, Best Male Performer award as Bobbinet in "La Vie Parisienne" at Waterford 1969. Also at Waterford 1964, Best Comedy Actor in "La Belle Helene", part of which was performed later on BBC TV when he played "King Menalaus".

Peter hosted his own radio show on BBC Radio Gwent between 1988 - 1992 during over 400 broadcasts.
He, along with The Fortunaires Singing Group, entertained in and won the UK Senior Citizens Talent Contest in Southport going on to win The Welsh & West of England Finals five times!

In 2000 Peter entered the finals at Southport as a solo comedian coming second, and when winning the Wales and West final in Swansea, he won a unique trophy presented by Whitbread for the Millennium year only - which was a statuette of Eric Morcambe.

Not an Oscar - but an Eric!
Still to be seen performing in 2002 and in demand as an after dinner speaker, Peter who was a widower in 1996 enjoys life with his son and two gorgeous grandchildren

Peter Hourahine
In Camelot.

Peter Hourahine - Actor, Singer, Comedian.

He's won first prize again!

Peter as Topole, Fiddler on the roof.

Peter giving it all he's got!

Peter with Ester Ransom.

Peter wins the Eric Morecambe award.

Peter broadcasting from Cwmbran BBC Radio Wales.

275

The Riverfront Theatre

The New Theatre, raising the roof

The Riverfront Theatre, to be named The Waterfront Theatre and will open in 2004

The New Theatre under construction.

"Up she goes and open she will".

The Southern Distribution Road Bridge

There she goes over the River Usk.

Looking at things from the Pill side of the River Usk.

The Southern distribution road Bridge near completion.

The bridge over troubled waters.

THE CAMPAIGN TO SAVE OUR SHIP

S.O.S. Save Our Ship S.O.S.

Timeline

May 8th 2002	Work began on the laying of foundations for the new 500 seat Theatre and Arts Centre on the riverside.
June 22nd 2002	The medieval trading vessel is discovered on the muddy banks of the River Usk by contractors sinking foundation piles, work is halted while a team from the Glamorgan-Gwent Archaeological investigate the find.
July 11th 2002	A campaign group under the leadership of Newport business-man Charles Ferris to save the ship said "The people of Newport feel quite adamant that the ship should be preserved, at the very least more time should be given to see what options are available."
August 1st 2002	Newport Council announces two open evenings for those interested in viewing the ship.
August 7th & 14th	Public interest increases as an estimated 10,000 people queued 2002 to view the ship. A public meeting was held at the Dolman Theatre by Save Our Ship campaigners where about 300 people attended.
August 16th 2002	S.O.S. launch a round the clock vigil to protect the ship. Mr Jan Preece of Pill Heritage Centre had collected well over 2,000 signatures to save the ship.
August 17th 2002	Culture Minister Jenny Randerson promises the ship will be saved.
August 19th 2002	Campaigners deliver a 6,000 name petition to Newport Borough Council and finally to the Welsh Assembly at Cardiff Bay in support of the ship's preservation.
Augusta 23rd 2002	The Welsh Assembly announces it will Save the Ship with a £3.5million preservation package to put the ship on display in the basement of the New Arts Centre.
September 2002	S.O.S. Committee was formed to maintain interest and liase with relevant bodies as to the final resting place and display centre for the vessel. Estimated viewers over a 2 month period to the ship is said to be in the region of 6,000.
2003	Announcement made by Newport Borough Council that the keel and bow of the ship was saved but they were unable to save the stern, as further excavations would have caused subsidence in the embankment. All timbers so far recovered are now being stored in water tanks at the Corus Site of Llanwern Steelworks.

Friends of the Newport Ship:

The elected Committee are as follows: -

Chairman :	S.C. Rutherford
Vice Chairman :	Ron McCormick
Treasurer :	Terry Underwood
Secretary :	Jean Gray
Membership Secretary :	Tracy Holder

Members :

Jeff Brooks
George Bullock
Charles Ferris
Rosi Hollister
Chris Plaister
Jan Preece
Bob Trett

Charles Ferris leader of the campaign to save the Medieval ship discovered on the banks of Newport's River Usk in the site of the New Theatre and Arts Centre in 2002.

A.M. member Rosemary Butler and Jan Preece of Pill Heritage signing the partition to save the Ship.

Terry Underwood chairs the first meeting of Friends of The Ship, August 2002.

Daily queues of people come to see the Medieval Ship discovered on the banks of the River Usk at Newport. Reported number of viewers were in excess of 50,000 in 2002.

Patiently waiting their turn to view the treasured ship.

Friends of the Ship encouraging suppoort from passing motorists.

Simon Ruthreford, Charles Ferris, Terry Underwood, Jan Preece at the Dolman Theatre in August 2002.

What a discovery isn't she great.

A.M. member Rosemary Butler addressing the audience at the Dolman Theatre on the finding of the Medieval Ship and its proposed restoration.

The first meeting of interested Newportians when the Ship was discovered.

Archeologists working on the ship.

Discovery of the ship
on site - View A.

View B of the ship.

View C of the ship.

Artist Paul Deakin with his painting
of how the ship would have looked
in its day, with a delighted Charles
Ferris, leader of the Campaign to
Save the Ship.

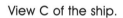

GEORGE STREET FURNISHERS (Est.1951)

Richard Sheppard, a one time apprentice upholsterer discovered at a very early age that he not only had the freedom of the road with his motorcycle, but had a head filled with dreams and ambitions.

Fifty-two years ago whilst living at Gaer Park Road Newport, Richard began to achieve his ambition by starting up his own company, an upholstery business. His first workshop was a then defunct back garden Air Raid Shelter at his home, which became the hub of his life.

The business grew rapidly and still eager to progress even further, Richard acquired new premises in Commercial Road where he began retailing in upholstery and furnishings. Very soon, Richard Sheppard was employing some twenty or more staff and running two small delivery vans.

Above: Graham Sheppard, Richard Sheppard (the founder of the company) and Martyn Sheppard
Right: Martyn Sheppard, son Adam and brother Graham

Twenty years later with his dreams come true, the entrepreneurial streak in Richard shone through as with all the confidence in the world, he purchased the now George Street Warehouse, with ample parking for customers and deliveries.

The premises are spacious with three floors which allowed for further expansion. The success of the company is obvious, occupying a prime spot close to George Street Bridge which straddles the River Usk.

Although Richard has always led the way, he would be the first to say, "Yes I did it, but not without the support of my loyal staff".

Today, George Street Furnishers are blessed with a 40 strong staff to meet the needs of their loyal customers.

On his retirement, Richard's two sons Martyn and Graham took over the business.

Martyn Sheppard is Managing Director and Graham the Principal Buyer for the Company.

And to quote the hard-working pair "This is a family business with Christian values that are an integral part of the firm. Those values are very much a part of our company and the fact that eighty per cent of our sales come from repeat business shows that people like the way we work."

Two of Richards pride and joys, his B.S.A. motorbike and his newly acquired premises.

284

The very first shop of Richard Sheppard, Commercial Road, Newport.

Richard Sheppard taking the front seat on his car, in Gaer Park Road.

The staff of George Street Furnishers (est 1951) with managing director Richard Sheppard seated front right.

George Street Warehouse in the year 2000.

And the computor vision of its present day appearance.

WILDINGS STORES

For the visitors to Newport, and of course the people who reside in the City, Newport has excellent shopping facilities with a number of major stores occupying prime sites in the main streets, a far cry from the Newport that existed in the eighteen hundreds.

In the year that Benjamin Disraeli become Prime Minister of Great Britain, and butter was fourpence a pound, the growing pains of Newport, then a small town, could be heard as far away as the Midlands and North Wales. The year was 1874, when a young man of twenty-one years of age arrived in the town to start a business – his name was Alfred Wilding. The streets of Newport were filled with horse-drawn trams and delivery trucks, handcarts and hansom cabs and of course, people. Messenger boys ran between High Street, Commercial Street and Dock Street relaying information from one business to another.

Newport in Monmouthshire in 1874 was a hive of activity. The town was experiencing the effects of tremendous growth. The population had risen from one thousand and eighty in the year 1800 to around thirty thousand in 1874. The rapid growth of the town was one of the main factors that inspired the young Alfred Wilding, who was born and lived in Winstanton, Shropshire, to come to Newport.

Halfway down Commercial Street and in the main shopping area, Alfred Wilding opened his first exclusive store, gentlemen's hatter and hosier, catering for the well-to-do and nobility of the town, with high-class merchandise.

The small, but well-stocked lock-up shop with living accommodation over at 154 Commercial Street, soon attracted the more affluent customer and in the first year of trading, Alfred soon realised that much larger premised were needed.

In 1882, the business transferred to premised at the bottom of Stow Hill which stood very much in the main Westgate Square.

Frederick Wilding, the son of Alfred was appointed a Director of Wildings following the death of his father in 1924. Frederick held the position he was to hold until his death in 1967 at the age of 89.

Newport-born Sheldon James joined Wildings at the age of 30 as Company Secretary and on Mr Frederick Wildings death became Managing Director, a position he held until his retirement in 1995. He still remains the Company Secretary and is a Director, and for Sheldon it is a great pleasure to see that his son, Peter, has taken over the reins of Wildings and progress is still being made keeping up with supplies and demands of the 21st Century.

Success in business has been with Wildings for the last 129 years, it will remain important not to lose sight of the fact that the fundamentals of retailing will always be the same. The one constant for Wildings has been the high calibre of its staff. They have been responsible for the success of the business and will surely be the making of the business in the future. Good quality products backed up by first rate service will be the basis on which Wildings will develop under the Managing Directorship of Mr Peter James.

If Wildings can continue to deliver these, then the future of the Company looks bright.

Wildings' store, Commercial Street.

New managing director of Wildings,
Mr. Peter James with Paul Flynn M.P.
for Newport and poet Geoff Margan.

Paul Flynn M.P. for Newport in Commercial Street
outside Wildings.

M.I.I. MR RAY BARTON
MECHANICAL INSTALLATIONS INTERNATIONAL LIMITED

Newport born Ray Barton lived in a modest terraced house just off the main Chepstow Road. The time, the early 1950's and like most young men he had a dream, he wanted to be successful in all that he chose to do.

In 1966 Ray became an apprentice at Girlings, Cwmbran, then served as a mechanical engineer. In the evenings he would perform on stage with the Standard Telephones Operatic Society and later with the New Venture Players Theatre Group. All of this activity gave him the confidence he was seeking to help fulfil his ambitions.

Working his way through the ranks, Ray developed a career in sales in the 1970's. By 1978 he had joined Stevens Engineering Company based in Pontypool where he met Glyn Stevens the Managing Director and owner of the company. Glyn Stevens was a prominent figure in the South Wales Industrial Circle. It was here that Ray worked his way up to becoming Sales Director. Working all day and performing on stage at night kept Ray very busy, however he found time to meet and marry his lovely wife Ruth. Whilst on honeymoon during 1984, the news came that Stevens Engineering Company had been forced to close.

Ray and Glyn quickly realised that they were not ready for the employment exchange, besides said Ray, we can't afford it. Within weeks of the bad news, together they established Mechanical Installations International Limited on Johnsey Estates, and in 1985 they secured their first international contract.

Employing their first secretary, a Y.T.S. apprentice who is now Company Secretary, M.I.I. developed as a leading mechanical installation contractor in the U.K. and Europe.

In 1987 they recruited Reg Baggard as Managing Director of the growing mechanical installation team which has at times reached 250 employees.

During 1991 M.I.I. moved premises from Johnsey Estates to Richmond House on Chepstow Road. They became preferred supplier of mechanical installation services to British Steel, Llanwern and Port Talbot in 1992.

By 1995 M.I.I. establishes maintenance division to generate additional work with existing customer bases. On reaching an age way past his retirement age, Glyn Stevens was finally persuaded to let go the reins and retire. However, Glyn maintains a keen interest in the company.

During 1999 work commenced on the Continuous Annealing Process Line at Corus Steelworks, Port Talbot, M.I.I.'s largest single project at the time. The company also worked on four other major contracts concurrently. Then in 2001, Ray Barton heads the restructuring of M.I.I. to challenge the downturn in work from Corus Steelworks.

From 2003, 6 new divisions were established, including pipework facilities, machinery relocation, electrical project management and C.D.M.

One of the new divisions includes a full Fire Protection Service headed up by Ray's son David – will history repeat itself ? But, as Ray Barton would say if asked "you may start off life with dreams but to achieve your ambitions stop dreaming, roll up your sleeves and get on with it."

Ray still performs on stage when he finds time, and is a great help in encouraging others by helping financially with many productions and theatre groups in the City. His love for starting blocks in life is still there and is recognised by all.

Ray Barton is President of Standard Telephones Musicals and Vice President of New Venture Players, and is a Benefactor of St Anne's Hospice.

Mr. Ray Barton magaing director of
MII Limited

Mr. Reg Baggard, managing director
of Mechanical Installations.

(L to R Standing)
Don Le Clare, Brian Jones, Dave
Miller, Peter Sands, Ray Barton, Rosso
Safavi
(L to R Seated)
Fiona Parsons, Brian Arnesen.
At the Launch of their Website
December 2002

Newport County AFC Club History

Newport County AFC were founded as Newport AFC in June 1989to replace the original Newport County which had folded less than four months earlier. Consequently the club's aim has always been, and will remain, progression through the English pyramid system to pursue a return t o the Football League status held by the original club.

The Exiles obtained their nickname as a result of the need to play their inaugural season in the North Gloucestershire town of Moreton in Marsh at which venue they won the Hellenic League & Cup double, winning promotion to the Southern League.

After two seasons back home in Newport at Somerton Park, football politics consigned them to a further two seasons of exile at Gloucester and the club was forced to resort to extensive, and expensive, legal action to protect themselves from being forced out of the English non-league pyramid.

That litigation proved successful, a landmark High Court verdict enabling them to have a permanent home in Newport at the newly built Newport Stadium. The club's first season back in Wales, in 1994-95, saw them promoted to the Southern League's Premier Division by the winning of the Midland Division Championship. That was achieved by a 14-point margin and, on the way to that championship, the club set a then Southern League record by winning fourteen successive league matches.

Despite a subsequent relegation, they bounced back with their third promotion in a decade. They followed their return to the Premier Division by reaching the highest ever position in the pyramid and last season claimed a top ten finish despite considerable mid season difficulties.

As a result of summer team strengthening and the local authority undertaking an upgrade of facilities to Conference standard, interest and support among the public of Newport and the surrounding area has been greatly increased. The club's away following is among the largest outside the Football League.

The club is probably unique in non-league football as many of its fans live far from Newport. The "Over the Bridge Exiles" (OBE's) were formed in 1996 and boast a membership of over 100 paying a £15 annual subscription. They produce a monthly newsletter.

The Amber Army, formed in the summer , is another major fund raising organisation for the club, with members contributing byu standing order. Information regarding both the OBE's and Amber Army can be obtained from the club at Newport Stadium, Spytty Park, Newport, South Wales NP19 0PT, or e-mail to obes@newport-afc.demon.co.uk

ALL TIME RECORD

		Pld	W	D	L	F	A	Pts	Pos
1989-90	Hellenic League	34	23	6	5	71	28	75	1st
1990-91	Beazer Homes (Midland)	42	19	6	17	54	46	63	7th
1991-92	Beazer Homes (Midland)	42	15	13	14	72	60	58	10th
1992-93	Beazer Homes (Midland)	42	23	8	11	73	58	77	5th
1993-94	Beazer Homes (Midland)	42	26	9	7	84	37	87	4th
1994-95	Beazer Homes (Midland)	42	29	8	5	106	39	95	1st
1995-96	Beazer Homes (Premier)	42	13	13	16	53	59	52	14th
1996-97	Beazer Homes (Premier)	42	9	13	20	40	60	40	21st
1997-98	Dr. Martens League(Southern)	42	21	6	15	83	65	69	7th
1998-99	Dr. Martens League (Midland)	42	26	7	9	92	51	85	2nd
1999-00	Dr. Martens League (Premier)	42	16	18	8	67	50	66	7th
2000-01	Dr. Martens League (Premier)	42	17	10	15	70	61	61	10th

Newport County Football Club.

At Whiteheads
- Newport County
players. David Hando
(chairman) pictured
extreme left.

League decider
celebrations with chairman
David Hando.

Newport Football team
at Somerton Park.

INAUGURAL COMPETITIVE MATCH

NEWPORT AFC v PEGASUS JUNIORS

MORETON-IN-MARSH

19th AUGUST, 1989

Dave Williams *(Trainer/Director)*   D.Graham Jones *(Doctor)*   Wallace Brown *(Director)*   Phil Burgess *(Director)*   Ian Bartlett *(Director)*   Ray Taylor *(Director)*   Mike Everett *(Director)*   Brian Toms *(President)*   David Hando *(Chairman)*   Hywel Rees *(Director)*

Marc Williams *(Director)*   Jayne Greenham *(Director)*   Martin Greenham *(Director)*   Dale Williams *(Director)*   Steve Pepperall *(Director)*   Colin Jones *(Director)*   David Hicks *(Director)*   Brian Preece *(Player)*   Tony Gilbert *(Physio)*

Mike Pratt   Graham Rogers *(Asst.Manage)*   Gary Spink   Richard Evans   John Relish *(Manager)*   Norman Parselle *(Captain)*   Tony Bird   Andrew Nelson   Dean Richards   Chris Stanton

Barrie Vassallo   Michael King   ChrisLillygreen

David Gibson *(Mascot)*

CHRISTIAN MALCOLM

Newport-born champion sprinter Christian Malcolm once said that Britain's athletic sprint facilities are the best on the planet. Living in the Maindee area of the city, over the years, Newport has produced great athletic talent and Christian has proved to be one of the best; in fact, the city of Newport sporting facilities are certainly the best in Wales with more on the way. By 2003, Newport will be the site of the seven million pound Welsh national Velodrome.

A cousin of Welsh International sprinter Kevin Williams, Christian has long shown exceptional promise, with a superb running style; a promise that came to a brilliant fruition in 1998, when he was the World Junior Athletic Champion.

He competed for three years in Britain's Junior International team, from 1996 to 1998, making great progress each year. Success followed success with every event that Christian took part in.

His mother, Yvonne Malcolm once said, "Christian has won so many medals and trophies that we have to store them in boxes in the attic because there is nowhere else for them to go on display".

Apart from being a credit to his family, Christian Malcolm, at only twenty-two years of age, has set an outstanding example to his generation.

Here are few of his sporting achievements taken from the internet: -

In 1996, aged 17, Christian was Britain's fastest junior over 200m and reached the world junior semi-finals in Sydney.

Two years later during the winter season, he broke the Welsh indoor record for 200m (21.26secs) at U20 level and pushed his good friend and rival Dwain Chambers all the way over 60m.

In what will undoubtedly be the one of many awards Christian received, the 1997 Junior Male Athlete Of The Year' award by the IAAF at their annual ceremony in Monte Carlo, an award they apparently re-established due to Christian's fantastic achievements.

Christian won three European junior medals; 200m Gold, 4 x 100m Gold and100m Silver. His 100m time of 10.24 beating Colin Jackson's long standing Welsh Senior record. Christian's arrival on the International circuit was against the legendary Carl Lewis at Zurich in 1997; Christian beat Carl who earmarked him as a future star.

In 1998 he became the World Junior 100m and 200m Champion, in 2000 he became the European Indoor Champion and came 5th in the Olympic Games at the age of 21. Arguably the most talented 200m runner in the world, Christian is quickly establishing himself as the sprinter to watch.

Christian's transition from a junior to a senior athlete was remarkable. He stormed into the indoor season taking the national 200m title and winning the 200m at the British Grand Prix. He went on to win his first senior Gold medal at the European Indoor Championships in Gwent in a Welsh record (20.54), and the Five Nations Classic in Glasgow against the best in the world to reaffirm his arrival on the senior circuit.

Christian's 1998 season underpinned Carl Lewis's remarks. After winning the 100m and 200m at the U20's AAA Championships, he went on to win the 200m at the Welsh Senior Championships. Christian's ultimate goal for 1998 lay at the World Junior Championships in Annecy, France. Christian not only won Gold at the 200m in a new UK Junior and Championship record of 20.44secs, but also won Gold at the 100m in 10.12secs, a personal best and Championship best.

Christian's maturity and experience has continued to grow as rapidly as his racing capability. He competed in Zurich and Lausanne in preparation for the Commonwealth Games. At the games, Christian with his first real taste of senior championships, ran superbly in the 200m final taking the Silver medal in a new personal best and European Junior record of 20.29secs.

Christian, keen to capitalise on his success of 1998, launched into the 1999 season with a new personal best time for the indoor 200m of 20.74 and just missed out on a place at the World Indoor Championships. However, his focal point for 1999 was the outdoor season and the European Under 23 Championships in Gothenburg. Christian delighted his fans by taking Silver in both the 100m and 200m sprints, and competing as part of the GB 4 x 100m relay. Christian came away with a European U23 Gold medal.

Christian has a superb 2001 season, just missing out on a medal at the World Championships in Edmonton in both the 100m and 200m, but impressed the world's media and fellow competitors by reaching the final in both events.

Christian's focus for the busy 2002 season was firmly set on three events. He began with the European Indoor Championships in Vienna (March), where he aimed to retain his 200m title. As firm favourite going into the final, Christian was desperately unlucky to pull his hamstring coming off the final bend and had to settle for the Silver medal.

Now in 2003, Christian is looking towards achieving more medals in this year's World Athletics Championships.

Keep going Christian !

Power driven Christian.

Ready for take off.

297

Christian Malcolm, champion sprinter.

Christian Malcolm, on the street where he lives.

Get set, get ready - go!

Mark Williams

Mark who regularly practices for his snooker tournaments in Newport is famous for winning the World Snooker Championship in 201.

His successful record as a Junior in Wales, and in particular, his great composure at such a young age, had the pundits marking their cards for the future, but Mark had other sporting interests at that age, which could have severely damaged his snooker career.

Mark's amateur career path also saw him in the boxing ring, but by the age of 17, he had decided that he didn't like getting hurt and he wisely chose to turn to professional snooker.

Mark's rise up the world rankings was nothing short of meteoric. In just four seasons, he climbed from 119th to 4th and following his most successful season ever in 1998/9 he had established himself at number three, and had become one of the few players to win three ranking tournaments in one season.

His 1998/9 season, after a rather inauspicious start blossomed into his best ever. Having reached two semi-finals, he went one better to lose the final of the German Masters to John Parrott and one better again to win the Irish Open. He followed this with the Regal Welsh title and the Thailand Masters, his season culminating with his first appearance in the final of the Embassy World Championship. By the end of the season his career earnings had reached £1,070,848. Just enough to pop out and treat himself to a brand new 'Flaming Red' Ferrari. Mark is restricted to keeping the car for fun, having discovered very quickly that he could fit neither his cue case, nor his golf clubs in the car!

He started the 1999/2000 season as the provisional number one, the first time a Welsh player had ever hel d that position and the three-way tussle for the top spot ran throughout the season, before Mark was eventually confirmed as the new No. 1at the Regal Scottish.

Beginning with the Champions Cup, Mark reached seven finals in 1999/00 and won three major titles. He took the UK Championship, retained the Thailand Masters and at the Embassy World Championship became the first Welshman for twenty years, and the first ever left-hander to take the game's greatest prize.

By the end of the 1999/2000 Season he had consolidated his position as number one in the rankings, with a huge 11,000 point lead over John Higgins, whom he beat in the semi-finals on the way to glory at the Crucible.

And this season, Mark has maintained his winning record, taking the Grand Prix title at Telford, beating Ronnie O'Sullivan 9-5, to gain revenge for his defeat at the hands of 'The Rocket' in the TSN Champions Cup final.

One of Williams' most memorable wins came in the 1998 Benson and Hedges Masters, when, after trailing 6-9, he clawed back to defeat Stephen Hendry on a re-spotted black in the deciding frame.

Mark stills plays in the same club, The Emporium, Bargoed, where he first picked up a cue. "I've been playing here for more than 10 years, I entered my first tournament at the Emporium as a 13-year-old. I think other people realised I could play the game before I did and it just went from there, really. There's a table in the corner that I practise on and I just get up and play. Everyone knows me and they just let me get on with it."

If Williams ever decides to hang up his cue, he could do worse than turn his hand to golf, on which he is very keen; he is one of the best snooker-golfers around and during the summer spends many hours on the course, often for the benefit of charity at pro-celebrity events.

Quite apart from snooker success in the year 2000, Williams also had extra reason to celebrate in December as he became egaged to girlfriend Joanne Dent.

Mark Williams. World Snooker
Champion, from Cwm.

Mark in play.

Mark wins the trophy.

Newport Boxer
Johnny Basham.

ROYAL
ALBERT HALL
Manager ... ... MR. HILTON CARTER.
On FRIDAY, OCTOBER 14th, at 8
Under the direction of J. ARNOLD WILSON.
Middleweight Championship
of Europe
20 Three Minute Rounds
TED (KID)
LEWIS
(ALDGATE)
V.
JOHNNY
BASHAM
(WREXHAM)
THEIR FIRST CONTEST AS
MIDDLEWEIGHTS.
OTHER SPECIAL CONTESTS.
Box Office.: WISDEN'S. 23. Cranbourn Street. W.C. 2. 'Phone:
Gerrard 2120. Also at Albert Hall and usual Agencies.
Prices (including Tax) ;
12/- £1/4/0 £2/7/0 £3/10/0 £5/16/0

Johnny Basham, Newport boxer in action.

THE NEW VENTURE PLAYERS

The King & I 1976

31 YEARS OF ENTERTAINING
THE CITY OF NEWPORT

No No Nanette 1977　　　*BIG*　　　*South Pacific 1979*

AND STILL GOING STRONG

Guys & Dolls 1984　　　*The Card 1980*　　　*Mr. Scrooge 1987*

The New Venture Players Theatre Group 1984.

The New venture Players c1997.

New Venture Players, ladies chorus 1985.

New Venture Players in rehearsal with director Gordon Colins (front) showing them how to do it.

Terry Underwood with... "Oh, so many."

Stan Stennett with me. "Now look Terry, I've got enough on my plate, I'll do the jokes as long as you'll keep laughing.

Town crier Terry Underwood shouting the odds in John Frost Square, to let the population of Newport know what's going on... well, one or two anyway.

Me starting the Jowett Car Rally on May 25th 2003. "Goodbye... was that Lord Lucan at the wheel?"

Lyn (The Leap) Davies, a member of the staff of the Noahs Ark Appeal, Vanessa Clarke, Stan Stennett and me.

With Sir Anthony Hopkins and his mother, Murial and my wife Hazel at the opening ceremony of Abbeyfield, Caerleon, in 1994.

Me with Anita Dobson, from the BBC programme Eastenders, 1996.

With Cliff Richards when appearing in Heathcliffe.

with Desmond Llewelyn who was Q in the James Bond series of films.

My wife and I with Dave Willetts, West End star of Phantom of the Opera and many other West End productions.

With Jimmy Johnston, on his Wedding Day.

With Alex Cordell, at 'The Hill', Abergavenny, six weeks before he died.

Terry and Leslie, whooping it up.

Hazel with Leslie Thomas, author of
Virgin Soldiers and many more.

Bruce Cambell now curator of the Newport Museum and Library, with me as extras in the 1980 film production of 'The Time Bandits' filmed at Raglan Castle and Keinsham near Bristol.

Five handsome fellas's - Peter Hourahine, Bob Pickard, Terry Underwood, Don Edwards and Harry Denham. Terry with the Fortunaires.

TERRY UNDERWOOD. A LIFE WELL LIVED.

Born in 1928 at 10 Clytha Square, Newport, Terry Underwood has entertained and contributed to the welfare of the people for over 60 years.

At the age of 13 as a boy scout he spent a day in July 1941 serving teas etc. to rescue workers when Eveswell Street and Archibald Street were bombed; and when 37 people died in the devastation.

A writer of 7 books on his home town of Newport and 8 musicals, he has entertained and given his time and energy to many charitable organisations as compere/comedian.

As Director to the New Venture Players he produced 74 musicals in his time and is now their President. Over the years, Terry has been an organiser for main tent events at Newport's Fetes and Carnivals, given slide shows on Newport to many Senior Citizen Clubs, Womens Guilds, University of 3rd age and the partially sighted.

As a young comedian Terry belonged to the Star Variety Concert Party who entertained troops of the army and airforce stationed in South Wales, visiting military camps at Nash, the Lighthouse, Chepstow, Bridgend, Llanover, Abergavenny, Llanmartin, Cowbridge, St Athens, Belmont, Caldicot and Cardiff.

His enthusiasm for the theatre and the love of his home town has kept him active all his life. He is currently Social Chairman at Eleanor Hodson House/Abbeyfield Nursing Home where he arranges, on a monthly basis, entertainment for the residents.

A life well lived - not a moment wasted.

His motto.....Spread a little happiness.....

 Scouts 16th Newport, St Johns, Maindee 1939 - 1941

 Young Venture Players President 2004 - on going

Newport Transporter Bridge Chairman 1998 - 2002

 Army Cadets 4th BTN. Monmouthshire Regiment 1941 - 1946

 Newport Carnival Committee 1957 - 1963

Newport Transporter Bridge Vice President March 2005 - present

Star Variety Concert Party 1942 - 1946

Founder Member Newport Pantomine and Musical Society 1970 - 1972

Christchurch Music Society- Committee 2004 - on going

Royal Armoured Corp 62nd Regiment 1946 - 1948

 Chartist Reinactment Group 1989 - 1991

Friends of the Newport Save our Ship Treasurer 2002 - 2004 2005 - Patron of the Newport Ship

Army Cadets (re-joined) as underofficer Underwood, then 2nd Lieutenant 1948 - 1950

 Town Crier 1980 - 1982

The Rotary Club of Newport 1998 - on going

Founder Member STANDARD TELEPHONES PANTOMIME AND REVIEW SOCIETY 1948 - 1957

(Founder / Artistic Director) 1972 - ongoing (President) 2002 - ongoing ESTABLISHED 1972

In 1960 started to direct for Caldicot Operatic Society, also till 1970 directed musicals for Chepstow Operatic Society

Founder Member STC MUSICAL SOCIETY 1957 - 1961

Abbeyfield Nursing Home Chairman entertainments 1994 - on going

DIRECTOR
TERRY UNDERWOOD

In 1979 until 1993 Started his company Unipak (Newport) Ltd Labels and Engraving

 1979 - on going
The Lord's Taverners Ltd

"Often called Mr Newport"

A Life Well Lived - Terry Underwood Time Line

Date	One Act Plays	Sketches	Pantonmines	Revues
1938	The Snuff Box			
1939		A Dog's Life*		
1940		Knocking Up Ginger* Kick the Can*		
1941		Handy Mum* Paws at the Kerb*		
1943			The Queen of Hearts	
1944			Babes in the Woods	
1947			Klinkerella*	
1950			Old Mother Hubbard*	
1953		Hyde Park Corner		
1955		The Bell Ringers		What a Performance*
1956	They're Off		Cinderella*	Out of the Blue*
1963				
1969				
1970			Dick Whittington*	
1971				Over the Footlights*
1972		My Umberella		
1975				
1980				
1981				
1984				
1992				
1995		School's Out		
1997				
1998				
1999				
2003		Wartime in Court-y-bella*		

Songs	Full Length Musicals	Books	
			} * Written for St. Johns Maindee 16th Newport Scouts Victoria Avenue
The 2.22 from Tooting			
Huggy Wuggie			
			* Written for the 62nd The Royal Armour Corp. Catteric
Here Comes Santa			* St. Patricks Church
Nice to be Home			
			} * Written for S.T.C. Operatic Society
	Gretna Green		
	Lorna Doone		} * Written for Newport Pantomine and Playgoers Society
A Touch Too Much			
Win or Loose			
	Uncle Gilbert*		* Written for New Venture Players
		Yesterday's Newport	
	Mister Scrooge*		} * Written for New Venture Players
	The Sunday Boys*	The Way We Were in Newport	
	Dodger*	Time to Remember, Time to Forget Once Upon a Time in Newport	
	Rape of Our Fair Country*		
		Wildings	
	Rise and Shine*	Newport Transporter Bridge Handbook	* Written for Lliswerry High School
		The City of Newport, Gateway to Wales	* Written for Pill Heritage

NICE TO BE HOME

Words and music by Terry Underwood © 2002

Written for Miss Tessie O'Shea

I've travelled the world
been everywhere
climbed many mountains
but nothing compares
to my homeland (homeland)
homeland

I've travelled the seas
with wind in my sails
but I'd rather be
in that place they call Wales
It's my homeland (homeland)
homeland

I'm going back to the land of my birth
where there's green hills, valleys and dales
It's called the land of song
and that is where I belong
I shall wander no more from my Wales

(chorus)

Oh it's nice to be home
nice to be home
back in Wales again
sat by a cosy fire
listening to the choir
singing songs oh so sweet
in the chapel down the street
Now I've been to old gay Paris
and this I must say
I prefer the girls in Tonypandy any day
Oh it's nice to be home
nice to be home
back in Wales again
yes, back in Wales again

(second chorus)

Oh it's nice to be home
nice to be home
back in Wales again
sat by a cosy fire
listening to the choir
singing songs oh so sweet
in the chapel down the street
I've been up to London town
and this I must say
I prefer the girls in Newport City any day
Oh it's nice to be home
nice to be home
back in Wales again
yes, back in Wales again

315

NICE TO BE HOME.

WORDS & MUSIC BY TERRY UNDERWOOD

I'VE TRAVELLED THE WORLD   BEEN EV'RYWHERE

CLIMBED MANY MOUN —TAINS BUT NOTHING COMPARES TO MY   HOME — LAND

(HOME — LAND)   HOME — LAND

I'VE TRAVELLED THE SEAS   WITH WIND IN MY SAILS

BUT I'D RATHER BE   IN THAT PLACE THEY CALL WALES IT'S MY

HOME — LAND   (HOME — LAND)   HOME — LAND

I'M GOING BACK TO THE

LAND OF MY BIRTH   WHERE THERE'S GREEN HILLS   VALLEYS AND DALES

IT'S CALLED THE LAND OF SONG AND THAT IS WHERE I BELONG   I SHALL

WANDER NO MORE FROM MY WALES. OH! IT'S NICE TO BE HOME

NICE TO BE HOME BACK IN WALES AGAIN

SAT BY A COSY FIRE LISTENING TO THE

CHOIR SINGING SONGS OH SO SWEET IN THE CHAPEL DOWN THE STREET/NOW)

1. I'VE BEEN TO OLD GAY PARIS AND THIS I MUST SAY I PREFER THE
2. I'VE BEEN UP TO LONDON TOWN AND THIS I MUST SAY I PREFER THE

GIRLS IN TONY-PANDY ANY DAY. {OH IT'S NICE TO BE HOME
GIRLS IN NEWPORT CITY ANY DAY.

NICE TO BE HOME BACK IN WALES A - GAIN,

YES BACK IN WALES A —

1st. C

— GAIN. OH! IT'S — GAIN.